Student Companion to

# Eugene
# O'NEILL

**Recent Titles in Student Companions to Classic Writers**

Student Companion to

# Eugene O'Neill

Steven F. Bloom

**Student Companions to Classic Writers**

GREENWOOD PRESS
Westport, Connecticut • London

**Library of Congress Cataloging-in-Publication Data**

Bloom, Steven F. (Steven Fredric), 1951-
   Student companion to Eugene O'Neill / Steven F. Bloom.
     p. cm.—(Student companions to classic writers, ISSN 1522-7979)
   Includes bibliographical references and index.
   ISBN–13: 978–0–313–33431–3 (alk. paper)
   ISBN–10: 0–313–33431–5 (alk. paper)
     1. O'Neill, Eugene, 1888-1953—Criticism and interpretation—Handbooks,
manuals, etc. I. Title.
   PS3529.N5Z5678 2007
   812'.52—dc22      2007003237

British Library Cataloguing in Publication Data is available.

Library of Congress Catalog Card Number: 2007003237

ISBN–13: 978–0–313–33431–3
ISBN–10: 0–313–33431–5
ISSN: 1522–7979


First published in 2007

Greenwood Press, 88 Post Road West, Westport, CT 06881
An imprint of Greenwood Publishing Group, Inc.
www.greenwood.com

Printed in the United States of America

The paper used in this book complies with the
Permanent Paper Standard issued by the National
Information Standards Organization (Z39.48–1984).

10  9  8  7  6  5  4  3  2  1

*For my parents,*
*who first took me to the theatre*
*. . . and for Margie, Rachel, and Daniel,*
*who keep going with me*

# Contents

# Series Foreword

This series has been designed to meet the needs of students and general readers for accessible literary criticism on the American and world writers most frequently studied and read in the secondary school, community college, and four-year college classrooms. Unlike other works of literary criticism that are written for the specialist and graduate student, or that feature a variety of reprinted scholarly essays on sometimes obscure aspects of the writer's work, the Student Companions to Classic Writers series is carefully crafted to examine each writer's major works fully and in a systematic way, at the level of the nonspecialist and general reader. The objective is to enable the reader to gain a deeper understanding of the work and to apply critical thinking skills to the act of reading. The proven format for the volumes in this series was developed by an advisory board of teachers and librarians for a successful series published by Greenwood Press, Critical Companions to Popular Contemporary Writers. Responding to their request for easy-to-use and yet challenging literary criticism for students and adult library patrons, Greenwood Press developed a systematic format that is not intimidating but helps the reader to develop the ability to analyze literature.

How does this work? Each volume in the Student Companions to Classic Writers series is written by a subject specialist, an academic who understands students' needs for basic and yet challenging examination of the writer's canon. Each volume begins with a biographical chapter, drawn from published sources, biographies, and autobiographies, that relates the writer's life to his or her work. The next chapter examines the writer's literary heritage, tracing the literary influences of other writers on that writer and explaining and discussing the literary genres into which the writer's work falls. Each of the following chapters examines a major work by the writer, those works most frequently read and studied by high school and college students. Depending on the writer's canon, generally between four and eight major works are examined, each in an individual chapter. The discussion of each work is organized into separate sections on plot development, character development, and major themes. Literary devices and style, narrative point of view, and historical setting are also discussed in turn if pertinent to the work. Each chapter concludes with an alternate critical perspective from which to read the work, such as a psychological or feminist criticism. The critical theory is defined briefly in easy, comprehensible language for the student. Looking at the literature from the point of view of a particular critical approach will help the reader to understand and apply critical theory to the act of reading and analyzing literature.

Of particular value in each volume is the bibliography, which includes a complete bibliography of the writer's works, a selected bibliography of biographical and critical works suitable for students, and lists of reviews of each work examined in the companion, both from the time the literature was originally published and from contemporary sources, all of which will be helpful to readers, teachers, and librarians who would like to consult additional sources.

As a source of literary criticism for the student or for the general reader, this series will help the reader to gain understanding of the writer's work and skill in critical reading.

# Preface

Eugene O'Neill, the only American playwright to receive the Nobel prize for literature, is America's greatest dramatist. He wrote more than 50 plays, including a number never completed to his satisfaction that he destroyed. Three of his completed works—*The Iceman Cometh*, *Long Day's Journey Into Night*, and *A Moon for the Misbegotten*—are arguably among the best of American and even world drama, and several others—including *The Emperor Jones*, *The Hairy Ape*, *Desire Under the Elms*, and *Ah, Wilderness!*— are remarkable works within their respective genres. Most significantly, although a few of his plays are awkward and unsatisfying, the dramaturgical reach and thematic scope of his entire varied canon changed the course of the American theatre forever.

The plays selected for this volume are those that are most commonly taught in high school and college courses. Although some instructors may neglect O'Neill's early one-acts for their lack of thematic or structural complexity, and his more ambitious, experimental plays for their demanding length and seemingly relentless somberness, many of these works will, in fact, reward further study, especially when considered, as all dramatic literature should be, with an eye toward their theatricality. In particular, both *Strange Interlude* and *Mourning Becomes Electra*, from O'Neill's middle period, are challenging works in which the playwright treats many of his recurrent themes with distinctive approaches, the bold use of spoken thoughts, in the first case, and the clever transmogrification of Greek tragedy, in the second. In addition, although the general perception of O'Neill is primarily as a writer of long dramas, several of his early one-act plays are highly evocative of the allure and mystique of the sea; and the late one-act *Hughie* captures and evokes much of the same existentialist angst of his longer mature plays, while also anticipating multimedia productions of today. Although these works are not treated in nearly the same detail as the eight that are featured in Chapters 3 through 9, the reader will find some commentary on these and others in Chapters 1 (biography) and 2 (literary heritage), as well as opportunities for further study in many of the critical studies and collections of critical essays listed in the bibliography.

Most of the information on O'Neill's life included in Chapter 1 is derived from the invaluable comprehensive biographies written by Louis Sheaffer and Barbara and Arthur Gelb. The year cited for each play at the beginning of Chapters 3 through 9 is the year O'Neill completed the work, based on the chronology in the Gelbs', *O'Neill: Life with Monte Cristo*, published in 2000. O'Neill often completed his plays some time before they were published or produced, so the date of completion is a more accurate reflection of O'Neill's development as a writer and the sociohistorical context in which that development took place. For example, 1941, the year O'Neill completed *Long Day's Journey Into Night*, provides a much more accurate context for the writing of that play than does 1956, the year of its publication and first production.

"O'Neill Play by Play," the downloadable electronic bibliography by Charles A. Carpenter (posted on www.eoneill.com in July 2006), is a remarkably user-friendly guide to virtually all that has been published by and about O'Neill, and it is the source for most of the entries in the selected bibliography. It does not, however, include theatre reviews; Jordan Miller's bibliography, *Eugene O'Neill and the American Critic*, is the source for those references to reviews before 1973.

At the time of his death in 1953, having been creatively stifled by ill health for a decade, O'Neill had been disregarded by much of the theatregoing public; however, the landmark productions of *The Iceman Cometh* and *Long Day's Journey Into Night* in 1956 restored his reputation and prominence in the American theatre. Since that time, much has been written about O'Neill's life and works. Scholarly activity was bolstered and nurtured by the creation of *The Eugene O'Neill Newsletter* in 1977 and the Eugene O'Neill Society in 1979. In 1989, under the stewardship of its founding editor, Dr. Frederick Wilkins, the *Newsletter* became *The Eugene O'Neill Review*, which retains its status today as the journal of record for O'Neill studies. The mission of both the Society and the *Review*, to promote the study and appreciation of O'Neill's life and works, has been complemented and catapulted into the twenty-first century by Harley Hammerman M.D., who in 1999 created a pioneering Web site, www.eoneill.com, which has become an invaluable interactive source of information and communication for O'Neillians in the computer age.

A glance at the bibliography in this book offers sufficient evidence that scholarship on O'Neill is extremely vibrant and healthy, with new articles and books being published every year. Many of our finest directors and actors continue to turn to O'Neill's dramas for challenging new ventures on the stage, resulting in a strong production history, on and off Broadway and in regional and university theatres in the United States and abroad. Since the 1980s, the Eugene O'Neill Society has regularly organized international conferences—in locales associated with O'Neill, such as Boston, Bermuda, Tours, and Provincetown—that have brought together numerous admirers of the dramatist from both the academic and theatrical worlds to discuss, perform, and critique his life and works.

One of O'Neill's homes—the Monte Cristo Cottage in New London, Connecticut—is a registered national landmark, and a second—Tao House, in Danville, California—has been designated a National Historic Site by the United States government. Both institutions pay tribute to O'Neill's legacy. Both are open to the public for educational purposes, and both support the continuing study and recognition of O'Neill's work by scholars and theatre professionals, while also nurturing new work by aspiring writers and theatre artists. Indeed, the Eugene O'Neill Theater Center in Waterford, Connecticut, which owns and operates the Monte Cristo Cottage, has become one of the premier sources of new plays for the American theatre, having helped to launch the careers of contemporary dramatists such as Wendy Wasserstein, John Guare, and August Wilson.

This book is the result of many years of studying and teaching about O'Neill's life and works. I am grateful to Fred Wilkins for first welcoming me into the ranks of O'Neillians with his friendly encouragement and good will. I am indebted to my many colleagues, especially those in the Eugene O'Neill Society, whose productions, publications, conference presentations, and lively conversations have been inspiring. I am also indebted to the numerous students, of all ages, in my classes over the years, whose ideas and insights have often been enlightening. I am grateful for research assistance provided by the staff at the Brennan Library at Lasell College. I truly appreciate the insistent, yet friendly, encouragement to meet my deadlines from my editor at Greenwood Press, Debby Adams. I am grateful to Vice President for Academic Affairs Jim Ostrow, President Tom de Witt, and the Putnam Faculty Development Fund at Lasell College for support of this project. Finally, thanks to my wife Margie for reading what I write and always asking such good, helpful questions, and to Margie, Rachel, and Daniel for making room for O'Neill at our family table for all these many years. Without my family, there would only be hopeless hope.

# 1

# The Life of Eugene O'Neill

Eugene O'Neill was the son of a popular nineteenth-century matinee idol and the father of American drama. O'Neill brought realism, expressionism, and lyricism to an American stage that was characterized mostly by superficial melodramas, light comedies, and entertaining musicals, and he changed it forever. Early in the twentieth century, O'Neill set the stage for a tradition of serious American drama that has grown and flourished into the twenty-first century. As one writer put it in *Time Magazine* after O'Neill's death, "Before O'Neill…the U.S. had theater; after O'Neill, it had drama" (Sheaffer, *S&P* 481). The impact he had on the American theatre is integrally, and interestingly, tied to the conflicted relationship he had with his own father, because of whom he both learned the language of theatre and resolved to transform what it had become in America in the hands of his father's generation.

The content of O'Neill's drama is intricately tied to his own past. His plays are populated with characters who strikingly resemble, in both appearance and behavior, people he knew in his life, from the citizens of New London with whom he was acquainted, to seamen with whom he sailed, to zealots and ne'er-do-wells with whom he caroused. In particular, though, O'Neill could not escape—neither in his own psychic development nor in his playwriting—from the conflicted relationships he had with all the members of his own family; virtually all of his plays are peopled with headstrong fathers, distant mothers, and rival siblings. These characters have different names and are disguised in different historical and social contexts until the very end of his career when he removed the disguises and transparently placed his own family front and center on stage as the Tyrones in *Long Day's Journey Into Night,* and then his brother as Jim Tyrone in a sequel of sorts, *A Moon for the Misbegotten.*

Although these late plays are not literal autobiographies, they are remarkably autobiographical; they are the culmination of a body of work that is testimony to O'Neill's extraordinary talent for creating universally moving drama from the painful details of his own life and the demons of his own psyche. In his 1999 biography of O'Neill, Stephen Black proposes that virtually all of O'Neill's creative output represented, for the dramatist, a protracted process of grieving the loss of his family: "O'Neill was obsessed with the losses, and with the process of mourning . . . . O'Neill found a way to use the writing of plays as a form of self-psychoanalysis. The analysis was successful to the extent that it allowed him to mourn his dead and to create in his last plays work that must have come very close to fulfilling even so large a talent as his" (xvi–xviii). Taken together, the works of Eugene O'Neill stand as a major artistic achievement, and familiarity with the life of Eugene O'Neill enriches one's appreciation of that achievement.

## THE EARLY YEARS

Eugene Gladstone O'Neill was born on October 16, 1888, in a Times Square hotel room in New York City, the first milestone on a lifelong road of itinerancy. His father, James O'Neill (1844–1920), the working-class son of an Irish immigrant, was a celebrated turn-of-the-century matinee idol who traveled around the country performing primarily in a popular melodramatic play, *The Count of Monte Cristo,* which earned him a fortune for those days. Eugene's mother, Mary Ellen (Ella) Quinlan (1857–1922), the middle-class daughter of a Midwestern businessman, reluctantly accepted theatrical life, accompanying her husband on the road and never settling down in a conventional home. The closest the family ever had to a home was a house that James purchased in New London, Connecticut, where they spent summers together between theatrical seasons.

Eugene was the third of three sons. The first, James O'Neill, Jr., was born in 1878. The second, Edmund, was born in 1883, but died 18 months later, after contracting measles from his older brother. The loss of her second son had a profound impact on Ella, not the least of which was her ambivalence about having another child, a crucial psychological factor in her relationship with that next child, Eugene, and one that is notably reflected in Mary's relationship with Edmund in *Long Day's Journey.* When

Eugene was born in 1888, his older brother, Jamie, was away at boarding school, and the new baby and his mother accompanied James as he toured with *Monte Cristo*. Ella had been given morphine, commonly prescribed at the time, to ease the pain caused by the birth of Eugene. She became addicted to the drug, and, as depicted so pointedly in *Long Day's Journey*, her addiction came to dominate the family dynamics from then on. The O'Neills hired a nurse named Sarah Sandy to care for Eugene during these early years, and the only time they really experienced anything resembling a normal family life was those summers in New London.

## FORMAL EDUCATION

At the age of seven, Eugene was sent to a strict Catholic boarding school, where he felt lonely, estranged from Sarah Sandy, rejected by his parents, and alienated by the school's rigid adherence to Catholic dogma. In 1902, relenting in the face of Eugene's adamant rebellion, his parents enrolled him in a more liberal and nonsectarian boarding school, Betts Academy, in Connecticut. In the summer of 1903, he witnessed, along with his brother and his father, Ella's attempt to drown herself in the river near the New London house. After this, he could no longer be protected from the truth about his mother. His father and brother informed him that she was addicted to morphine, which was the final piece of evidence of the futility of religious faith that the young Eugene needed to turn his back on Catholicism. He spent the rest of his life, and a good part of his creative output as a playwright, searching for something to replace his lost religious faith.

In his four years at Betts, he read voraciously, becoming familiar with the classics, which the Betts curriculum emphasized, while continuing to cultivate his taste for modern literature (Gelbs, *O'Neill: Life* 187). He completed his formal education with a nine-month stint at Princeton University, where he spent more time drinking and carousing than studying. His proximity to New York City enabled him to frequent bars and brothels with his brother Jamie, but it also gave him relatively easy access to the theatre. In 1907, he returned to see Ibsen's *Hedda Gabler* 10 times (226), evidently sowing the seeds of his later determination to bring the experimentation of European theatre to the American stage. Needless to say, his lifestyle detracted from his studies, and although there is some evidence that he was asked to leave Princeton for conduct code violations, he clearly was no longer interested in enduring this kind of institution-based education. So he set out on a mission to make life experiences his school, and over the next few years, he did so with a vengeance.

## ADRIFT ON LAND AND AT SEA

With financial support from his father, he was able to live, unemployed (except for a brief run as a mail-order clerk), in New York City, where he spent much of his time frequenting bars, brothels, and bookstores. He spent his days reading the works of writers who were most popular among the radicals of the time and his nights drinking, consorting with prostitutes, and dallying with women of more substance. His reading brought him to the works of Nietzsche, whose *Thus Spake Zarathustra* he would later acknowledge as the book that had the greatest influence on him (219–220). His dalliances brought him to the bed of Kathleen Jenkins, the woman who would bear his first child, Eugene Jr., and of whom, later in life, he would say, "the woman I've given the most trouble to has given me the least" (Gelbs, *O'Neill* 191).

His father disapproved of his relationship with Kathleen and arranged to send Eugene off to Honduras on a mining expedition, where his journey into the jungle would form the basis for the jungle setting of *The Emperor Jones* years later; before he left, however, knowing that Kathleen was pregnant, Eugene married her. Although he returned from Honduras within a few months, stricken by malaria, he did not return to settle down with Kathleen. He did not even meet his son, Eugene Jr., who had been born while he was away. Rather, his father swept him away to work for his theatre company, and when that failed, Eugene decided to pursue his desire to be a seaman and set sail aboard the *Charles Racine* for Buenos Aires. He found the feeling of being at sea exhilarating (later to be expressed by characters in the early sea plays, *The Hairy Ape*, and most especially by Edmund in *Long Day's Journey*), but he also suffered the greatest physical deprivation during this time, barely surviving in Buenos Aires, where he more often than not slept on park benches.

When he returned to New York in 1911, he was on a downward trajectory that landed him at a seedy rooming house called Jimmy-the-Priest's, where he would continue to drink heavily. Within a few months, he attempted suicide by taking an overdose of a barbiturate called Veronal, only to be saved by his friends, who discovered him in his room and brought him to the hospital to have his stomach pumped. This failed suicide attempt in 1912 marked an important turning point in O'Neill's life, and it is no coincidence that he set *Long Day's Journey Into Night* in that year. Having seen his first piece of writing in print (a poem in a little-known journal with a modest circulation), having put his relationship with Kathleen Jenkins behind him (the divorce was granted in the summer of 1912), and having purged himself of some demons through his failed suicide attempt, he finally agreed to return to New London for a summer with his family. Here, he allowed his father to use his influence to help him acquire a position on the local newspaper. Illness would curtail his journalism career but send him down another path as a writer.

## THE TURNING POINT, 1912

During the fall of 1912, Eugene was diagnosed with tuberculosis, and he checked into the Gaylord Farm Sanatorium, where he remained for six months. During his stay there, with nothing much else to do besides read, he became more familiar with the works of European dramatists and philosophers, and he began to write his own one-act plays. When he left the sanatorium, he returned to New London, where he continued to write. It was during this period that he became aware of the famous playwriting course offered by George Pierce Baker at Harvard, and he applied to Professor Baker for admission. In his letter of application, he claimed to aspire to be "an artist or nothing" (Gelbs, *O'Neill: Life* 433). Baker accepted him, and thus, in 1914, O'Neill moved to Cambridge, Massachusetts, to begin his first formal training as a dramatist.

Although in retrospect he regarded most of what he wrote (primarily one-acts) during his eight months in Baker's class as "rotten" (463), O'Neill acknowledged in private that "Baker had, more than anything else, given him faith in himself" (*O'Neill* 279). Although Baker accepted him for a second year in the playwriting course, O'Neill did not return to Harvard, but instead, after spending the summer in New London, he moved to New York City to write for a magazine. When that position did not pan out, he joined the ranks of the bohemian artists and intellectuals in Greenwich Village and spent much of his time brooding and drinking at an establishment called the Golden Swan, better known as the Hell Hole (*O'Neill: Life* 502). The Hell Hole, along with many of its inhabitants, would later figure into a number of his plays, most especially *The Iceman Cometh*.

It was during this year in the Village that O'Neill met the free-spirited, left-wing activists Jack Reed and Louise Bryant. O'Neill was attracted to Bryant, who was already Reed's lover, but theirs was an open relationship, so it did not deter O'Neill from pursuing her, nor did she discourage him. When Reed and Bryant announced that they were going to spend the summer of 1916 in Provincetown on Cape Cod, O'Neill decided to join them there. This would be a fateful move, as it was in Provincetown that O'Neill would meet another couple, George Cram Cook and Susan Glaspell, who were the combined guiding force behind the Provincetown Players, a group of artists committed to producing theatrical works that challenged all the assumptions of the commercial American theatre.

## THE EARLY YEARS AS PLAYWRIGHT

The Provincetown Players had been producing plays on Cape Cod and in Greenwich Village but were still searching for a distinctive voice.

O'Neill arrived in Provincetown with a collection of one-act plays that he had written during and since his Harvard days. He brought one called "Bound East for Cardiff" for the Players to read aloud and consider for production. A simple play about a sailor named Yank who dies aboard ship, the play evokes a haunting sense of the inevitability of death, the mystery of life, and the power of companionship. After the reading ended, Glaspell is reported to have said of that moment, "Then we knew what we were for" (558); the Players knew they had found their voice. With the production of "Bound East for Cardiff" at the Wharf Theater in Provincetown that summer, O'Neill began his ascent as America's premier dramatist.

The next few years brought productions by the Provincetown Players of several one-act plays written by O'Neill, including those that were subsequently grouped together with "Bound East for Cardiff" as the "Glencairn Plays"—"In the Zone," "The Long Voyage Home," and "Moon of the Caribbees"—as well as other "sea plays," including "Ile" and "Where the Cross is Made," all of which were drawn from O'Neill's experiences at sea. Many of the characters were composites of the men whom he had known aboard ship and in portside saloons. The sea plays were all characterized by a deemphasis of a conventional plot, depending for their effect instead on atmosphere and mood. In these plays, O'Neill captured the ironically lonely camaraderie of men at sea, the frustrating repetition of their confined lives, and the perpetual reality of death. There was a dark, cosmic irony hanging over all of O'Neill's early plays, including others set at sea, such as "Thirst" and "Fog," as well as those not set at sea, such as "The Rope" and "Before Breakfast." This ironic tone would continue to characterize O'Neill's plays throughout his career.

During this period, O'Neill lived in Provincetown in the summers and in Greenwich Village the rest of the time. Soon after he first arrived in Provincetown, in 1916, he became more involved with Louise Bryant and indeed fell in love with her, while she remained in her relationship with Jack Reed. This arrangement proved awkward and difficult for O'Neill, but it continued until Reed and Bryant departed for Russia to observe and write about the Revolution there in the summer of 1917. Then in the fall, at the Hell Hole in New York City, O'Neill met Agnes Boulton, an aspiring pulp fiction writer who resembled Louise Bryant. Within six months, they were married. They soon moved to a house, purchased for them by O'Neill's father, on a section of the dunes in Provincetown known as Peaked Hill Bar; the house had been converted from an abandoned Coast Guard life-saving station. In 1919, their son, Shane, was born.

By 1920, O'Neill had written more than 25 plays, most of them one-acts, and many of them unremarkable in their own right, but of interest, retrospectively, for the signs of what was still to come from the dramatist. Many, but not all, of these plays were produced by the Province-town Players on Cape Cod or in Greenwich Village between 1916 and 1920. Some were produced and then forgotten; others have enduring interest, especially some of the sea plays. By this time, O'Neill was finding the one-act form rather limiting and he began to expand his repertoire. In 1920, O'Neill's first full-length play to be produced, *Beyond the Horizon*, was also his first play to be produced on Broadway. It is the story of two brothers, one suited to a life on the farm and the other to a life at sea, who switch roles for the love of a woman, which leads to disappointment and despair for all concerned. It was both a critical and commercial success, earning O'Neill his first Pulitzer prize and heralding a new era in the American theatre. Even O'Neill's father acknowledged that his son had arrived, proudly congratulating him at the end of the opening performance and tacitly acknowledging the impact the play had had on him. Upon leaving the theatre, the senior O'Neill could not help remarking to his son, "Are you trying to send the audience home to commit suicide?" (*O'Neill* 408).

Ironically, O'Neill's great moment of personal success would be followed by a long period of personal loss. Soon after the opening of *Beyond the Horizon*, James O'Neill suffered a stroke and died, beginning a period of four years during which O'Neill would endure the deaths of all three members of his family of origin. Some time after his father died, his mother (who, contrary to what is suggested in *Long Day's Journey*, had regained her religious faith and overcome her addiction to morphine) and his brother (who had stopped drinking after his father had died) moved to California, where, early in 1922, Ella died, also after suffering a stroke. Her illness and death drove Jamie back to the bottle, and within less than two years, in the fall of 1923, he died of complications from alcoholism. Years later, O'Neill would depict, with a sense of compassion, his brother's final despair in *A Moon for the Misbegotten*.

## THE MIDDLE YEARS OF EXPERIMENTATION

During this period of familial loss, O'Neill completed a number of important plays, including the bold expressionistic experiments *The Emperor Jones* (1920) and *The Hairy Ape* (1921) and the more realistic *Anna Christie* (1920). Opening in Greenwich Village in 1920 and 1922, respectively, and then transferred for successful runs on Broadway, *The Emperor Jones* and *The Hairy Ape* are both evocative, episodic theatrical works that explore the human psyche, taking on provocative social issues regarding race, in the one case, and class, in the other. *Anna Christie* is a more conventional drama, but with a strong female character—a prostitute to boot—at its core, and with its ambiguous ending, it also broke new ground at the time. Some critics, finding more hope in the ambiguous ending than O'Neill intended, condemned the playwright for selling out, an accusation that represented to him a complete misunderstanding of his play, and that led him later to renounce it (Sheaffer, S&A 68). Nevertheless, it was a commercial success on Broadway in 1921 and earned him his second Pulitzer prize.

Aside from stylistic innovations, O'Neill also brought new subject matter to the American stage, both off and on Broadway. In 1923, he completed *Welded* (first produced in Greenwich Village in 1924), an intense drama about marital relations generally believed to reflect aspects of his own marriage to Agnes Boulton, and *All God's Chillun Got Wings* (first produced in Greenwich Village in 1924), a daring drama about miscegenation. In 1924, he completed *Desire Under the Elms* (also first produced in Greenwich Village in 1924), a modern transmogrification of Greek tragedy (primarily drawing on the story of Phaedra and Hippolytus) with highly Freudian overtones. The latter two were the first of O'Neill's plays to cause censorship controversies, in the first case, over a white woman kissing a black man's hand on stage (134–143), and in the second, over what was perceived as the vulgar language and immoral behavior of the characters (164–166). More than 20 years later, a similar controversy accompanied the out-of-town tryouts of O'Neill's final play in his lifetime, *A Moon for the Misbegotten* (595–596).

Although none of these dramas produced in 1924 directly depict O'Neill's own family, each reflects in some way O'Neill's struggle with familial issues, which he was experiencing with particular intensity during these years of personal loss. These plays mark the beginning of what has come to be considered O'Neill's experimental middle period, a time of great productivity for O'Neill. That he was so prolific was perhaps a result of the sublimation of his grief and mourning into his creative work, a process that, as Stephen Black has persuasively argued in his biography, *Eugene O'Neill: Beyond Mourning and Tragedy*, endures for the next two decades and culminates in the highly autobiographical works of his final years.

In the early 1920s, the O'Neills spent summers in Provincetown and winters in New York or Ridgefield, Connecticut. In 1924, O'Neill determined that he did not write as well while living in a cold climate (Sheaffer, S&A 154), so the family moved at the end of that year to Bermuda, in search of an ideal environment to support his writing. The decision to relocate to a warmer climate proved propitious, as O'Neill completed a number of plays there that were highly ambitious in both theatrical form and thematic content. The first of these was *The Great God Brown*, written in 1925 (first produced in Greenwich Village in 1926). In this play, O'Neill experimented most elaborately with masks, using them to convey the distinction between the external and internal lives of his characters. This was followed by *Marco Millions* (first produced on Broadway in 1928), a complicated work that pits East against West in a satire on American capitalist values, and then by *Lazarus Laughed*, a pageant drama set in biblical times with a cast of hundreds, that was virtually impossible to produce (it was mounted in 1928 at a community theatre in California). Together with *The Fountain*, another historical pageant play (which O'Neill completed in 1922 and was produced in Greenwich Village in 1925), which is about the life of Juan Ponce de Leon and the Fountain of Youth, these works constitute a daring attempt by O'Neill to defy the physical limitations of the theatre to capture on stage deep philosophical truths, based largely on the writings of Nietzsche. In these plays, O'Neill challenged stage directors and designers to create theatrical worlds with stunning visual potential, but they had muddled ideas and little of the human drama that had made many of his earlier works so compelling, leaving audiences puzzled and frustrated.

In 1925, O'Neill's second child with Agnes, Oona, was born, and although O'Neill expressed delight at her birth, he by no means adopted a domesticated identity. If anything, by all evidence, he seemed unsuited for fatherhood. In Bermuda, O'Neill left most of the housekeeping and childrearing to Agnes while he devoted himself to writing and unwound by drinking. A binge drinker, O'Neill would remain sober while working on his current project, and when it was complete, he would drink heavily for days and weeks on end. Sometimes he would travel without Agnes and the children to New York to attend to the details of productions of his plays, clearly preferring drinking and carousing with old friends to caring for and playing with his children. Agnes, a writer herself, grew increasingly resentful of the arrangement that allowed O'Neill to nurture his craft, while she was abandoned, with time only to nurture the children.

During this period, in speaking with several psychiatrists and medical doctors and reading materials they provided, O'Neill came to recognize that his habitual excessive drinking was going to kill him; he could either drink or write. His determination to be "an artist or nothing" was strong enough that he was able to stop drinking in 1926. His sobriety became an additional source of tension between him and Agnes, as her enjoyment of drinking was now in conflict with her husband's need to abstain.

In 1927, O'Neill completed *Strange Interlude*, a long drama, more conventional than its immediate predecessors in its focus on identifiable contemporary characters, yet still unconventional in its use of spoken asides to convey the characters' unspoken thoughts. The central character is Nina Leeds, another in a line of O'Neill's complex and captivating female characters, and the play depicts the impact of her grip on the men around her. It was produced on Broadway in 1928. In spite of its extraordinary length—nine scenes, performed in four-and-a-half hours of playing time plus an intermission for dinner—*Strange Interlude* was O'Neill's greatest commercial success during his lifetime, and it earned him his third Pulitzer prize.

As his success and fame grew, and he continued to spend extended periods of time away from the family, his relationship with Agnes suffered, but through all these troubled years, there is no evidence of his infidelity to Agnes until the summer of 1926. While on vacation in Maine, he met a beautiful actress named Carlotta Monterey (who, coincidentally, had appeared as Mildred in *The Hairy Ape* in 1922). Carlotta's attraction to O'Neill led her to pursue a relationship with him. At first he resisted, but flattered by her attention and sensing in her some of the very qualities he found lacking in Agnes (not the least of which was a keen curiosity and concern about his work), he gradually relented. O'Neill claimed that he and Carlotta had not yet slept together at this time, and according to Sheaffer, Agnes accepted that (234–236). O'Neill began to spend a great deal of time with Carlotta whenever he traveled to New York to attend to business regarding publication or productions of his plays, leaving Agnes behind in Bermuda with the children.

The next few years were marked by severe inner turmoil for O'Neill as he struggled with his growing attraction to and involvement with Carlotta and his sense of obligation to Agnes and his family. As his attraction to Carlotta blossomed into love, his obligation to Agnes became less compelling, and he became increasingly alienated, both physically and emotionally, from Agnes and his children. O'Neill's romance with Carlotta began to stir gossip in the press, so early in 1928, to curtail a scandal, O'Neill secretly fled with Carlotta to Europe, which, in those days, would protect them from the gossipmongers in the American media. During their initial stay in England, O'Neill completed *Dynamo*, another expressionistic experiment with technical stage effects in the interest of philosophical discourse, in which the central character, Reuben Light, attempts to find a replacement for God in science and technology. Bogged down by both the machinery and the hazy philosophy, when produced on Broadway in 1929, *Dynamo* was a failure.

Toward the end of 1928, after several months of successfully evading the press while living in England and France, O'Neill and Carlotta sailed to

Asia, where they spent time traveling, and where he fell off the wagon and went on a drinking binge, causing a temporary estrangement from Carlotta and attracting the press coverage he was trying to avoid (314–322). The new year (1929) found them back in Europe, residing on the French Riviera. Because this locale was not isolated enough for O'Neill, however, within a few months, they moved to a château near Tours called Le Plessis. In the summer of 1929, legal proceedings initiated by Agnes finally led to a divorce agreement, which opened the door for Eugene and Carlotta to make official what had now been *de facto* for some time. On July 22, 1929, the couple was married in a simple ceremony in Paris. O'Neill's marriage to Carlotta would be his third and last and would endure for 24 years. In Carlotta, O'Neill finally found what he needed in a woman because she was willing to devote the rest of her life to the support and nurturing of Eugene O'Neill, the artist. O'Neill remained sober for the rest of his life.

From the very beginning, Carlotta began to create the environment that O'Neill needed, as she saw it, by isolating him from those friends and companions whom she perceived as bad influences on him, including most of those from his years in Provincetown and Greenwich Village. This planned isolation began in France and continued after the couple returned to the United States until O'Neill's death. During the two years they lived at Le Plessis, thanks to Carlotta, O'Neill found the solitude he needed to complete a complex new drama that was based on Aeschylus's *Oresteia*. Transferring the story of the House of Atreus to post–Civil War America, O'Neill conceived *Mourning Becomes Electra* as a trilogy that would run over five hours plus a dinner break, once again making great demands on his audiences. Focusing on the story of Electra, O'Neill's version depicts the murder of a Civil War hero, Ezra Mannon, on his return home to New England, by his wife and her lover, who is a cousin of Mannon's. Lavinia (O'Neill's Electra), who loves her father and resents her mother, conspires with her brother to avenge their father's murder. At the end of the trilogy, after a series of murders and suicides, all of the Mannons are dead, except Lavinia, who entombs herself in the family mansion to await her own death. In its concern with fate and free will, passionate feelings, and familial feuds, *Mourning Becomes Electra* presents a dark vision of the human condition in a powerful theatrical package.

As comfortable and isolated as Le Plessis was, as had happened before and would happen again in his life, O'Neill grew restless and needed to move on. Soon after he completed writing *Mourning Becomes Electra*, producers in New York were eager to mount it; and so it was, in this case, the playwright's need to assist with this production that brought the O'Neills back to the United States in 1931. This production garnered the most positive reviews that O'Neill received for any production of any of his plays during his lifetime (387–390).

Once *Electra* opened on Broadway, O'Neill again sought refuge from the distractions of New York City, and on the recommendation of a friend, in March 1932, he and Carlotta moved to Sea Island, Georgia, which Carlotta compared to the "Blessed Isles" of which O'Neill had written in *Mourning Becomes Electra* (Gelbs, *O'Neill* 759). In the home there that Carlotta designed, Casa Genotta, O'Neill labored over *Days Without End*, which he had begun in 1931 and would complete, after many revisions, in 1934. In this play, O'Neill returned to the philosophical and religious themes of *Dynamo* and used expressionistic techniques such as masks, which recall *The Great God Brown*, to depict his characters' dualities and inner realities. Through the plight of the central dual character, John Loving, O'Neill depicts the human quest for faith and meaning, ending with an awkward affirmation of Catholicism that led some observers to wonder if the playwright had regained his faith, a conclusion he denied. Rather, the ambiguities of the play suggest the dramatist's continuing frustrated quest to discover meaning, not just in religion, but in human existence. *Days Without End* was a critical and commercial failure on Broadway, and it was O'Neill's final experiment with expressionism.

In September 1932, O'Neill directed his attention away from that serious play to write *Ah, Wilderness!*, his only comedy. The plot for this play had come to him in a dream (only the second of his plays to be inspired by his unconscious in this direct way, the other being *Desire Under the Elms*). He completed *Ah, Wilderness!* in six weeks and then returned to *Days Without End* (761–762). *Ah, Wilderness!* was produced on Broadway in the fall of 1933 and became O'Neill's second greatest commercial success in his lifetime after *Strange Interlude*. The critics were mixed in their reception of the play, some finding it a surprisingly refreshing change of pace, but others believing it to be disappointingly lightweight (Sheaffer, *S&A* 421). It was a self-confessed nostalgic glimpse at the family life O'Neill wished he had had as a young boy, but neither audience nor critics could know then that it was merely a comic prelude to the more tragic vision of family life that was still to come after an extended period of retreat from the public eye during which he immersed himself in the past.

## THE FINAL WORKS: RETURN TO THE PAST

At first, O'Neill became absorbed in an ambitious project that has come to be known as the cycle plays. Originally conceived as a three-play cycle, called "The Calms of Capricorn," about an Irish family in America from the time of the American Revolution to O'Neill's own time, the project gradually became more focused on the period between the 1850s and his own time, while expanding in scope from three to nine plays. O'Neill changed the cycle title to "A Tale of Possessors, Self-Dispossessed." Although he would complete only one of these plays before his death (*A Touch of the Poet*), he developed elaborate scenarios and wrote drafts of many of them, and a great deal of this work was painstakingly accomplished while O'Neill lived at Sea Island. He settled into a routine at Casa Genotta that consisted of rising early in the morning and writing until past midday; swimming, reading, gardening, fishing, and/or sunning after lunch; conversing with Carlotta over tea in the late afternoon; socializing, reading, or playing cards with Carlotta after dinner; and then retiring early (Gelbs, *O'Neill* 795–796). This routine enabled O'Neill to meet the formidable challenge he had imposed on himself in conceiving and writing the cycle: "A lady bearing quintuplets is having a debonair, carefree time of it by comparison" (805). The hot climate in Georgia did not make the grueling work he was doing any easier. By the end of the summer of 1936, the O'Neills once again packed their bags and moved on, this time crossing the country to live in the cooler Northwest, settling initially in Seattle, Washington.

They rented a house near Seattle and while living there in the fall, O'Neill received word that he would be the recipient of the 1936 Nobel prize for literature, which that year carried a monetary award of $40,000. O'Neill was only the second American (the first being Sinclair Lewis in 1930) and the first American dramatist to receive the Nobel prize. To this day, he remains the only American dramatist to be so honored, and remarkably, at the time of the award, he had not yet written his greatest works. Not feeling up to making the journey to Stockholm to receive the prize at a ceremony in December, O'Neill wrote a speech that was read for him, in which he paid tribute to August Strindberg, the native son of the Nobel host country, Sweden, as the major influence on his own work as a dramatist: "For me, [Strindberg] remains...the master, still to this day more modern than any of us, still our leader" (814). A week after his speech was read in Stockholm, the playwright and his wife, having decided that Washington State was too damp and cool for them, headed south to make a new home in northern California.

With the $40,000 from the Nobel prize, the O'Neills built yet another house, in the San Ramon Valley east of Oakland, designed by Carlotta, this time with an Eastern influence and called Tao House. During his years at Tao House (1937–1943), O'Neill found the seclusion he needed to retreat fully into his past, putting aside the cycle plays and focusing his attention on three dramas that were extremely personal and explicitly autobiographical. These three dramas—*The Iceman Cometh, Long Day's Journey Into Night,* and *A Moon for the Misbegotten*—would come to be regarded as his masterpieces. How fitting it was that the money from the 1936 Nobel prize was used to build the house in which he would write the works that would ultimately confirm the wisdom of the Nobel committee in awarding him the prize.

In *The Iceman Cometh,* O'Neill drew on his memories of the Hell Hole and other such establishments in New York City, and the desperate people who frequented them, to create a complex ensemble drama in which the characters try to make their miserable lives meaningful by believing in "pipe dreams." The central character, Hickey, challenges their self-deceptions, and through the resulting conflicts, O'Neill, more compellingly than in any of his other dramas, brings to the stage the philosophical core of the mystery of the human condition in the twentieth century. Like some of O'Neill's middle plays, *The Iceman Cometh* is long, running approximately four hours. Some observers have disparaged it as long and repetitious, but O'Neill steadfastly refused to cut it and defended its length as integral to its effectiveness.

In *Long Day's Journey Into Night,* the dramatist looked back at his own troubled family of origin—as he himself put it in his dedication of the former play to Carlotta, "with deep pity and understanding and forgiveness" (O'Neill 714)—and created a family drama rich in insights into family dynamics, human behavior, and again, the human condition. In this play, the four members of the Tyrone family (unmistakably based on the four O'Neills) endure a single day in the summer of 1912 (that fateful year in the playwright's own life) during which the mother relapses into an addiction to morphine, the younger son is diagnosed with tuberculosis, and the three men—alcoholics all—drink excessively, all of which triggers and facilitates familiar patterns of denial, guilt, and blame that lock all four characters together in what appears to be a hopeless descent into lonely despair. Once again, O'Neill would try his audience's endurance; in production, *Long Day's Journey Into Night* would run more than four hours.

*A Moon for the Misbegotten* is the lyrical story of the doomed love affair between Jim Tyrone (a very close likeness of O'Neill's brother Jamie) and Josie Hogan (the final and most compelling of the playwright's female characters, ultimately representing the all-forgiving mother that O'Neill so desperately sought in his own life). The drama reaches its climax in a long monologue in which Tyrone confesses his transgressions against his mother after her death and reveals the intense self-hatred that has frozen his spirit. The forgiveness and blessing that Josie bestows upon Tyrone in the end enable him to die in peace, and on another level enable O'Neill himself to die in peace 10 years later, never having written another word for the stage after Josie's final blessing.

In addition, during the Tao House years, O'Neill put the finishing touches on the only completed cycle play that survived him, *A Touch of the Poet*, which stands on its own as a minor masterpiece. He also completed one shorter play, *Hughie*, in a projected cycle of one-acts that was to be called "By Way of Obit." *Hughie* similarly stands well on its own, independent of its projected cycle, and is very much akin to *The Iceman Cometh*.

Set in the early nineteenth century, *A Touch of the Poet* marks the time in the planned sequence of plays when the Yankee Harford family meets the Irish Melody family through the union of Sara Melody and Simon Harford. Simon remains unseen offstage throughout the play, but Sara anticipates the social advancement that her marriage to Simon will mean for her and her family. Meanwhile, however, her father becomes the central figure in the play, as he struggles mightily with the conflict between his presumptuous identity as a gentleman and his status in America as an immigrant Irish peasant. In the dynamic between father and daughter, O'Neill anticipates both the philosophical debate about pipe dreams in *The Iceman Cometh* and the moving father-daughter dynamic in *A Moon for the Misbegotten*.

A remarkably modest work in length at this stage in O'Neill's writing, but just as remarkably ambitious in its dramaturgy, the one-act *Hughie* marks the playwright's return to the dramatic form with which he had launched his career, now with the full powers of his mature dramaturgical skills at his command. As in *Iceman*, in *Hughie*, O'Neill draws on his memories of the seedy New York City hotels and rooming houses of his nomadic youth. Here in the lobby of such a hotel, Erie reminisces about his relationship with the former night clerk, Hughie, who has died, while the new night clerk, Hughes, listens, distracted by the sounds of the city and his own thoughts. Ahead of its time, O'Neill's concept demands a multimedia production for a complete depiction of the consciousness of each character and the loneliness of the individual within the modern urban environment. O'Neill reiterates in this play what is implicit at the end of *The Iceman Cometh*, that loneliness can be relieved by companionship and the mutual reinforcement of illusions that give meaning to life.

O'Neill's productivity during the Tao House years has been largely attributed to Carlotta's stewardship. She played the gatekeeper at Tao House, vigilantly keeping most visitors away and approving the few people who could visit and when. She established an environment in which O'Neill was able to occupy himself in the daily routine necessary for his writing, similar to the routine he had established at Casa Genotta. The O'Neills rarely traveled and barely ventured beyond the gates of their property during this period. Because Tao House was not near the ocean, they built a swimming pool so that Eugene could have his daily swim on the grounds, looking out over the San Ramon Valley. He also found great pleasure in the companionship of their Dalmatian, Blemie, who had been their loyal pet since their days at Le Plessis in France, as well as in the music he played on the antique player piano called Rosie, which had been a birthday gift from Carlotta while they still lived in Georgia (Gelbs, *O'Neill* 776).

Although O'Neill did not meet his first son, Eugene Jr., until the boy was 12 years old, their relationship grew as the two grew older, and in fact, O'Neill helped pay for his son's education at Yale. Just before the O'Neills moved to Tao House, in 1936, Eugene Jr. earned his doctorate in classics and then gained a position on the classics faculty at Yale, where he began to establish a reputable career as a scholar in his own right. Eugene Jr. visited several times at Tao House. O'Neill had less of a relationship with his other two children, partly because of the uncomfortable nature of his divorce from their mother and partly because Carlotta had no fondness and little tolerance for anyone associated with the playwright's turbulent earlier years who might somehow threaten the tranquility she had established and maintained. In spite of her trepidations, Carlotta did allow his children to have some contact with their father, and during the Tao House years, both Shane and Oona visited them, although neither received very much attention from their father.

In 1942, O'Neill expressed annoyance when he learned that Oona, in her last year of high school, was getting press coverage as a debutante, which he considered frivolous, and he resented her exploitation of his name recognition for such purposes (842). Within a year, O'Neill would turn his back entirely on his daughter after learning that she had married Charlie Chaplin, a man his own age. He had no comment for the press about the wedding, and he never spoke to his daughter again (852). Oona and Chaplin had eight children, but O'Neill never knew these grandchildren. Oona died in 1991.

O'Neill and Carlotta continued to have intermittent contact with Shane. After he married, Shane and his wife Catherine occasionally had dinner with the O'Neills, but the relationship came to an end in 1946 after Shane's two-month-old son, Eugene O'Neill III, died of asphyxiation (which today would have been identified as sudden infant death syndrome or SIDS) (868–869). The last O'Neill heard of his youngest son was in 1948, when he learned of Shane's heroin addiction. O'Neill did not offer to help him (896); in 1977, Shane committed suicide by jumping from the fourth-floor window of an apartment building in New York (Shepard 44).

These years at Tao House were difficult for O'Neill. His health was failing, as he suffered from a number of different ailments, Most significantly, the tremor that had begun to plague him some years before was becoming more severe, symptomatic of the progressive disorder, originally diagnosed as Parkinson's, that would eventually prevent him from writing altogether. O'Neill was also deeply troubled by deteriorating conditions in the world, as Hitler marched through Europe, the Japanese bombed Pearl Harbor, and the United States entered World War II. The intensely personal nature of the plays he was focusing on during these years, however, made the creative process itself hardly an escape from these external sources of woe; in fact, his work seemed to deepen his malaise. The Gelbs cite Carlotta's observation: "'At times I thought he'd go mad,' Carlotta recalled. 'It was terrifying to watch his suffering'" (*O'Neill* 836).

In spite of his emotional anguish and physical debilitation, however, and driven by the need to write these plays, O'Neill completed *The Iceman Cometh* in 1939, *Long Day's Journey Into Night* in 1941, *A Touch of the Poet* and *Hughie* in 1942, and *A Moon for the Misbegotten* in 1943. By the time he completed all of these works in 1943, he had not had a play of his produced in 10 years. He was awaiting the end of the war to have *The Iceman Cometh* produced, and he had no intention of ever having *Long Day's Journey Into Night* produced. In fact, he stipulated that it was not to be published until 25 years after his death. At this time, his tremor was worsening significantly, and he now found it nearly impossible to write. In the summer and fall of 1943, he suffered several illnesses and required increased medical attention, and Carlotta found it increasingly difficult to maintain the house. So once again, the O'Neills became unable to remain in the home that they had created, and by the end of 1943, they had put Tao House up for sale and planned to move to a hotel in San Francisco. The six years they lived at Tao House was their longest stay in any single residence; it was to be the last house they would live in that would give them any semblance of "home" for any significant amount of time. When World War II ended in 1945, the O'Neills headed back East to live once again in New York City.

## THE FINAL YEARS

Over the next few years, while living in New York, O'Neill was somewhat reinvigorated by the prospect of seeing productions of three of the Tao House plays. His anticipation of renewed activity on the theatre scene, however, was frustrated, by lukewarm critical receptions, threatened censorship, and his own failing health. *The Iceman Cometh,* produced on

Broadway in 1946, was not critically well received and closed after 136 performances; and *A Moon for the Misbegotten*, causing controversy in Detroit and St. Louis, closed out of town. O'Neill was too ill to travel to the tryout locations, and after these initial setbacks, he insisted that the productions of both *Moon* and *A Touch of the Poet* be delayed until his health improved (884–885). This was never to happen, and neither play would be produced before his death in 1953. In fact, no play of his would again be produced in his lifetime.

Life in New York City brought turbulence, and even separation for a time, to the relationship between O'Neill and Carlotta. In 1948, they agreed to another attempt to restore their life together by seeking the kind of seclusion that had previously brought them more peace, so in October of that year, the O'Neills moved into a house on the ocean north of Boston in Marblehead, Massachusetts, where O'Neill hoped to begin writing again. He still had voluminous notes and drafts for the cycle, which had by this time, in his mind, expanded to 11 plays, as well as outlines for other plays. His tremor was so severe at this time, however, that he eventually had to accept that writing was impossible. He was doomed to spend his time in Marblehead sitting and gazing out at the sea, perhaps "beyond the horizon"; virtually his only pleasure was entertaining occasional visitors.

As his own physical and mental status deteriorated during the time at Marblehead, he received news in the summer of 1950 that his eldest son, Eugene Jr., had committed suicide. O'Neill had had great respect for his son's academic and intellectual accomplishments and might have seen more of him had it not been for Carlotta's increasingly exclusionary control of his life. Like his father, Eugene Jr. struggled with alcoholism, but unlike his father, he was unable to escape the grip of his addiction. Although alcohol was not the cause of his death (he slit his wrists and ankle in the bathtub), the note he left behind with an empty bourbon bottle tellingly stated, "Never let it be said of O'Neill that he failed to finish a bottle" (904). His son's suicide deepened O'Neill's melancholy during this trying time in his own life. Most of the time that he and Carlotta spent in Marblehead was tense and explosive. It ended in the winter of 1951 with both of them being hospitalized, he for treatment of a broken leg and she for treatment of mental distress.

After a few months of separation, during which both Carlotta and O'Neill were under doctors' care, they were reconciled again, and in May, they moved into the Shelton Hotel (today a Boston University dormitory) overlooking the Charles River in Boston. Here O'Neill would live out the last days of his life, passing much of his time looking out the window at the Charles River. Three significant events occurred during their two-and-a-half years at the Shelton. First, O'Neill rewrote his will, excluding his children and making Carlotta his sole beneficiary and executor, which gave her singular authority over all his surviving works. Second, to ensure that no one would ever try to complete his unfinished plays, he and Carlotta tore all his remaining manuscripts up and burned them, except for a draft of one drama, *More Stately Mansions*, which somehow survived. It was to be the play that would immediately follow *A Touch of the Poet* in the cycle, focusing on the struggle between the poet and the materialist in American culture, represented by Simon Harford, whose self-identity is complicated by his conflicted relationships with his wife, Sara, and his mother, Deborah. In 1967, with Carlotta's permission, *More Stately Mansions* was published and produced on Broadway as a "new play by Eugene O'Neill," much to the chagrin of those who do not consider the edited version to be truly O'Neill's, even if based on the playwright's notes. Finally, in November 1953, as O'Neill lay dying from complications of pneumonia, according to Carlotta, he sat up in bed and spoke his final words: "Born in a hotel room—and God damn it—died in a hotel room!" (939). O'Neill died on November 27, 1953, and with Carlotta keeping details from the press, he was buried in a very small private ceremony at Forest Hills Cemetery in Boston.

After his death, an autopsy revealed that O'Neill had not suffered from Parkinson's disease, as his malady had originally been diagnosed, but rather, from a rare neurological disorder, symptomatically similar to Parkinson's, which caused gradual degeneration of motor functions, but had no effect on mental activities. The autopsy report merely confirmed what Carlotta, in particular, had witnessed during the last decade of the playwright's life, which was the pained frustration of a man in full control of his extraordinarily fertile and active mind, yet physically unable to perform those operations necessary to bring the products of that active mind to fruition (941).

By the time of his death in 1953, then, it had been a full 10 years since he had written any new plays and 7 years since anything new he had written had been produced, the last having been poorly received productions of *The Iceman Cometh* and *A Moon for the Misbegotten*. Although there had been some press coverage of his stormy marriage with Carlotta, she had managed to keep him out of the public eye and to keep his death and funeral arrangements sufficiently private so that his passing went remarkably unnoticed by the American public, especially for a man who was still the only American dramatist to have ever won the Nobel prize for literature.

## POSTSCRIPT

This public neglect would change in 1956, when a director named José Quintero visited Carlotta and received her permission to mount a new production of *The Iceman Cometh* at the Circle in the Square in New York City. That production, which would launch the career of an unknown actor named Jason Robards Jr., was a huge success and rekindled interest in O'Neill. That interest was fully ignited after Carlotta agreed to allow Quintero to direct *Long Day's Journey Into Night* later in 1956.

O'Neill had decreed that *Long Day's Journey Into Night* was never to be produced and to be published only 25 years after his death. Carlotta claimed, however, that O'Neill had insisted on delaying publication and prohibiting production only to protect Eugene Jr.'s privacy, but that after his son's death, the playwright had approved its earlier release. O'Neill never communicated any such change of heart to executives at Random House, which is where he originally sent the manuscript with the instructions to seal it. Insisting on her authority as the sole executor of his estate, including all of his written and published works, Carlotta brought the manuscript to the Yale University Press for publication (for whom it became a bestseller) and agreed to allow the Royal Dramatic Theatre in Sweden to produce the play in 1956. She then granted permission to Quintero to direct it at the Circle in the Square in New York City the same year. O'Neill was posthumously awarded his fourth Pulitzer prize for *Long Day's Journey Into Night* in 1957. The careers of both Quintero and Robards (who played Jamie) would become forever linked to the works of O'Neill, as both seemed to discover a profound connection to the playwright and the man.

Many other accomplished actors would hone their craft and scale new heights confronting the challenge of performing in O'Neill's plays, including Geraldine Fitzgerald, Colleen Dewhurst, Katharine Hepburn (on film), Vanessa Redgrave, Frederic March, Sir Lawrence Olivier, Jack Lemmon, Al Pacino, Brian Dennehy, Peter Gallagher, and Kevin Spacey. During O'Neill's lifetime, several of his plays were made into movies, including *The Emperor Jones, Anna Christie, Desire Under the Elms,* and the Glencairn plays. O'Neill was not involved in writing the screenplays for, or in other aspects of, these productions; he had mixed reactions to them, but he did earn some profits from them. Among these films, *Anna Christie* is probably the most notable, but more because it was the first "talkie" in which Greta Garbo appeared than because it was based on O'Neill's play. The most well-known and critically acclaimed of all the film versions of his plays is the posthumous 1962 production of *Long Day's Journey Into Night* directed by Sidney Lumet and featuring Katharine Hepburn and Jason Robards.

Although to this day, there is still disagreement and uncertainty about whether or not Carlotta was justified in overturning the stated wishes of her husband, most scholars agree that the course of American drama would likely have been very different had *Long Day's Journey* not been published until 1978, as the playwright originally had stipulated. Whether or not she had her husband's blessings to do so when Carlotta released the play in 1956, she gave the American theatre, indeed the world theatre, a tremendous gift. With the publication and production of this monumental drama, O'Neill's stature in the American theatre was revived and his legacy ensured.

## WORKS CITED

Black, Stephen A. *Eugene O'Neill: Beyond Mourning and Tragedy.* New Haven: Yale University Press, 1999.

Gelb, Arthur and Barbara. *O'Neill.* New York: Harper & Row, 1962.

———. *O'Neill: Life With Monte Cristo.* New York: Applause Books, 2000.

O'Neill, Eugene. *Complete Plays 1932–1943.* Ed. Travis Bogard. New York: Library of America, 1988.

Sheaffer, Louis. *O'Neill: Son and Playwright.* Boston: Little, Brown, & Co., 1968.

———. *O'Neill: Son and Artist.* Boston: Little, Brown, & Co., 1973.

Shepard, Richard F. "Shane O'Neill, Playwright's Son, Suicide; Life was Dominated by Father's Themes." *New York Times*, 7 Dec. 1977, 44:1.

# 2

# Literary Heritage

## IN AND OUT OF THE SHADOW OF THE FATHER

To understand Eugene O'Neill's literary heritage, one need not look much further than the two plays he wrote about his youth in New London. Both *Ah, Wilderness!* and *Long Day's Journey Into Night* are rife with allusions to the literary works that gripped and inspired the aspiring young writer. In *Ah, Wilderness!* all of the books in Richard's library that shock his mother—including those by Wilde, Shaw, Kipling, and Khayyam—are validated by his literate and relatively open-minded father; and when Richard returns home drunk, he pays tribute to Ibsen with a reference to "vine leaves in his hair" from *Hedda Gabler.* In *Long Day's Journey,* there are quotes and references to some of these and other writers, and the dramatist actually places many of the works themselves, as if in tribute, on display in the bookcases on stage. From the three sets of Shakespeare in one case to the philosophical writings of Nietzsche and the plays of Ibsen and Strindberg in the other, an observer might discern the vast and eclectic range of styles and ideas represented there and therefore in the minds of the people who have read them. The stage directions indicate that all of these books "*have the look of having been read and reread*" (CP 1932–1943 717), and although the young O'Neill himself may not have read every single one of them, there is ample evidence that he read many of them; those he did not read, his brother or father most certainly read and quoted from. More than anything else, this book collection and his relationship with the man who lorded over it—his father, as suggested by the depiction of James Tyrone—had the greatest influence on the writer that Eugene O'Neill was to become.

For all of the intense bickering that dominates so much of *Long Day's Journey Into Night*, one of the bonds that ties the Tyrone family together (or at least the male Tyrones) is a love of literature. This affection is revealed through the many literary allusions and recitations throughout the drama, surely among the fonder memories that the mature playwright drew on when recalling his own family "with deep pity and understanding and forgiveness" (714). The other bond, of course, is the theatre itself. For the offspring of James O'Neill—not just an actor, but a proud and demonstrative man of the theatre—talk of the theatre and indeed performance itself were as much a part of the atmosphere of their youth as the air around them. Both sons rebelled against their father and his theatre. Jamie O'Neill vacillated, and at times tried to adapt, but in the end, he rejected (and was rejected by) his father's world. Eugene O'Neill, steadfast in his rejection and rebellion at first, ironically adapted in the end in a way that was to change that world forever. Just as the portrait of Shakespeare hanging over the bookcase in the Tyrones' living room suggests the undeniable influence of the Bard (Berlin 5), so, too, does the depiction of James Tyrone suggest the formidable influence of O'Neill's father and his theatre (i.e., nineteenth-century melodrama) on the development of America's preeminent dramatist.

O'Neill wrote a good deal of poetry as a young man before and during the time when he began writing plays, and he wrote a few short stories as well during his early years as a playwright. His plays, with their voluminous and detailed stage directions, sometimes read like novels, yet it was his keen sense and affinity for theatrical effect and character development that made him most comfortable with dramatic form, and it was his conflicted relationship with his father that made the dramatic form simultaneously the most familiar and the most challenging to him. He was determined to move beyond the superficialities of the American theatre of his time and to delve more deeply into the realities of human experience and consciousness. Although he was influenced in his approach to this challenge by contemporary European dramatists who were experimenting with techniques of realism, expressionism, and symbolism, he also knew that there were aspects of his father's melodrama that made for gripping theatre, and he did not hesitate to use these. It is ironically fitting, then, that underlying many of O'Neill's most daring experiments with form are plots built on some of the basic elements of melodrama, such as contrived plot twists (*Anna Christie, Mourning Becomes Electra*) and heightened passions (*Strange Interlude, Desire Under the Elms*).

O'Neill learned the tricks of the theatrical trade at his father's knee, but he also inherited a love for literature and reading that empowered him to use these practical devices in new and interesting ways. Those 50 volumes of "the World's Best Literature" and the three volumes of Shakespeare in his father's bookcase, along with a heavy dose of the classics in his four years at Betts Academy and an early affinity for modern literature, sowed the seeds for a lifelong love of reading. O'Neill's extensive reading expanded his intellectual reach beyond the limitations of a short-lived formal education to help shape a body of work that exhibits threads of influence by and confluence with a broad range of literature and discourse, from Greek tragedy and philosophy through American transcendentalism and Freudian psychology.

## MELODRAMA

In the late nineteenth century, at the time of O'Neill's birth, melodrama dominated the American stage. Simply put, melodrama emphasizes plot over character; uncomplicated bad characters threaten uncomplicated good characters, and through a contrivance of circumstances, the good characters triumph in a happy ending. Melodramatic situations provoke heightened emotions in the characters, fear and revenge being the most common. O'Neill was too interested in and perceptive about character to subordinate it entirely to plot, and none of his characters is simply good or bad. His early one-acts were mostly character sketches and atmospheric plays. When he began to write longer plays, he still did not write melodramas, but he turned to some of the devices of melodrama to engage his audiences in stories that were to reveal depth of character and provoke thought about timely social issues, as well as timeless universal questions about the human condition. The scholar Michael Manheim, who has written extensively about O'Neill's use of melodrama, has implicitly associated this development in the dramatist's style with his complicated relationship with his father James O'Neill by noting his increased use of these melodramatic devices in the years after his father's death.

In *Beyond the Horizon,* two brothers, in effect, exchange identities for the love of a woman, leading the one to sea who should remain at home. In *Anna Christie,* a young woman who has turned to prostitution because of mistreatment by relatives in the Midwest returns to the East Coast and her father, who believes she is a wholesome Midwestern girl; she falls in love with a hearty Irish seaman rescued aboard her father's barge in a storm. In *Desire Under the Elms,* a young man lusts after, and falls in love with, his father's new young bride; the young lovers have a child, whom the mother murders to prove her love in the face of accusations of betrayal and deceit. In *Mourning Becomes Electra*, a woman, after having fallen in love with her husband's estranged cousin, plans the murder of her husband when he returns from war; her children then avenge the murder of their father by killing their mother's lover, which leads their mother to kill herself, and subsequently her son, wracked by guilt, does the same. Even the final play O'Neill wrote, *A Moon for the Misbegotten*, has melodramatic plot elements: a landlord threatens to foreclose on the property of a tenant farmer and his daughter, so the farmer conspires with his daughter, who is in love with the landlord, to trick him into sleeping with her in order to blackmail him into allowing them to keep their farm.

Although each of these stories has the makings of a melodrama, in O'Neill's hands, they become more complicated dramas, and even reach for tragedy, on a very basic level, because the characters are not simply black or white and the endings are not simply happy. Although *Anna Christie* appears to have a happy ending when Anna and Burke agree to marry, on more careful consideration, the ending is understood as ambiguous, which defies melodrama. The misinterpretation of the ending as happy was a source of great frustration for O'Neill. Also, there are no bad guys who are responsible for the plight of the good guys in these plays. The suffering of the central characters in these plays has a source outside of the cast of characters. In *Anna Christie*, that source is identified clearly and repeatedly by Chris, as "dat ole davil, sea," but it is less explicitly understood in O'Neill's other plays as something akin to the ancient Greek notion of Fate.

## GREEK TRAGEDY

O'Neill's drama has several marks of a writer who studied classical literature, which he did as a young boy at Betts Academy; he was especially familiar with Greek tragedy. The notion of the unities of time, place, and action, based on the writings of Aristotle, is apparent throughout much of O'Neill's drama. Although several of his lesser works, such as *Marco Millions* and *Lazarus Laughed*, and even some of the better ones, such as *The Hairy Ape* and *Strange Interlude*, have multiple and far-flung (in a few of these cases, some might even say far-fetched) settings, many, and especially his last, and greatest, full-length plays—*A Touch of the Poet*, *The Iceman Cometh*, *Long Day's Journey Into Night*, and *A Moon for the Misbegotten*—have a single set. Furthermore, the action of all of these final plays takes place within no more than 48 hours, and three—*Poet*, *Long Day's Journey*, and *Moon*—within 24 hours. Just as in *Oedipus Rex*, on which

Aristotle modeled his theories, although the single action of each of these plays takes place within the span of a single day, or at most, two, a lifetime of behavior and interactions unfolds. As in the Greek tragedies, the past is key to understanding the present, and the family is the microcosm through which much of human behavior can be observed. In Greek tragedies, the gods influence human actions and fate is predetermined. In O'Neill's plays, no gods pull the strings, but human beings do struggle with the conflict between free will and a sense of predetermination, not imposed by any gods, but by some force seemingly beyond human knowledge and control.

Like Arthur Miller after him, O'Neill was inspired by the challenge of writing modern American tragedy, which means imagining ordinary people as tragic figures, as America, by its very nature, disavows royalty, a prerequisite for a tragic hero in Greek drama. In facing this challenge, during his middle period of experimentation, O'Neill wrote two plays about ordinary Americans that explicitly pay homage to the classical Greek notion of tragedy, drawing specifically on the myths and mythical characters of Greek drama.

In *Desire Under the Elms*, O'Neill used the story of Phaedra and Hippolytus, as well as that of Medea, and to some extent, Oedipus, as the basis of his tale of greed and lust in nineteenth-century New England. In the first myth, a woman lusts after her stepson, kills herself rather than face public humiliation and rebuke, and then leaves behind a note accusing the stepson of raping her. In the second, a woman kills her children in vengeance against her husband. In the third, in attempting to defy a holy oracle, a man fulfills it, killing his father and marrying his mother. O'Neill incorporates all of these storylines, with slight variations, and the heightened passions that drive them, in his story of the Cabots. Abbie Putnam lusts after her stepson, Eben, who hates his father and has an intense attachment to his late mother; Abbie provokes the jealousy of her husband by lying about Eben's unwanted advances and in the end kills her own child to prove that she loves Eben.

*Mourning Becomes Electra* is O'Neill's most ambitious, and to a large degree, most successful attempt to modernize a Greek tragedy by transporting the story of the House of Atreus to New England just after the Civil War, and focusing on the character of Electra to tell a modern story of familial strife, jealousy, love, hate, sin, and repentance. In this case, O'Neill adapts the story almost wholesale, in trilogy form: the war hero (Agamemnon/Mannon) returns home to betrayal and murder at the hands of his wife (Clytemnestra/Christine) and her lover (Aegisthus/Brant), then to be avenged by his two children (Electra and Orestes/Lavinia and Orin), one of whom (Orestes/Orin) will subsequently be tormented by guilt. In the original, Orestes and Electra murder both Clytemnestra and Aegisthus, whereas in O'Neill's version, Orin and Lavinia murder only Brant, which drives Christine to kill herself. Similarly, in the original, the Furies drive Orestes mad, whereas in O'Neill's version, Orin's guilt drives him to commit suicide. In the most important and interesting variation from the original, whereas the central character of *The Oresteia* is Orestes, the central character of O'Neill's drama is the Electra figure, Lavinia. The only surviving member of the family at the end, she entombs herself in the family mansion, closing all the doors and windows and vowing to terminate the family curse by doing penance alone with the family ghosts until the end of her days, thus imbuing the female with the power to determine the family's ultimate fate.

Both plays have formal elements that further highlight the association with Greek tragedy. For one thing, in both, the townspeople play the role of the Greek chorus. In *Desire Under the Elms*, they appear only in part 3, scene 1, as the guests at Cabot's party to celebrate the birth of his son. In this scene, much like the chorus in a Greek tragedy, their suspicions about the truth of the situation foreshadows the strife and misery to come. This is their only function in the play, and although several speak individually, each serves only the choral function of the group.

O'Neill expanded the use of this device in *Mourning Becomes Electra*, in which each of the three plays in the trilogy begins with a fairly lengthy scene involving a group of townsfolk. These townsfolk not only provide exposition about the Mannons that helps the audience follow the storyline, but they also comment on the behavior of members of the Mannon family in ways that suggest the sociocultural and moral context of their actions and help to guide the responses of the audience. O'Neill has gone so far in *Electra* as to create a figure who does stand out from the group, thus approximating the role of the choragos in Greek tragedies. Seth, the Mannons' groundskeeper and handyman, appears in all three parts of the trilogy. He interacts not only with other townsfolk as part of the choral interludes but also with the main characters, and in particular, provides counsel to the central figure, Lavinia, whom he seems to favor among all the Mannons. Although no gods intervene in human affairs in O'Neill's drama, his ordinary characters experience the same heightened passions and commit the same awful acts as the characters of Greek mythology, thus elevating them to a similar tragic stature.

Another favorite device of O'Neill's that seems to be derived from Greek drama is the mask. Although O'Neill's preoccupation with masks speaks more to his desire to capture modern psychological insights on stage than the influence of classical literature, some influence is culturally undeniable. In his oft cited "Memoranda on Masks," O'Neill argues that "the mask *is* dramatic in itself, *has always* been dramatic in itself, *is* a proven weapon of attack" (407). Although he refers to the traditions of masks in Japanese Noh drama, Chinese theatre, and African culture, but omits any explicit reference to ancient Greek drama, it seems unlikely that he meant to exclude the Greek use of masks when he claims that the "main values" of mask drama are "psychological, mystical, and aesthetic" (407). In fact, he explicitly cites the Greeks in his defense of the use of masks against those who object that they belittle the skills of actors: "After all, masks did not extinguish the Greek actor, nor have they kept the acting of the East from being an art" (411).

O'Neill argues for the usefulness of masks to the modern dramatist, as they help to "express those profound hidden conflicts of the mind which the probings of psychology continue to disclose to us." He observes further that "one's outer life passes in a solitude haunted by the masks of others; one's inner life passes in a solitude hounded by the masks of oneself" (406–407). Beginning with *The Emperor Jones* in 1920 and ending with *Days Without End* in 1933, O'Neill used actual masks on stage to convey the split consciousness of individual characters, the most elaborate experiment with this device being *The Great God Brown*. In other plays, he used devices that reflected the same dramaturgical goals, such as the spoken asides in *Strange Interlude*. In *Mourning Becomes Electra*, the dramatist made a conscious decision *not* to use actual masks (409), but instead, throughout the drama, describes characters' faces as "mask-like" and makes a point of the facial resemblances among members of the Mannon family.

## SHAKESPEARE

Based on the exchanges between the father and his two sons in *Long Day's Journey Into Night*, it is more than reasonable to expect to find a connection between the works of O'Neill and the works of William Shakespeare. Tyrone is Shakespeare's advocate throughout the play, quoting him several times, and the sons are most often countering their father's optimistic read of Shakespeare's philosophy with their own cynicism taken from modern writers. A fine example of this occurs in act 4, when Edmund tries to express his affinity for the fog, and his father recommends Shakespeare's "We are such stuff as dreams are made on, and our little life is rounded with a sleep." Edmund then reframes Shakespeare to capture his feeling more accurately: "We are such stuff as manure is made on, so let's drink up and forget it" (CP *1932–1943* 796). The most moving revelation in Tyrone's monologue later in act 4 is that he now regrets having bought the rights to the commercial melodrama that has enslaved him financially to a single role and prevented him from realizing his potential as "one of the three or four young actors with the greatest artistic promise in America," and he cites the praise he received from Edwin Booth for his performance as Othello 38 years in the past as the high point of his career (809). Finally, Edmund (who represents the playwright in his younger days) reveals his own facility with Shakespeare's verse when he reminds his father of the time he won a bet by learning and reciting perfectly the whole role of Macbeth (799), which surely seems like an implicit acknowledgement by the mature dramatist that Shakespeare's works live within him and inform his drama.

The scholar Normand Berlin has written extensively on this connection in his book *O'Neill's Shakespeare,* in which he documents numerous allusions to Shakespeare's plays in the plays of O'Neill. He discusses *Long Day's Journey* at length and finds many connections in O'Neill's other works, as well. In his discussion of Mary in *Long Day's Journey,* Berlin points out that in addition to the obvious association Jamie makes between his mother and *Hamlet's* Ophelia when he announces her entrance late in the play with, "The Mad Scene. Enter Ophelia!," there is also an allusion here to Lady Macbeth (220–221). Lady Macbeth can also be recognized in the earlier *Mourning Becomes Electra* as Lavinia urges Orin on to murder Brant in retribution for his adulterous affair with their mother that has led to the murder of their father. Orin has misgivings and is later wracked by guilt over his actions, yet Lavinia, like Lady Macbeth in the early going, seems driven to take action, unperturbed by any moral questions. Unlike Lady Macbeth, however, Lavinia never struggles to wash her hands of the blood of her victims. She refuses to consider suicide as an option, but rather faces a crueler self-inflicted punishment in the end when she locks herself within the darkness of the family home to live with her demons until the time of her natural death. Berlin's book provides a wealth of fascinating evidence of the O'Neill-Shakespeare connection.

O'Neill was not the master of the English language that Shakespeare was, but he had a similarly acute instinct for what works in the theatre. In his ambition to write plays exploring the larger questions about the human condition (the relation between man and God), and with his psychological insights into family conflicts, as well as in his overarching desire to be "an artist or nothing" as a dramatist, O'Neill was certainly inspired by Shakespeare and his works. O'Neill is arguably one of only two dramatists writing in the English language (George Bernard Shaw being the other) whose canon reflects a variety of characters and content and a breadth of dramaturgical talent comparable to that of William Shakespeare.

## MODERN DRAMA: NATURALISM AND EXPRESSIONISM

Realism in European drama lagged behind the realistic movement in fiction. Many of the novels by the French realists Balzac, Stendhal, and Flaubert, for instance, had appeared by the 1850s, whereas Ibsen first introduced social realism to the theatre in the late 1870s. Similarly, realism in American drama lagged behind the realistic movement in American fiction. The works of novelists like Mark Twain, William Dean Howells, and Henry James in the last few decades of the nineteenth century, and Jack London in the first decade of the twentieth, had already shifted the direction of American fiction toward realism. By the turn of the century, several playwrights, including Howells, James A. Herne, and William Gillette, were producing drama with some characteristics of realism. Howells, however, was much more accomplished as a novelist than a dramatist, and the others were theatre professionals whose talents as playwrights were limited, and their plays are of only historical interest. It was not until O'Neill's sea plays were first produced by the Provincetown Players in 1916 that realism, modeled on the European version pioneered by Ibsen and Strindberg, truly arrived on the American stage.

An avid reader, inclined to be a writer, nurtured on theatre culture, and disillusioned with the melodramas of his father's theatre in America, the young O'Neill was inspired by new developments in European theatre, and especially by the works of those two Scandinavian playwrights who brought realism and expressionism to the stage. When O'Neill received the Nobel prize for literature in 1936, he paid homage to the Swedish dramatist, August Strindberg, as he recalled in his acceptance speech: "It was reading his plays when I first started to write, back in the winter of 1913–1914...that above all else, first gave me the vision of what modern drama could be, and first inspired me with the urge to write for the theater myself" (Gelbs, *O'Neill: Life* 404). It was around the same time, in the late 1930s, that O'Neill similarly acknowledged the impact on him of Strindberg's Norwegian contemporary, Henrik Ibsen, as he recalled the experience of seeing a production of *Hedda Gabler* repeatedly for 10 nights in 1907: "It gave me my first conception of a modern theater where truth might live" (226). It can be said that Ibsen and Strindberg, the fathers of modern drama, begat O'Neill, who was to become the father of American drama.

Ibsen's realistic plays like *A Doll's House* and *Ghosts* challenged traditional Victorian notions about marital gender roles and sexual behavior. Respectable middle-class characters suffered from venereal disease, and truthful revelations provoked reactions that did not necessarily lead to happy resolutions. It is fair to say that when Ibsen's Nora slams the door on her husband and their marriage at the end of *A Doll's House*, Ibsen opened the door for a long line of fiercely independent, although often conflicted, female characters on the world stage, including those of O'Neill. The reverberations of Nora's slammed door can be heard most explicitly in Anna's vernacular in act 3 of *Anna Christie* when she rebukes both her father and her lover for assuming they can control her:

> You was going on 's if one of you had got to own me. But nobody owns me, see?—'cepting myself. I'll do what I please and no man, I don't give a hoot who he is, can tell me what to do! (*CP 1913–1920* 1007)

This declaration underlies the independent thinking and behavior of other O'Neill women, including Nina Leeds in *Strange Interlude*, Lavinia Mannon in *Mourning Becomes Electra*, and Josie Hogan in *A Moon for the Misbegotten*. In addition to challenging traditional notions of gender role identity, O'Neill did not hesitate to confront audiences with socially uncomfortable situations that they were unaccustomed to seeing depicted on stage, such as the marriage of a black man and a white woman in *All God's Chillun Got Wings*. In these characters and situations, O'Neill's plays reflect the social realism introduced by Ibsen.

Naturalism is a form of realism that is distinguished largely by its partiality to the seamier side of life and its adherence to a Darwinian belief in determinism. In his early drama, Strindberg was inspired by the naturalist movement, especially regarding the philosophical orientation, most apparent in plays like *The Father, The Stronger,* and *Miss Julie*. In *Miss Julie*, a socially forbidden love affair between a young woman and her servant unavoidably ends in her fall (and presumed suicide), the conclusion predetermined by the social and psychological forces driving the two characters. This pattern is evident in many of O'Neill's plays. For instance, from the outset, the illicit relationship between Eben and Abbie in *Desire Under the Elms* seems doomed, and, as in *Miss Julie*, the social and psychological forces inevitably drive the characters into extreme actions, in this case, Abbie's murder of their baby son.

Like Strindberg, O'Neill was interested in the apparent paradox between the belief in free will and the role of predetermination in human affairs. It is implicit in Hickey's confessional monologue at the end of

*The Iceman Cometh*, as he explains how he came to murder his wife, Evelyn, and it is a source of continuous inner turmoil for Mary Tyrone in *Long Day's Journey:*

> None of us can help the things life has done to us. They're done before you realize it, and once they're done they make you do other things until at last everything comes between you and what you'd like to be, and you've lost your true self forever. (*CP 1932–1943* 749)

This metaphysical dilemma—inherent to naturalism—lies behind the struggle of many of O'Neill's characters to understand their own actions.

O'Neill's drama also shares with that of Strindberg a fascination with the so-called battle between the sexes. The most commonly noted parallel is the one between Strindberg's *The Stronger* and O'Neill's early one-act play, "Before Breakfast" (1916), in which a nagging woman, Mrs. Rowland, drives her husband, who never appears on stage (except for his hand reaching out from the bathroom at the end), to suicide. The scholar Travis Bogard has elaborated on the ways in which the sexual battle revealed through her extended monologue (an interesting dramaturgical experiment in itself, which paved the way for O'Neill's later use of lengthy monologues) seems to have been directly inspired by O'Neill's familiarity with the Strindberg play (76–78). In *Welded* (1923), O'Neill drew on aspects of his own relationship with Agnes in another naturalistic drama of marital strife written, as Bogard puts it, "in Strindberg's vein" (184).

One of the devices O'Neill used for naturalistic effect in *Welded* is the pause, a device that is integral to the naturalistic drama of turn-of-the-century Russian dramatist, Anton Chekhov. Through stage directions that repeatedly indicate pauses and silences, Chekhov calls attention to the inarticulateness of his characters and to the reality that conversations among people rarely consist of eloquent and witty repartee, but more often, are characterized by extended periods of awkward silence. Often the unspoken subtext reveals more than the spoken text. Similarly, for O'Neill, silence provides a means by which to probe beneath the realistic surface and into the depths of his characters' consciousness. In this movement beyond what O'Neill saw as superficial realism to what he called "supernaturalism," he cast his work in the same mold as much of the naturalistic drama of Strindberg and Chekhov (186–187).

O'Neill followed another tenet of naturalism in his depiction of the lower strata of society, especially in his early sea plays, set aboard ship and in seedy saloons, and then finally, and most elaborately, in *Hughie* and *The Iceman Cometh*, the latter most strikingly similar to *The Lower Depths* by another Russian naturalistic playwright, Maxim Gorky. The realistically detailed depiction of common people is also a feature of the ethnic drama with which O'Neill is most closely associated by his Irish ancestry. The scholar Ed Shaughnessy has cited a remark O'Neill once made to his son, claiming that "the most important thing about me and my work [is] the fact that I am Irish" (137).

O'Neill's deep sense of fatalism and his resulting dark sense of ironic humor are firmly rooted in his Irish heritage, as is his disdain for the arrogance of (Yankee/British) privilege and his intolerance of oppression. In 1911, while he was barely surviving on the streets of New York, he made a point of seeing all the productions by the Abbey Players of Dublin, who were touring the United States. Among the works by Irish dramatists such as Yeats, Lady Gregory, and T. C. Murray, those by J. M. Synge, such as *Playboy of the Western World* and *Riders to the Sea*, had the greatest impact on O'Neill. This influence is observable in the commonplace settings of his plays and the ordinary people who populate them and speak the local vernacular. Furthermore, in *Riders to the Sea* in particular, the characters have a fateful, almost mystical, bond to the sea, born of their island-bound culture, with which O'Neill strongly identified and which is crucial to understanding a number of his characters from Chris Christopherson to Edmund Tyrone. Finally, O'Neill was enchanted and inspired by the naturalistic acting style of the Abbey Players (Sheaffer, *S&P* 205). Later in his life, O'Neill would express admiration for the works of the Irish playwright Sean O'Casey, who once told O'Neill, "You write like an Irishman, not like an American," a remark that the American dramatist reportedly took as a great compliment (Gelbs, *O'Neill* 788).

Many of the naturalistic dramatists whom O'Neill admired eventually turned to techniques of expressionism and symbolism to continue their theatrical explorations beneath the surface of human behavior. So, too, did O'Neill. Like Strindberg and Ibsen, he created a dreamlike atmosphere in some plays, like *The Hairy Ape* and *The Emperor Jones*, which also adhered to the episodic structure and, to some extent, the use of archetypes for characters, typical of German expressionism. Although these two plays are the purest examples of O'Neill's foray into expressionistic drama, most of the experimental techniques he used in the plays of his middle period—masks, spoken asides, episodic structure, archetypal characters, sound effects—were indicative of O'Neill's dedicated attempts to plumb the depths of consciousness through expressionistic staging.

Also, like both of his Scandinavian idols, as well as the Russian Chekhov and the Irish Synge and O'Casey, O'Neill overlaid his naturalistic dramas with heavy doses of symbolism, often conveyed through visual and aural stage effects. In Chekhov, it is the orchard and the sound of an ax cutting down trees; in Synge, it is the sight and sound of women keening; in O'Neill, it is the fog and the sound of a foghorn, or the sound of a beating tom-tom. In all cases, these sounds can be traced to realistic sources, while at the same time representing something deeper and richer, like the unavoidable march of progress, the cruel certainty of death, or "hopeless hope." In all of this, O'Neill conceived his plays as "behind-life" drama, a term he applied to the movement toward expressionism in modern drama launched by Strindberg (Bogard 187).

## AN AMERICAN VOICE

O'Casey's comradely praise notwithstanding, there are many aspects of O'Neill's drama that place him firmly within the American literary tradition. For one thing, many of his plays focus on an individual on some kind of quest, either one that involves conquest and subordination of others, such as that of Marco Polo in *Marco Millions* and Brutus Jones in *The Emperor Jones,* or one of self-discovery, such as that of Yank in *The Hairy Ape* and Hickey in *The Iceman Cometh.* Sometimes, as in the cases of both Jones and Yank, the quest functions on both an external and internal level (and O'Neill accomplishes this dual effect by means of expressionistic devices). The stories of these characters are not unlike those of some of the best-known heroes of American fiction, such as Huck in Twain's *Huckleberry Finn* and Captain Ahab in Melville's *Moby Dick.* The concept of "rugged individualism," popularized by Herbert Hoover in 1928, and valuing self-sufficiency above all else, vividly comes to life in the character of Ephraim Cabot in *Desire Under the Elms,* and the socialistic brand of rugged individualism associated with the heroes of Jack London's fiction emerges in Yank of *The Hairy Ape.* In fact, Yank and the men in the sea plays, as well as several later characters such as Adam Brant and even Edmund Tyrone to some extent, suggest the strong influence on O'Neill of London's romantic spirit of adventure, which O'Neill admired and emulated as a young man. (Joseph Conrad, although not an American, was another writer whose adventurous life and stories inspired the young O'Neill and had a lasting impact on his works.)

Many of O'Neill's characters are spiritually nourished by another current in American cultural history, transcendentalism, which is most closely identified with a group of nineteenth-century New England writers, Ralph Waldo Emerson and Henry David Thoreau being the best known of them. The transcendentalists, drawing their inspiration from the British romantic poets, sought spiritual fulfillment by striving beyond the limitations of the flesh and the physical world into a state of oneness with nature. Many of O'Neill's characters express this kind of sentiment or experience this feeling, from several of the seamen in the sea plays to Robert Mayo in *Beyond the Horizon* and Paddy in *The Hairy Ape*; the reclusive Simon Harford in *A Touch of the Poet* and *More Stately Mansions* is also conceived in this tradition of the romantic American hero/poet. It is Edmund Tyrone in *Long Day's Journey Into Night* who captures the sentiment most eloquently. Speaking of his experience lying on the deck aboard ship at night, he tells his father in act 4:

> I became drunk with the beauty and singing rhythm of it, and for a moment I lost myself—actually lost my life. I was set free! I dissolved in the sea, became white sails and flying spray, became beauty and rhythm, became moonlight and the ship and the high dim-starred sky! I belonged, without past or future, within peace and unity and a wild joy, within something greater than my own life, or the life of Man, to Life itself! To God, if you want to put it that way. (*CP 1932–1943* 812)

Although Edmund dismisses his own words as "stammering...the native eloquence of us fog people" (812–813), it is hard to imagine a passage that conveys the spirit of American transcendentalism more effectively. Edmund's eloquence would have appealed to Walt Whitman, another American poet associated with transcendentalism, but also with the democratic ideal that encourages the spirit to soar in all Americans, from those who live in the mountains to those who dwell in the fog.

In his fascination with the power and mystery of the sea, O'Neill certainly displays an affinity with Melville that goes beyond the idea of the quest, with echoes of the voluminous *Moby Dick* in the obsessive behavior of Captain Keeney in the simple one-act "Ile," and of the shorter Melville work *Typee* in Orin's yearnings to escape to the south sea islands in O'Neill's voluminous *Mourning Becomes Electra*. Although O'Neill never found a place to call home during his lifetime, from the dialect of many of his characters to the settings on farms and at or near the sea to the themes of guilt, retribution, and salvation to the quest for self-knowledge, self-sufficiency, and indeed for home itself, his works unmistakably identify him as a New England writer.

## PHILOSOPHICAL COMRADES

Whereas Strindberg was O'Neill's dramaturgical master, Friedrich Nietzsche was his philosophical guru. Disillusioned with Catholicism at an early age, O'Neill was searching as a young man for a belief system to help explain what he experienced as the mysteries of existence, and he found the basis for such a system in the works of Nietzsche, *Thus Spake Zarathustra* and *The Birth of Tragedy* in particular. The nineteenth-century German philosopher wrote of the Apollonian/Dionysian dichotomy and balance within human consciousness (equated broadly with the human impulses toward the rational and emotional). The conflict between the Dionysian and Apollonian spirits is played out in many of O'Neill's dramas, but it lies at the heart of *The Great God Brown,* in which he used masks to represent the Nietzschean schism within his central character, Dion Anthony. O'Neill sought to integrate the Dionysian and Apollonian to achieve the effect that Nietzsche admired in Greek tragedy. One vivid example of this effect is the final scene of *The Iceman Cometh,* depicting simultaneously the Dionysian revelry of the patrons of Harry Hope's and the Apollonian contemplation of Larry Slade.

O'Neill identified strongly with Nietzsche's notion that human beings can realize truly meaningful insights only while in a Dionysian state of exhilaration (not unlike intoxication). The mystical experience of Dionysian transcendence is expressed by a number of O'Neill's characters, but it is conveyed most articulately by Edmund in *Long Day's Journey Into Night,* as he recalls the feeling he has had several times in his life while "swimming far out, or lying alone on a beach" (presumably reflecting O'Neill's own experiences and feelings as a young man):

> For a second you see—and seeing the secret, are the secret. For a second there is meaning! Then the hand lets the veil fall and you are alone, lost in the fog again, and you stumble on towards nowhere, for no good reason! (CP 1932–1943 812)

Complete with its allusion to the veil of Mâyâ, this Nietzschean passage acknowledges O'Neill's frustration and disappointment with the transient nature of the transcendent experience. It also suggests the conflict between Eastern and Western religious thought that the scholar James A. Robinson has identified throughout O'Neill's canon in his book, *O'Neill and Oriental Thought: A Divided Vision.*

Nietzsche's philosophy was derived to a large degree from Eastern religious beliefs, which undoubtedly was in part responsible for O'Neill's interest in Hinduism, Buddhism, and Taoism, all of which he studied. As Robinson observes, the tenets of these religions inform many of O'Neill's plays:

> From the early sea plays through the final tragedies…O'Neill's affinity to Eastern mysticism informs his dynamic vision of reality, influences the values and attitudes of his protagonists, and shapes the symbolism and structure of entire plays. (3)

These Eastern belief systems figure most prominently in the plays of O'Neill's middle period, such as *The Fountain, Marco Millions,* and *Lazarus Laughed.* It is also, of course, no accident that O'Neill named his final home in Danville, California, in which he wrote his last and greatest plays, Tao House.

One of Nietzsche's best-known statements—"God is dead"—underlies the origins of existentialist philosophy, which became popularized by the French philosopher Jean-Paul Sartre and others in the mid-twentieth century. As the scholar Linda Ben-Zvi points out, *Thus Spake Zarathustra* is an important work cited by Martin Esslin as an inspiration in developing his theory about the "theatre of the absurd," a dramaturgical movement linked closely to existentialist philosophy. As Ben-Zvi observes, there is much evidence in O'Neill's works that the playwright was sympathetic to the tenets of existentialism, although the specific term had not yet been coined at the time, and that his drama, with its Nietzschean undertones, anticipates Esslin's theatre of the absurd: "His plays have within them the awareness of modern futility and the need to find dramatic articulation of this nullity.... They are also important as historical foreshadowings of the theater that was to follow, the theater of Beckett, of Pinter, and later of Shepard and Mamet, a theater that O'Neill may in part be responsible for foretelling, even for influencing" (54).

O'Neill's extensive reading led him down diverse and interesting philosophical paths, including those that were emerging as the dominant strains of Western thinking in the early twentieth century. Darwin's ideas about evolution were already current by the turn of the century, and their impact on O'Neill is evident in his use of naturalism, with all its implications about the predetermined nature of human actions, and the nagging feeling conveyed by characters in so many of his plays (sometimes explicitly and sometimes not) that some fatelike force is shaping human affairs. This force is, in some cases, represented by an external entity, such as "dat ole davil, sea" in *Anna Christie,* but it manifests itself mostly as psychological determinism, functioning within the characters' psyches; in *Long Day's Journey,* it is identified as "the past." Darwin's theories are at the core of the quandary that plagues a number of O'Neill's characters. The moral implications of Darwinian determinism suggest that human beings cannot be held responsible for their actions and therefore have nothing about which to feel guilty or to blame others. Yet, a profound and persistent sense of sin and guilt (perhaps born of the playwright's Catholic upbringing), as well as empirical evidence of free will, makes exoneration unattainable. Mary Tyrone explains to Edmund: "It's wrong to blame your brother. He can't help what the past has made him. Any more than your father can. Or you.

Or I" (*CP 1932–1943* 751). Yet it is impossible for Mary not to feel guilty and blame others.

Although not primarily a political writer, O'Neill was not unaffected by the ideological reverberations that rattled the world during his lifetime, most of which were based on, or in reaction to, the writings of Karl Marx. As a young man, O'Neill traveled in leftist circles, read the works of radical thinkers, and was associated most famously (and to some, infamously) in those days with Louise Bryant and Jack Reed, the journalist who wrote *Ten Days that Shook the World*, a sympathetic account of the Bolshevik revolution in Russia in 1917. Marxist/socialist ideology is explicitly (if not always most articulately) espoused or at least implicitly couched in anticapitalist rhetoric in several of his plays, such as *The Hairy Ape, Marco Millions, Ah, Wilderness!*, and *The Iceman Cometh*. The works of Marx are among the books that appear in the smaller bookcase on the set of *Long Day's Journey Into Night*, evidently suggesting a formative role in the intellectual development of the younger generation of Tyrones and therefore reflecting Marx's place in the intellectual life of the playwright himself.

In various letters and communications with friends and associates, O'Neill often expressed his disappointment with American society for its failure to live up to its potential, a failure he attributed to the spiritual and moral price of the hegemony of materialistic values in a capitalist society. This theme is apparent to some degree in almost all of O'Neill's plays and is highlighted in such works as *The Emperor Jones, The Hairy Ape, Desire Under the Elms, Marco Millions*, and *The Iceman Cometh*. It was to be the central focus of the projected cycle, "A Tale of Possessors, Self-Dispossessed." O'Neill once observed that his theme for the cycle is most clearly captured in a biblical passage: "For what shall it profit a man if he gain the whole world and lose his own soul?" (Sheaffer, *S&A* 442).

Next to Darwin and Marx, the third major current of twentieth-century thinking flows from the works of Sigmund Freud, and given the primacy of psychology in O'Neill's drama, it is not surprising that the Freudian current is the most dominant of the three. O'Neill read Freud's work, which was especially popular with his friends and colleagues in his days with the Provincetown Players. Furthermore, he consulted with psychiatrists on several occasions about his drinking and his nerves, and he underwent brief psychoanalytic treatment with one of them. Sheaffer reports that when this psychiatrist who treated him informed him that he had an Oedipus complex, O'Neill joked that the doctor could have learned that by reading his plays (190).

Indeed, his plays are populated with characters who seem like textbook case studies of Freud's theories regarding the ego, id, and superego;

transference and countertransference; the pleasure principle; the death wish and of course, the Oedipus complex. During his middle experimental period, O'Neill seemed particularly engaged by the latter concept, as both Eben Cabot in *Desire Under the Elms* and Orin Mannon in *Mourning Becomes Electra,* and in a different way, Charles Marsden in *Strange Interlude,* all display symptoms of the Oedipus complex (in addition, Lavinia personifies the so-called Electra complex, a term coined by Freud's disciple, Carl Jung, to categorize a girl's infatuation with her father and hatred of her mother, the female equivalent of the Oedipus complex). In addition, as the Gelbs point out, a number of the spoken asides in *Strange Interlude* incorporate Freudian language to analyze the behavior of other characters, using terms such as *love objects, realizes subconsciously,* and *taboos* (O'Neill 631).

On several occasions, especially in relation to *Desire Under Elms* and *Strange Interlude,* O'Neill denied Freud's influence on his writing. Regarding himself as an "intuitively keen analytical psychologist" (577), he resented the notion that he needed to know Freud's theories to write his plays as he had: "I feel that although [*Interlude*] is full of psychoanalytical ideas, still these same ideas are age-old to the artist and that any artist who was a good psychologist...could have written 'S.I.' without ever having heard of Freud, Jung, Adler & Co." (631). Even granting that there may have been more direct influence than acknowledged by O'Neill, the confluence between Freud's ideas and O'Neill's theatrical depiction of human behavior is remarkable. Both men had astute insights into the human psyche, but each channeled those insights into a different medium. Although surely merely a coincidence, it is interesting to note in this context the initials of the playwright's full name: E.G.O.

## O'NEILL'S INFLUENCE ON AMERICAN DRAMA AND CULTURE

From 1916, when his first play was produced, until 1936, when he received the Nobel prize, it is difficult to imagine that anyone writing for the theatre in the United States could not have been influenced, in some way, by O'Neill. Those in the Provincetown Players with whom he collaborated in the early years—most notably, Susan Glaspell—benefited most immediately and directly from his innovations and success, and he paved the way for others to write serious drama later in the period and beyond, among them Elmer Rice, Maxwell Anderson, Clifford Odets, Lillian Hellman, William Saroyan, and Thornton Wilder. In the 7 years or so before O'Neill's death, during which time nothing new of his was produced, his reputation waned somewhat. Simultaneously, two new playwrights established themselves as major voices on the American stage. By 1953, Tennessee Williams had made a distinctive mark with *The Glass Menagerie*(1944) and *A Streetcar Named Desire* (1947), and Arthur Miller had produced *All My Sons* (1947) and made theatrical headlines with *Death of a Salesman* (1949).

Some were quick to dismiss O'Neill in those days, but the critic John Gassner came to the playwright's defense in 1951, as reported by Sheaffer:

> Noting that some of the new generation thought that O'Neill's crown had descended on Tennessee Williams...or Arthur Miller...Gassner was reminded of "the neo-classic playwrights who succeeded the 'noble brood' of Shakespeare and his fellow Jacobeans after 1660. They are free from the awkwardness of the giants," Gassner adds, "but they are not giants." (*S&A* 662–663)

In the mid-1930s, Miller himself had considered O'Neill's work "archaic," but by the late 1940s, in spite of the poor 1946 production of *The Iceman Cometh*, Miller recognized more to admire in O'Neill (Miller 228–229). Later in life, in an interview in *Humanities* magazine, he acknowledged O'Neill as a model in the struggle to overcome the forces of commercialism in the American theatre to produce serious plays (Miller, Interview). Williams was impressed from an early age with productions of O'Neill's plays that he saw, and he later paid tribute to O'Neill's triumph over his internal demons in the service of his art with words that the Gelbs chose to conclude the first volume of their revised O'Neill biography: "O'Neill gave birth to the American theater and died for it" (*O'Neill: Life* 640).

Both Williams and Miller continued to write poignant and evocative plays well into the second half of the twentieth century, and in Miller's case, even into the early years of the twenty-first. Their drama shares with O'Neill's a seriousness of purpose characterized by, among other things, a focus on families and family dynamics, an attempt to define tragic vision in the lives of ordinary Americans ("Attention must be paid," as Miller's Linda Loman puts it), and the depiction of the human struggle to find meaning in an apparently meaningless existence. Many theatre historians and critics now group Williams and Miller with O'Neill as the dominating triumvirate of American drama, although some would still agree with Gassner that O'Neill remains the giant among them, if for no other reason than that he was the first.

It has become impossible to write for the theatre in America without, in some way, confronting the shadow of O'Neill; all the major dramatists of the second half of the twentieth and early twenty-first centuries have done so, either explicitly in their comments or implicitly in their plays. It is not necessarily a matter of direct influence, but rather, the delineation of a wide dramaturgical and theatrical path down which all American dramatists now walk.

Edward Albee has written several intense family dramas, and the use and effects of alcohol influence the behavior of a number of his characters. In addition, an important theme in his plays is the notion that people depend on illusions to protect them from the painful reality of their lives. All of these O'Neillian ingredients are combined with greatest effect in Albee's best-known play, *Who's Afraid of Virginia Woolf?* Similar dramaturgical heights are scaled by Sam Shepard in his powerful family dramas, such as *True West*, in which sibling rivalry erupts in violence only suggested by O'Neill in *Long Day's Journey*, and *Buried Child*, in which, like Albee, Shepard links illusion and hope with family offspring, but in a way that places the dead baby at the center of the family more than O'Neill did with Eugene in *Long Day's Journey*. In a different vein, David Mamet has created a potent and vulgar drama centered around male characters who speak a crude and obscene language that makes O'Neill's seamen, bums, and derelicts sound like schoolboys. His real estate brokers in *Glengarry Glen Ross* clearly mark the sociocultural descent of the American salesman, both literally and as a metaphor for human beings within the capitalist system. They trace their theatrical lineage through Willie Loman in Miller's *Death of a Salesman* to their progenitor, O'Neill's Hickey in *The Iceman Cometh*.

August Wilson boldly imagined a historical cycle of plays chronicling the African American experience in the United States in the twentieth century, much like O'Neill's projected cycle about the Irish American experience in the United States. Unlike O'Neill, Wilson was able to complete the 10-play cycle, culminating with *Radio Golf*, produced in 2005, the year of Wilson's death. Within this cycle, Wilson has written moving family dramas, such as *Fences*, that raise philosophical/spiritual questions about the meaning of an individual life and the man-to-God relationship within a specific ethnic milieu. Even Neil Simon, a popular playwright who mostly writes in a mode very different from that of O'Neill, has found his way to O'Neill's path in his series of family plays—*Brighton Beach Memoirs, Biloxi Blues,* and *Broadway Bound*—in which the central character is (coincidentally?) named Eugene, and the three plays combined are called "The Eugene Trilogy." In the final play, in particular, the comic dramatist treads into O'Neillian territory in depicting, more seriously than he usually does, the marital strife between the father and mother, as well as the tender, but somewhat conflicted, relationship between mother and son.

Surely O'Neill's truthful depiction of alcoholism and its effects in so many of his plays and of morphine addiction and its effects in *Long Day's*

*Journey Into Night* opened the door for numerous dramatic writers to portray the lives of alcoholics and addicts seriously and with graphic detail on stage. This influence is seen in such plays as Jack Gelber's *The Connection* (1959), Albee's *Who's Afraid of Virginia Woolf* (1962), and even Jonathan Larson's musical *Rent* (1996), and on screen, in films like *Easy Rider*(1969), *The Panic in Needle Park* (1971), and *Trainspotting* (1995).

O'Neill's currency in popular culture during his own time is evident in the Marx Brothers' 1934 film, *Animal Crackers*, at the moment when Groucho turns to the camera and does a deadpan imitation of the spoken asides from *Strange Interlude*. No less impressive is the reference to O'Neill in Cole Porter's hit song, "You're the Top." In a litany of items valued by the singer to which he compares the object of his affection, is "an O'Neill drama." O'Neill has had an unexpected impact on popular culture in more recent times, as well. Although the language of O'Neill's plays is often leaden and awkward, as several critics (most pointedly, Mary McCarthy) have charged, and few lines from his plays are well known or often quoted, as, for instance, are so many of those of Shakespeare, yet O'Neill's unique play titles have made their mark in popular culture. The O'Neill scholar and founding editor of *The Eugene O'Neill Review*, Frederick Wilkins, once called on readers to note newspaper and magazine headlines that use, or allude to, O'Neill's titles, yielding numerous examples such as several ice hockey stories headlined with some version of "The Iceman Cometh," a story about tax evasion called "The Taxman Cometh," and a weather forecast of continuing cloudy weather entitled "Long Daze Journey."

Finally, perhaps O'Neill's legacy lies most notably in the story of the American family as it has been depicted on stage and screen. A common notion in American culture is that the American family has become dysfunctional in the modern era. As industrialization and technology, as well as other social forces, have imposed new strains on the fabric of the American family, the resulting bruises and scars have been substantial, and an emerging openness in the culture has allowed those wounds to be exposed. Films like *The Great Santini* (1979), *Ordinary People* (1980), *American Beauty* (1999), and *Little Miss Sunshine* (2006) have joined the ranks of the dramas of Miller, Williams, Albee, and Shepard, and more recently, of playwrights such as Nicky Silver, Adam Rapp, and Jon Robin Baitz in an ongoing dramatic dissection—tragic, comic, and satiric—of the so-called dysfunctional American family. Unlike family sitcoms of the 1950s and 1960s that idealized family life, popular television programs of recent years—dramas, comedies, and "dramadies"—about the family, such as *Married . . . with Children*, *The Simpsons*, *Desperate Housewives*, *Six Feet Under*, and *The Sopranos*, are more truthful. They recognize that although bonds are strong, families are flawed, and they depict the struggles with self-identity that inevitably threaten to tear families apart, in spite of those strong bonds. Before there were the Simpsons, the Sopranos, and the desperate families on Wisteria Lane, there were the Tyrones.

One of the most interesting and important dramatists at the turn of the twenty-first century is Tony Kushner, whose major opus to date, *Angels in America: A Gay Fantasia on National Themes*, about AIDS and the political/ moral/spiritual corruption of America in the 1980s and at the end of the millennium, is as dramaturgically bold and thematically challenging as O'Neill's most ambitious dramas were. In 2003, Kushner wrote an essay in the *Times Literary Supplement* called "The Genius of O'Neill," in which he pays tribute to O'Neill:

> Much that an American playwright needs to know can be learned by study-ing Eugene Gladstone O'Neill's life and work....He exhorted himself to write better, dig deeper, and he did.
>
> ...in a play called *Fog*, O'Neill wrote a stage direction which could be used now to describe Eugene O'Neill's centrality in American drama, his inescapable presence in our national theatrical imagination, earned by vir-tue of his identification of our "native eloquence": "...the genius of the fog...broods over everything." (248, 256)

Before Williams, Miller, Albee, Shepard, Wilson, Kushner, and all the oth-ers, there was Eugene Gladstone O'Neill.

## WORKS CITED

Ben Zvi, Linda. "O'Neill and Absurdity." *Around the Absurd: Essays on Modern and Postmodern Drama*. Eds. Enoch Brater and Ruby Cohn. Ann Arbor: The University of Michigan Press, 1990. 33–35.

Berlin, Normand. *O'Neill's Shakespeare*. Ann Arbor: University of Michigan Press, 1993.

Bogard, Travis. *Contour in Time: The Plays of Eugene O'Neill*. New York: Oxford University Press, 1988.

Gelb, Arthur and Barbara. *O'Neill*. New York: Harper & Row, 1962.

———. *O'Neill: Life With Monte Cristo*. New York: Applause Books, 2000.

Kushner, Tony. "The Genius of O'Neill." *The Eugene O'Neill Review* 26 (2004): 248–256.

Manheim, Michael. "O'Neill's Transcendence of Melodrama in *A Touch of the Poet* and *A Moon for the Misbegotten*." *Critical Approaches to O'Neill*, edited by John H. Stroupe. New York: AMS Press, 1988 <http://www.eoneill. com/library/on/ manheim/mfm_crit.htm>.

Miller, Arthur. Interview with William R. Ferris. *Humanities* Magazine, March-April 2001 <http://www.neh.gov/ whoweare/miller/interview.html>.

———. *Timebends: A Life*. New York: Grove Press, 1987.

O'Neill, Eugene. *Complete Plays 1913–1920*. Ed. Travis Bogard. New York: Library of America, 1988.

———. *Complete Plays 1932–1943*. Ed. Travis Bogard. New York: Library of America, 1988.

———. "Memoranda on Masks." *The Unknown O'Neill: Unpublished or Unfamiliar Writings of Eugene O'Neill*. Ed. Travis Bogard. New Haven: Yale University Press, 1988. 406–411.

Robinson, James A. *Eugene O'Neill and Oriental Thought: A Divided Vision*. Carbondale: Southern Illinois University Press, 1982.

Shaughnessy, Edward L. "O'Neill in Ireland: An Update." *The Eugene O'Neill Review* 22 (1998): 137–156.

Sheaffer, Louis. *O'Neill: Son and Playwright*. Boston: Little, Brown, & Co., 1968.

———. *O'Neill: Son and Artist*. Boston: Little, Brown, & Co., 1973.

# 3

# *Anna Christie* (1920)

With only a few exceptions, in his earliest efforts at playwriting, O'Neill developed his dramaturgical skills within the relatively modest context of the one-act play. In many of his early naturalistic one-acts that are set at sea, O'Neill created characters based on people he had met in his seafaring days, several of whom were to reappear in more complex guises in his later plays. He also explored many of the ideas that were to become major thematic concerns in his more mature and ambitious dramas. Although he won his first Pulitzer prize for his first successful and critically acclaimed full-length play, *Beyond the Horizon*, it was *Anna Christie*, for which he won his second Pulitzer prize, that gained O'Neill more widespread popularity (albeit somewhat ironically). *Anna Christie* also marks the transition from his early naturalistic period to his middle experimental period, with its bold depiction of a realistic, strong female character at the center of a metaphysical drama set aboard a barge where the firm security of the land meets the mysterious force of the sea.

A few of O'Neill's plays, such as *Desire Under the Elms* and *Ah, Wilderness!*, came to him virtually ready-made, requiring little revising and completed within weeks. Most others, such as *Mourning Becomes Electra* and *Long Day's Journey Into Night*, involved months, even years of conceiving, writing, and revising. *Anna Christie* is the earliest example of a work with which O'Neill struggled long and hard, in this case, even publishing an earlier version of it with a different title. In 1919, O'Neill completed a play called

*Chris Christopherson*, later shortened to *Chris*, which depicted the story of a bargeman and his daughter, a stenographer, who falls in love with an American sailor against the wishes of her father. Considering *Chris* a failed "technical experiment" (Sheaffer 10), O'Neill put that play aside, and within the next year, he began again with the same basic story. Now, though, he made the daughter a prostitute who had been abused by the family to whom her father had sent her for safety, and her love interest became a charismatic Irish stoker, rather in the tradition of J. M. Synge's Christy Mahon in *The Playboy of the Western World*. The new version took its title from the female character, Anna Christie, suggesting a shift in perspective in the dramatist's approach to the material (Gelbs 435). Both plays—*Chris* and *Anna Christie*—exist in print, but only the dramaturgically superior *Anna Christie* continues to be produced. *Chris* remains interesting primarily as an early draft of the better play, which reveals insights into the playwright's craft.

*Anna Christie* has proven to be one of O'Neill's most enduring plays, certainly of his earliest works. It forever has a place in American cultural history, for it is the 1929 film version of *Anna Christie* in which Greta Garbo, in the title role, spoke her first words on the silver screen: "Gimme a whiskey—ginger ale on the side.... And don't be stingy, baby" (O'Neill 968). Beyond that, however, for its fine storytelling, its rich characters, its striking theatricality, and its suggestive ambiguities, it is often produced and it rewards further study.

## SETTING AND PLOT DEVELOPMENT

*Anna Christie* is a sea play; three of its four acts are set aboard the barge *Simeon Winthrop*. Although the barge is not "at sea," but rather, "at dock"—first in Provincetown, Massachusetts, and then in Boston—in all three acts, the stage directions include auditory reminders of the sea setting. In act 2, in Provincetown, "*The doleful tolling of bells, on Long Point, on ships at anchor, breaks the silence at regular intervals*" (979); in act 3, in Boston, "*From the harbor and docks outside, muffled by the closed door and windows, comes the sound of steamers' whistles and the puffing snort of the donkey engines of some ship unloading nearby*" (993); and in act 4, still in Boston, "*The whistles of steamers in the harbor can be heard*" (1013). Although the locale changes from New York to Provincetown to Boston, the sounds of the harbors, as well as Chris's repeated mantra, "dat ole davil, sea" and complaints about the fog, provide reminders for the audience of the constant and eternal presence of the sea in the lives of the characters. Although they move from port to port, these characters never leave the sea—except, of course, to drink.

Act 1, the only act *not* set at sea, takes place in a saloon near the harbor (i.e., the sea) in New York City. By setting the first act on land, O'Neill establishes the tension between land and sea that is at the heart of his drama. All of the characters who enter the saloon in act 1—except one—live at sea. The longshoremen, Chris, and Marthy, are all associated with the seafaring life. The exception is Anna Christie, who enters midway through the act, and, having arrived from the heartland of the country—from Minnesota—clearly comes from the land.

Much of nineteenth-century drama was set in the drawing rooms of the well-to-do. Inspired by the turn-of-the-century naturalistic plays of British and European dramatists like Shaw and Gorky, in his early sea plays, and especially in *Anna Christie,* O'Neill made barrooms and ships' cabins acceptable settings, and the lives of the underprivileged patrons of such places acceptable subjects, for serious American drama. The description of the saloon is evidently based on the numerous saloons that O'Neill patronized in his own seafaring days, and he uses it again in bar scenes in future plays, most notably as the single set of one of his longest, most complex, and most interesting dramas, *The Iceman Cometh.*

Set at Johnny-the-Priest's, a saloon near the waterfront in New York City, act 1 establishes the bar as a popular drinking hole for seamen and introduces the audience to Chris and Anna, two of the three main characters, while also providing a great deal of exposition. When the act opens, a postman delivers a letter from Minnesota, in a woman's handwriting, for Chris, a barge captain who frequents Johnny-the-Priest's whenever he is "in port." Soon after, Chris enters, accompanied by Marthy, a lively and streetwise woman who has been living with Chris on his barge. When Chris reads the letter, he discovers that his daughter, Anna, is on her way to New York to stay with him after 15 years of separation. Chris explains to Marthy and the bartender, Larry, that Anna had moved to the United States from Sweden as a little girl when her mother became tired of waiting at home for Chris to return from the sea, something he rarely did. When Anna's mother died, Chris decided that Anna would be better off staying on the farm with her cousins in the Midwest than moving back East to be with him. He was obsessively determined to keep his daughter away from the sea and therefore to free her from her mother's fate of meeting and marrying a seaman only to be left alone when he goes to sea, and ultimately, when he dies at sea, as most of the men in Chris's family have done. Sensing Chris's anxiety about his daughter's return, Marthy volunteers to move off the barge so that Anna may move on board.

As Chris and Marthy celebrate their continuing friendly feelings toward each other with more drinks, Chris imagines that his daughter is a "good, strong gel" (967), made more wholesome and pure by her land-bound, Midwestern upbringing. This speculation sets the stage for Anna's entrance, one of the most ironic delayed entrances in all of drama, the one made famous on-screen by Greta Garbo. As Marthy sits alone in the back room, Anna appears at the family entrance, "*showing all the outward evidence of belonging to the world's oldest profession*" (968). When she realizes who Anna is, Marthy, amused by the irony, strikes up a conversation with Anna, in which Anna tells Marthy her story of exploitation and abuse by her male relatives on the farm, as well as by other men when she worked as a "nurse girl," caring for other people's children. All of this exposition explains that becoming a prostitute was Anna's way to escape a life of abuse, and it has only reinforced her hatred of men. Yet with nowhere else to turn, she has come to New York in search of a man—her father—"as good an old guy as ever walked on two feet" (971), according to Marthy, who Anna hopes will provide her with a place to rest and start over.

When they finally meet, Chris is so blinded by the joy of being reconciled with his daughter that he does not recognize any of the outward signs of his daughter's occupation. He is, as Marthy has described him to Anna, "a simple old guy" (973), and Anna finds herself in the uncustomary position of being treated kindly by a man. He offers her the respite she seeks, and although she has reservations about living on a barge, she agrees to consider his offer.

When act 2 begins, it is 10 days later and Anna is on board the barge, which is now docked in Provincetown, shrouded by thick fog. The stage directions indicate that Anna looks "*transformed*" (979), which she almost immediately attributes to the effects of life at sea, and especially to the fog: "It makes me feel clean—out here—'s if I'd taken a bath" (980). After Chris confirms their family legacy of men going to sea and women waiting eternally for them to return, Anna reiterates how happy she feels now that she has, in effect, come "home" to the sea, which leads Chris to curse "dat ole davil, sea," in fear of the doom he always expects it to bring.

At that moment, the sea brings a call of distress from a group of sailors stranded after their steamer was destroyed. One of these sailors is Mat Burke, a big, strong, handsome Irishman, who is attracted to Anna as soon as he sees her. At first he tries to win her with sheer brawn, but when she resists, he turns to wooing her with verbal bravado about his exploits at sea. Anna's initial repulsion at his physical presence gradually turns to curious attraction, as they engage in a flirtatious exchange that leads Burke to propose marriage. Anna does not reject his proposal. Rather, she offers him her bed in which to rest and recuperate, which leads her father to curse "dat ole davil, sea" again, this time for bringing Anna and Burke together, as he fears that if his daughter marries Burke, she will be forever doomed to the lonely life of a seafarer's wife.

In act 3, Chris's barge, the "Simeon Winthrop," has moved on from Provincetown to Boston, where it is now anchored, and the scene takes place inside the cabin on the barge. Anna has been going ashore to movies and shows with Burke, much to the chagrin of her father, Chris. Anna tells her father how much she likes Burke, but also, rather mysteriously, confesses that she will not marry him because she is not "good enough for him" (996). Chris does not understand her reason, but it reassures him and provides him with ammunition against Burke. When Anna goes down to the end of the dock to watch the ships, Burke enters, and finding Chris alone, he takes the opportunity to announce his intention to marry Anna. Chris mocks him, taking courage from Anna's own confession to him moments before. This confrontation escalates into a heated argument about the relative superiority of stokers (Burke) and square-heads (Chris), with each man challenging the other's manhood, until finally Chris physically attacks Burke. Burke defensively repels the attack, restraining himself from harming his older and weaker opponent, at which point Anna returns to the cabin.

Burke proceeds to propose marriage to Anna, in spite of Chris's protests. Anna does declare her love for him, kissing him passionately to prove it, but she also says that she cannot marry him. Her refusal prompts Burke to press harder, and soon, the two men are shouting orders at her, each claiming to have authority over her. Their attitudes and words lead her to lose her patience—"You can go to hell, both of you!" (1007)—and she declares her independence from both of them:

> You was going on 's if one of you had got to own me. But nobody owns me, see?—'cepting myself. I'll do what I please and no man, I don't give a hoot who he is, can tell me what to do! I ain't asking either of you for a living. I can make it myself—one way or other. I'm my own boss. So put that in your pipe and smoke it! You and your orders! (1007)

She then proceeds to tell them the true story of her abuse by the men on the farm that eventually drove her to prostitution, and in spite of her pleading with Burke to believe that she has changed, that her love for him has "cleansed" her, Burke reacts with violent anger. He curses her for deceiving him and then leaves the barge to get drunk, promising to sail away on board a new ship that will take him as far away from her as possible. Chris reacts with a combination of repulsion and guilt, as Anna blames his failure as a father for her situation. Chris, though, puts it all in the context of his belief that "dat ole davil, sea" is to blame for everything. Then he too departs, to get drunk and forget, leaving Anna alone on the barge.

When act 4 begins, it is two days later, and Anna still sits alone in the barge's cabin, but now she is dressed for traveling, and a suitcase sits on the floor nearby. Chris enters, returning for the first time in two days, and showing signs of having been drunk. He apologizes to Anna, and she accepts, relieving him of his guilt with a sentiment not unlike his own belief in fate: "It ain't your fault, and it ain't mine, and it ain't his neither. We're all poor nuts, and things happen, and we yust get mixed in wrong, that's all" (1015). Anna admits to Chris that she has been waiting there hoping that Burke would return. Chris informs Anna that he has signed on to sail away on a steamer, and that his earnings will be paid directly to her, so that she will not have to work as a prostitute anymore, his way of making restitution for all his wrongs against her. Anna discovers that Chris has a revolver, which he confesses he originally purchased to use against Burke, but never bought the bullets. Anna takes it from him, as he exits to sleep off his hangover.

Within a few moments, Burke returns to the cabin, exhibiting physical signs of heavy drinking and fighting, as well as "wild mental turmoil" (1017). At first, Anna defends herself by raising toward Burke the revolver she has confiscated from her father, but she soon drops it in response to his claims of anguish, from which she surmises that she is not in any physical danger from him. Burke has returned because he cannot get Anna out of his mind, both in anger and in love (although he does not yet explicitly admit the latter). He is searching for a way to allow himself to accept her. First, he asks her to tell him it has all been a lie, which she will not do. Then, when he accuses her of being in love with all the other men with whom she has had relations, and when she vehemently denies it, he finds his rationale for accepting her. He reasons that, if she has never loved anyone else before, then the power of his love will surely be enough to change her into a new woman, leaving both of them with no recollection of her past, which, he further reasons, was not her fault anyway, given the irresponsibility of her father. He then asks her, and she agrees, to swear on a cross given to him by his mother that he is the only one she loves, and that she is leaving her sordid past behind her forever. When he realizes that Anna is not a Catholic, meaning that the oath she swears on his mother's cross is empty, he accepts her "naked word for it" anyway, confirming that he loves her deeply, which he proves with a "fiercely" passionate kiss (1025).

As Anna and Burke embrace, Chris reenters and proposes a toast to the couple's reconciliation and impending marriage. Anna informs them that both men have, ironically, signed on to sail on the same ship, so they will be bound together aboard ship, while she intends to live in a house on land and wait for them to return. Distressed when he learns that Anna and Chris are Lutherans by birth, Burke, for the first time, expresses some reservations about their fate:

CHRIS— It's funny. It's queer, yes—you and me shipping on same boat dat vay. It ain't right. Ay don't know—it's dat funny vay ole davil sea do her vorst dirty tricks, yes. It's so.

BURKE— (*nodding his head in gloomy acquiescence—with a great sigh*) I'm fearing maybe you have the right of it for once, devil take you. (1026)

Anna, however, who has painted a picture of domestic happiness, continues to cling to that vision: "Aw, say, what's the matter? Cut out the gloom. We're all fixed now, ain't we, me and you? . . . Come on! Here's to the sea, no matter what! Be a game sport and drink to that! Come on!" (1026). Yet, it is the skeptical Chris who gets the last word in the play:

(*looking out into the night—lost in his somber preoccupation—shakes his head and mutters*) Fog, fog, fog, all bloody time. You can't see vhere you vas going, no. Only dat ole davil, sea—she knows! (*The two stare at him. From the harbor comes the muffled, mournful wail of steamers' whistles.*) (1027)

Thus the play concludes with ambiguity, with hope in the face of anticipated inevitable doom.

## CHARACTER DEVELOPMENT

*Anna Christie* is essentially a three-character drama. The bartender, bar owner, longshoremen, and postman who appear in act 1 all remain undeveloped beyond their function in that scene, which is to provide the realistic setup for the reunion of Chris and Anna. Someone has to serve the drinks; someone else, besides Chris, has to patronize the saloon; and someone has to deliver the letter from Anna. Chris needs someone to talk to so that O'Neill can provide exposition for the drama that is about to unfold. The only secondary character in this opening scene who is developed somewhat beyond her functionality is Marthy, Chris's live-in girlfriend. Marthy provides humor, as well as a perspective on Chris that is important to the audience's perception of the relationship between Chris and Anna.

Marthy is a strong, confident woman who takes advantage of a good situation when it presents itself, but does not become too dependent on what she has. She is adaptable and fun-loving. Although she is demanding of

Chris in the scene at the saloon, her demeanor is quite good-natured; she is clearly fond of Chris, but this is not a romantic relationship. When Chris learns that his daughter is coming to visit, he is determined to have her stay with him on his barge, which means that he must ask Marthy to leave. Chris likes Marthy, and he is not just a little afraid of her, so he is hesitant to broach the subject, which creates an opportunity for Marthy to have some fun at Chris's expense.

As Chris awkwardly and meekly attempts to begin the conversation, she immediately attacks him for trying to break up with her, but when she observes Chris's fear and misery at the prospect of fighting with her, she lets him off easily by breaking up with him first:

> I'm wise to the game, up, down, and sideways. I ain't been born and dragged up on the water front for nothin'. Think I'd make trouble, huh? Not me! I'll pack up me duds an' beat it. I'm quittin' yuh, get me? I'm tellin' yuh I'm sick of stickin' with yuh, and I'm leavin' yuh flat, see? There's plenty of other guys on other barges waitin' for me. Always was, I always found.... So cheer up, Dutchy! I'll be offen the barge before she comes. You'll be rid o' me for good—and me o' you—good riddance for both of us. (966)

At the same time, she assures him that they will remain good friends, which she proves a few minutes later when she testifies to Anna about his uprightness. When Anna declares her hatred of all men, Marthy takes a more moderate, forgiving stance: "There's good ones and bad ones, kid. You've just had a run of bad luck with 'em, that's all. Your Old Man, now—old Chris—he's a good one" (972). Marthy's testimony on behalf of Chris gives Anna hope that he will provide the safe retreat she seeks; it also reassures the audience that Chris is as simple and good-hearted as he has appeared to be in the opening scene.

Marthy is the first character in the play to interact with Anna. It is Marthy to whom Anna first confides about her desperate past, and it is in Marthy that there may be some hope for Anna's future. Anna herself recognizes the possibility of change when she tells Marthy, "You're me forty years from now" (970). What she sees is an aging woman alone in a saloon, but Marthy is a companion to seafaring men (not a prostitute), and in Marthy's strong feelings of camaraderie with men like Chris, perhaps Anna unconsciously recognizes the chance that she will ultimately be reconciled with men, at least the good ones.

When Chris Christopherson first appears at the saloon, he seems to be a typical seaman (in his case, though, captain of a coal barge) spending time in port, carefree and drunk. Within minutes, an "*insistent ring from the doorbell*" (962) introduces Marthy as the woman who lives with Chris, suggesting that an unexpected level of responsibility and commitment may also be part of Chris's character. When moments later Chris reads the letter in a woman's handwriting that has arrived for him from Minnesota, and he announces not only that he has a daughter but that she is coming to visit him, his reaction—"*an expression of mingled joy and bewilderment*" (963)—suggests the inner conflict that makes him a much richer character than the audience might be led to believe when he first enters the saloon.

Exposition in the first act reveals the driving force behind all of Chris's behavior—"dat ole davil, sea." The sea is the only life he knows. Based on his experience and that of his family, he associates the sea with certain death, and therefore he fears it. This fear of the sea has justified his decision to try to protect his only daughter by keeping her inland with his wife's family, even though this means his own separation from her, about which he also feels sad and guilty. These conflicting emotions plague Chris throughout the play. He appears to be a caring father toward Anna, yet she clearly does have good reason to accuse him of abandoning her, rather than protecting her, especially as the protection he intended actually led her into a life of abuse and prostitution.

Similarly, although he takes her in and provides her with the rest she needs, which cleanses and renews her spirit, he is also overprotective of her and painfully unaware of who she really is and what she wants from life. Chris can appear to be a controlling and unreasonable man, yet there is also something comically and infuriatingly naïve about him. After Anna reveals the truth about herself to him and Burke in act 3, instead of accepting some of the responsibility for her situation, he just chants his refrain about the sea and wishes for blissful ignorance:

> It's dat ole davil, sea, do this to me! (*He shakes his fist at the door.*) It's her dirty tricks! It was all right on barge with yust you and me. Den she bring dat Irish Fallar in fog, she make you like him, she make you fight with me all time! If dat Irish fallar don't never come, you don't never tal me dem tangs, Ay don't never know, and everytang's all right. (*He shakes his fist again.*) Dirty ole davil! (1012)

One of the nagging questions about Chris throughout the play is whether he is a selfish, superstitious man or a selfless, pragmatic one. In his efforts to keep Anna safe from "dat ole davil, sea," Chris tries to intervene between Anna and Mat Burke, the sailor whom Anna meets aboard the barge. On the one hand, his objection to their relationship seems irrational and insensitive to his daughter's feelings; on the other hand, it seems perfectly reasonable and justified for a father, given the life that Burke lives. In the end, Anna and Burke together embrace the hope of beating the odds against their love, but Chris remains unchanged in his dread of the sea. Ironically, he finds himself signed on to set sail on the same steamer as his future son-in-law: "it's dat funny vay ole davil sea do her vorst dirty tricks" (1026). Through his choral-like repetition of the "ole davil sea" mantra, Chris comes to symbolize fate, a strong sense that human beings are subject to a higher force that determines what happens to them. It is not insignificant that Chris's familiar words are the last ones spoken in the play: "Fog, fog, fog, all bloody time. You can't see where you vas going, no. Only dat ole davil, sea—she knows!" (1027).

When Mat Burke first appears, he is a powerful force emerging from the fog, representing both the threat of the sea, as Chris perceives it, and the cleansing promise of the sea, as Anna perceives it. As Travis Bogard has observed, "Mat is like a personification of the sea, and he brings to crucial test Chris's conception that the sea is evil" (161). Burke is immediately perceived in terms of his physical strength, as described in the stage directions—"*He is about thirty, in the full power of his heavy-muscled, immense strength*" (984)—and his Irish ethnicity, as revealed in the syntax of his first line—"Is it dreaming I am?" (984). Sheaffer observes that Burke is "drawn with vitality and personal color, but his Irishness is painted on so thick that he sometimes verges on being a stage Irishman" (27). Beneath the stereotypical boozing, blarney, and bragging is a real human being in turmoil.

When Burke first discovers Anna on the barge, he takes his customary approach to the women he meets in port and attempts to have his way with her by impressing her with his strength and braggadocio. Anna, however, strongly rejects his advances. When she informs him that she is the daughter of the barge captain, he changes his manner and begins to woo her, still with a high dose of swagger and bombast. By the end of act 2, he has declared his intention to marry Anna, and in act 3, he persists in his pursuit of this end, which brings him into physical conflict with Chris, who is determined to prevent Anna from marrying him. As Burke's determination to defeat Chris stiffens his resolve, his tone toward Anna becomes more authoritarian, and she recoils. When Anna reveals the truth about her past as a prostitute, Burke turns on her in anger and disdain, and then, stopping short of harming her, he abandons her. In all of his responses thus far, Burke has behaved in a stereotypically male fashion, selfishly, and always to protect his own ego and self-identity.

In act 4, however, Burke's character seems to turn in a different direction. Unable to walk away entirely from Anna, he returns to the barge after a drunken binge, obviously struggling to find a way to overcome his moral confusion about Anna's revelation and reclaim his love without losing face. He accomplishes this by reassuring himself that Anna loves only him when she swears on his mother's crucifix. The irony is that Anna is not Catholic, and Burke does not understand that she is sincere in her vows to him, with or without religious oaths. In spite of his misgivings, Burke accepts Anna's "naked word for it" (1025) and declares his intention to marry her and to be happy.

Although Burke has evolved, beyond the stereotype of the sailor with a woman in every port, as a man with feelings and the need for a woman's love, he never quite makes a complete evolution. As he indicates, mostly nonverbally, in the final moments of the play, he retains his suspicions of Anna. More significantly, when he learns that he has signed on to set sail on the same ship as Chris, he acknowledges, for the first time, that there may be some justification for Chris's fear of the sea and of fate. Although he drinks to Anna's hopeful toast for the future, he does so with "superstitious premonitions" (1027) nagging at him, suggesting a fear that, in marrying Anna, he may be making a terrible mistake.

An earlier version of this play was called *Chris*, so when O'Neill reconceived it as *Anna Christie*, there was obviously a shift in perspective; he may have begun to write a play about Chris, but he ended up writing a play about Anna. There is no question that Anna Christie is at the center of this drama. O'Neill signals her importance at the outset by delaying her entrance, and building anticipation for it, through half of act 1. Her centrality is no more clearly indicated than in the scene in act 3 in which Chris and Burke stand on either side of her, barking orders at her, and, metaphorically at least, tugging her in two different directions.

As he does with the other main characters in the play, O'Neill bases the development of Anna on a stereotype. When she enters in act 1, she exhibits the outward trappings of a prostitute: "*Her youthful face is already hard and cynical beneath its layer of make-up. Her clothes are the tawdry finery of peasant stock turned prostitute*" (968). When she first speaks, the words made famous on film by Greta Garbo sound like those of a prostitute: "Gimme a whiskey—ginger ale on the side. (*then, as Larry turns to go, forcing a winning smile at him*) And don't be stingy, baby" (968). When she tells Marthy of her life of abuse and desperation in the Midwest, it sounds like the background of a prostitute. Anna, however, has arrived in New York seeking to escape from a life of prostitution, and although she claims to hate men, she seeks protection from her father.

When she moves aboard Chris's barge, she unexpectedly experiences the cleansing power of the fog and the sea, which allows her to wash away the memories of her sullied past. When she meets Burke, she is defensive about being treated like a prostitute, and she gains the assurance of a woman with a great deal more to offer than her body. Thus when Chris and Burke bark contradictory orders at her in act 3, she stands her ground and declares her independence from both of them and from men in general, sounding rather like Nora in Ibsen's *A Doll's House*, but uniquely American in O'Neill's vernacular: "But nobody owns me, see?—'cepting myself" (1007). It is this part of Anna to which Burke may be oblivious when he accepts her declaration of love for only him. Anna loves Burke, and she will do whatever it takes, including swearing a Catholic oath, to win him. As they attempt to negotiate a life together, with Burke instinctively giving orders and Anna instinctively resisting, their strong wills are likely to cross again before too long. At the end of the play, Anna is a resolute, independent woman agreeing to live a dull, land-bound life, perennially awaiting the return of her father and husband, who expect her to serve them; Anna may very well be marrying the wrong man.

## THEMATIC ISSUES

Given the relative contemporaneity of the writing of *Anna Christie* with the death of O'Neill's parents and brother, as well as with the birth of his son Shane, it is not surprising that family matters are such compelling thematic issues in the play. *Anna Christie* is both a quirky romance about Anna and Burke and a revealing family drama about Anna and her father, Chris. When Anna first appears in the saloon in act 1, she reveals that she has been abandoned by her father and is now seeking reconciliation with him. They each approach this reunion with false impressions of the other. Chris thinks Anna is a nurse girl, and Anna thinks Chris is a janitor. He has admitted leaving her with relatives in Minnesota, but he believes it was for her own good, to keep her away from "dat ole davil, sea." Because of this superstition, he has deprived his daughter of a normal parental relationship, for which she has harbored a good deal of resentment toward him.

When confronted with the truth about each other, Anna recognizes that, as Marthy has informed her, Chris is "a good one" (973), but Chris continues to see what he wants to see in his daughter. In spite of all the outward evidence of her profession, Chris treats her as if she were a "good girl." For example, when she asks for a drink at the end of act 1, he apologizes that they don't have "fancy" drinks at this saloon, like ginger ale and sarsaparilla, although the audience has already observed her order a whiskey when she first enters, and it is clear that she is a seasoned drinker.

When Anna finally reveals the truth about her past to both Chris and Burke in act 3, Chris's need to believe otherwise is so desperate that he curses the sea for bringing Burke to his barge in the fog, not because Anna is becoming involved with Burke, but rather because the fighting between Anna and Chris over her relationship with Burke leads her to reveal the truth about herself to Chris. He would prefer to believe in his own illusion: "Ay don't never know, and everytang's all right" (1012).

Chris attempts to control whom his daughter marries, which transforms their hopeful reunion into a strained battle. In the end, Chris apologizes for his role in her unhappiness and vows to stand aside if marrying Burke will make her happy, thus following the path of many parents who struggle as they instinctively attempt to protect their children until the children strike out on their own and reject the parents' protection. In this case, Chris doubts that marrying Burke will bring Anna happiness, yet he ultimately accepts his impotence and irrelevance in setting the course of his daughter's adult life.

This struggle for control between father and daughter is, of course, part of a larger metaphysical question that is raised in many of O'Neill's works, which is who or what controls the course of human lives. When Chris asks Anna for forgiveness in act 4, she says: "There ain't nothing to forgive, anyway. It ain't your fault, and it ain't mine, and it ain't his [Burke's] neither. We're all poor nuts, and things happen, and we yust get mixed in wrong, that's all" (1015). The implication of Anna's statement is that her father's belief in the power of "dat ole davil, sea" may not be so crazy, after all. According to Chris, the sea makes bad things happen, and the sea is therefore to blame for everything, so people, like Chris, cannot be blamed.

The questions of guilt and blame place O'Neill's drama firmly in the tradition of twentieth-century existential drama, in which the issue of personal responsibility defines the struggles within and between the characters. If things just "happen" that are beyond the individual's control, then no person has to take responsibility for his or her behavior. Many of O'Neill's characters want to believe in some higher power like the sea to relieve themselves of the awesome responsibility that comes with free will. Yet these same characters continue to be nagged by guilt, as is Chris. Is it true to say that Chris had no choice but to leave his daughter on the farm in Minnesota, or for that matter, that Burke has no choice but to return to the barge after Anna's revelation, or that Anna has no choice but to marry Burke? Could they each have behaved differently? Each must take responsibility for his or her action, which contributes to the ambiguity at the end of the play. It would be easy to blame the sea if things do not work out for Anna and Burke, but each has made a choice to be together, and each is responsible for making it work. To relinquish that responsibility and blame someone else, or the sea, would be living in "bad faith," as Sartre and the existentialists would have it.

## STYLISTIC AND LITERARY DEVICES

*Anna Christie* is characterized by a number of rather traditional plot elements. It begins with extended exposition in act 1, continues with the development of a complication with the appearance of Mat Burke in act 2, reaches a climax when Anna lashes out at both Chris and Burke in act 3, and is resolved when Burke returns to marry Anna in act 4. It is this formulaic approach, in part, that leads audiences to see the ending as happy, when O'Neill intended something more ambiguous. In this case, the form works against the content. O'Neill knew formulaic drama very well from his familiarity with his father's theatre (i.e., *The Count of Monte Cristo*), but he also knew realistic modern drama from his familiarity with the works of the European dramatists of his time.

Like his early sea plays, *Anna Christie* is naturalistic in style, but informed by expressionistic imagery, not unlike the drama of Chekhov, Ibsen, and other European playwrights at the turn of the twentieth century. *Anna Christie* is one of O'Neill's earliest efforts to develop a full-length play in this style. One characteristic of this dramaturgical approach is the rich and nuanced use of imagery. The sea is a dominant motif in many of O'Neill's early plays, and he developed it with both verbal and visual imagery. In *Anna Christie* the sea is a constant presence, and its significance is heightened by its contrast with the land.

Although the play begins on land, at Johnny-the-Priest's saloon, the longshoremen who come and go immediately provide the flavor of a seafaring venue, which is reinforced by the entrance of Chris Christopherson, singing "My Yosephine, come board de ship" (961) and speaking of his voyage from Norfolk: "yust fog, fog, fog, all bloody time!" (962). All of this sea talk is offset in the middle of act 1 by the entrance of Anna, coming all the way from the landlocked state of Minnesota. When she talks about traveling, it is by train, a land mode: "day and a half on the train. Had to sit up all night in the dirty coach, too. Gawd, I thought I'd never get here!" (968–969), and when she learns that her father is not a janitor (a land job), but rather a barge captain, she cannot imagine living aboard the barge with him (972).

It takes only a few days of living on the barge for Anna to discover the cleansing power of the fog. When Chris calls it the "vorst one of her [the sea's] dirty tricks" (979), Anna declares her love for the sea: "I never thought living on ships was so different from land" (980). Anna even acknowledges her preference for sea language over land language: "Funny I don't know nothing about sea talk—but those cousins was always talking crops and that stuff. Gee, wasn't I sick of it—and of them?" (980). Eventually, after she meets Burke, she states her preference in men in these terms, as well: "I sized you up as a different kind of man—a sea man as different from the ones on land as water is from mud—" (1010). The rest of the play is spoken much more in sea language than land language, with words such as *landlubber, stokehole*, and *drownded* dominating the vernacular. Even at the end, when Anna envisions her future in "a little house somewhere" (1026), although it is clearly on land, the house is imagined more as a safe harbor to which Chris and Burke will return from their sea voyages.

In contrast to all of the positive sea imagery, mostly associated with Anna, is Chris's constant lament about the fog and "dat ole davil, sea." From his earliest defense of leaving his daughter on the farm in Minnesota after her mother died, so that she (Anna) "don't know dat ole davil, sea" (964) to the very last words of the play, when Chris worries aloud about "Fog, fog, fog, all bloody time. You can't tell vhere you vas going, no. Only dat ole davil, sea—she knows!" (1027), the sea represents a formidable force that Chris believes dooms him and his family at every turn. O'Neill supplements the verbal imagery with the visual image of the fog, as indicated in the opening stage directions of acts 2 and 4, and with the aural imagery of bells tolling, steamers' whistles blowing, and ship engines snorting. It is not insignificant that the last sound heard at the end of the play is "*the muffled, mournful wail of steamers' whistles*" (1027). The sea imagery in *Anna Christie* sets the scene, establishes the mood, and subtly evokes the metaphysical dilemma faced by the realistic characters in the play. It is a highly effective merging of theatrical naturalism and expressionism.

## ALTERNATE PERSPECTIVE: READER-RESPONSE ANALYSIS

Reader-response theory evolved as a response to the new criticism of the mid-twentieth century, which posited that meaning derives exclusively from the text itself. On the other hand, reader-response, or reception, theory posits that meaning depends on the reader and the circumstances surrounding the act of reading. That is, meaning emerges from the interaction between reader and text, and therefore any single text is polysemic, or open to multiple interpretations, depending on the reader and what he or she brings to the text. Reader-response theory is particularly rich when applied to dramatic literature, because the full experience of drama depends on performance. The impact and meaning of a play can differ from production to production, depending on the actors, directors, and designers, and how they have responded to the text. Furthermore, the impact and meaning of any given production can differ every night, depending not only on the performances but also on the audience and how it responds to the play. O'Neill's conflicts over the years with various actors about their performances in his plays (e.g., Charles Gilpin in *The Emperor Jones*) are illustrative of the first application of reception theory. O'Neill's experience with the reception of *Anna Christie* by critics and audiences when it was first produced is illustrative of the second, which is more consistent with and suggestive of the theory's application to written texts.

When Anna stands up for herself against her father and Burke in act 3, she does so in response to their bullying attitude toward her. As she says, they speak of her as if she were a piece of furniture (1007), and each man seems determined to impose his will on Anna, which she will not tolerate. The bullying attitude toward women and the intolerance of it are essential characteristics of Burke and Anna, respectively, and these traits seem inherently at odds with each other. Anna's subsequent revelation about her past and Burke's enraged reaction to it provide additional evidence of potential incompatibility between these two characters. His inability to forgive her for her past transgressions in the light of the love that has been kindled between them does not bode well for their future together. Even when Burke returns in act 4, seeking a way to reconcile the woman Anna was with the woman he wants her to be, he seems to overlook the woman she is right now, a woman who loves him, but is strong-willed and determined to live her life on her own terms. When he does accept her vow to love only him, it is based on an oath that he knows is false and empty, yet he would prefer that to her "naked word" (1025). These are hardly the terms of a happy marriage.

Anna, as well, in her need for love, overlooks the reality of Burke's short-sighted and short-tempered character, as well as her own need for independence, when she agrees to marry Burke. He accepts her in spite of her past for egocentric and patriarchal reasons that should give Anna pause: "For I've a power of strength in me to lead men the way I want, and women, too, maybe, and I'm thinking I'd change you to a new woman entirely, so I'd never know, or you either, what kind of woman you'd been in the past at all" (1023). Anna, however, ignores the implications and encourages his egocentrism, even enduring his distrust of her "naked word." It is Burke, not Anna, who makes the final decision to marry, using terms of possession when he claims that he will "have" her, and sounding very much like the bully she protested against in act 3 when he declares publicly, not necessarily to her, but to the world, that they will marry: "We'll be wedded in the morning, with the help of God" (1025). His unromantic prosaic style is matched by his physical expression, as he "*crushes her to him and kisses her again*" (1025).

The play ends with Anna painting a picture of domestic tranquility, with her making a home on land where her father and husband will return from their voyages at sea, while Chris strikes his reliable refrain of doom about the fog and "dat ole davil, sea," and Burke squirms uncomfortably between the two visions. When Anna leaves for a few moments, Burke "*relapses into an attitude of gloomy thought*" (1026), clearly a revelation of his true feelings. At the last moment, Anna proposes a toast "to the sea" (1026), and significantly," *Burke banishes his superstitious premonitions with a defiant jerk of his head, grins up at her, and drinks to her toast*" (1027). "Dat ole davil, sea" has the last word in the play, accompanied by those "*muffled, mournful*" (1027) steamers' whistles. This is clearly not the stuff of happy endings.

Although *Anna Christie* brought O'Neill greater popularity than he had experienced until that time, to his mind, it was for the wrong reasons. Audiences responded positively to what they perceived as the happy ending of *Anna Christie*, which led some critics to accuse the usually somber O'Neill (whom they had up until then acclaimed for his seriousness in defying Broadway's commercial pressures) of "selling out": "Burns Mantle, for one, called it [*Anna Christie*] the first work in which 'the morbid young genius compromised with the happy ending all true artists of the higher drama so generously despise'; and Stephen Rathbun, not alone in his suspicion, wondered whether the author 'is gradually degenerating into a Broadway playwright'" (Sheaffer 67).

O'Neill, however, recognizing and acknowledging that he had written what could be construed as a happy ending, conceived its significance differently:

> The happy ending is merely the comma at the end of a gaudy introductory clause, with the body of the sentence still unwritten. (In fact, I once thought of calling the play *Comma*)…My ending seems to have a false definiteness about it that is misleading—a happy-ever-after which I did not intend.… A kiss in the last act, a word about marriage, and the audience grows blind and deaf to what follows. (67–68)

Because he believed that audiences misunderstood the ending of the play, he considered *Anna Christie* a failure, noting ironically that "its success depends on the audience believing just what I did not want them to" (Sheaffer 68; Gelbs 481). In fact, he felt so strongly about it that when Joseph Wood

Krutch was putting together a collection of O'Neill's "representative" plays sometime later, the dramatist insisted that *Anna Christie not* be included (Sheaffer 68; Gelbs 482).

In spite of O'Neill's disparagement of the play, its interest lies, in part, in the very quality for which the dramatist rejects it. He has written about characters with ambiguous and ambivalent feelings, which leave the audience/reader with many unresolved questions. There are reasons to hope that Anna and Burke might live happily ever after, even perhaps with Chris contentedly bouncing a grandchild on his knee, and there are reasons to doubt that this will ever happen, either because of the inherent incompatibility of Anna and Burke, or because of those larger, mysterious forces, represented by "dat ole davil, sea," which rule the lives of human beings. How a reader or viewer interprets it depends largely on the internal and external world of that individual viewer. Whatever O'Neill's intentions, once his work is published and/or produced, its meaning is out of his hands, and as reader-response theory would have it, even outside of the text itself. Only dat ole davil, reader, he or she knows!

## WORKS CITED

Bogard, Travis. *Contour in Time: The Plays of Eugene O'Neill* (Revised Edition). New York: Oxford University Press, 1988.

Gelb, Arthur and Barbara. *O'Neill*. New York: Harper & Row, 1962.

O'Neill, Eugene. *Complete Plays 1913–1920*. Ed. Travis Bogard. New York: Library of America, 1988.

Sheaffer, Louis. *O'Neill: Son and Artist*. Boston: Little, Brown, & Co., 1973.

# 4

## *The Emperor Jones* (1920) and *The Hairy Ape* (1921)

In the early 1920s, O'Neill wrote two plays that marked a distinct departure from his initial naturalistic works. Although he claimed that he wrote *Jones* "long before I had ever heard of Expressionism" (Sheaffer 76), both plays have characteristics (i.e., episodic structure, dehumanized characters, a dreamlike quality) that place them firmly in the expressionistic mode. It is true, however, as O'Neill contested, that the central figure in each of these two plays (Jones in *The Emperor Jones* and Yank in *The Hairy Ape*) has much more depth of personality than is the norm for purely expressionistic characters who tend to be mechanistic and faceless. As O'Neill justifiably asserts, "the character of Yank [in *The Hairy Ape*] remains a man and everyone recognizes him as such" (76). Still, these two plays are the closest O'Neill came to writing purely expressionistic drama.

It is useful to study these two plays together not only because of their common expressionistic style, but also because of O'Neill's purpose in using this style. In 1924, the dramatist wrote:

> The old "naturalism" no longer applies. It represents our Fathers' daring aspirations toward self-recognition by holding the family Kodak up to ill-nature. But we have taken too many snapshots of each other in every grace-less position; we have endured too much from the banality of surfaces…we have been sick with appearances and are convalescing; we "wipe out and pass on" to some as yet unrealized region where our souls, maddened by loneliness and the ignoble inarticulateness of flesh, are slowly evolving their new language of kinship. (124)

In both *The Emperor Jones* (1920) and *The Hairy Ape* (1921), O'Neill was experimenting with a new theatrical language. In both, he uses the theatre in non-realistic ways, not so much to "tell a story" as to probe beneath the surface of human experience.

In both cases, the dramatist turned to the same nonrealistic style to probe into the consciousness of a male figure on the fringes of society, in the first case, an African American ex-convict, and in the other, a stoker working in the dark stokehole of an ocean liner. Both characters end up dead, and in death, perhaps find peace. Furthermore, in both plays, O'Neill, not commonly regarded as a sociopolitically minded playwright, explicitly and boldly challenges traditional notions in society; in *Jones*, he takes on racism, and in *Ape*, capitalism.

## THE EMPEROR JONES (1920)

*The Emperor Jones* holds an important place in American theatre history as the first play in which an African American actor was cast in a leading role by a white theatre company (32). Admittedly, the character has traits consistent with old negative stereotypes of African Americans, such as superstition and shiftiness, and his dialect makes him sound uneducated. Furthermore, even though he is a black man himself, his use of the derogatory term "nigger" may be shocking for some audiences. Although he is clever and persuasive, qualities that land him on the Emperor's throne, in the end, he is brought down and his decline and descent may be seen as putting an uppity black man back in his rightful place. So, Brutus Jones is a controversial character, perhaps even more so today, when political correctness demands that writers avoid these kinds of depictions.

How did an Irish American writer come to create an African American character like Brutus Jones in 1920? Throughout his travels, O'Neill was open to meeting people from all walks of life, and he placed himself in situations in which he would do so. Many of these people later became characters in his plays. Like so many of O'Neill's other characters, Jones was a conglomeration of a number of people he had met in his travels as a young man, among them a gambler he knew in Greenwich Village, Jamaicans with whom he had worked at sea, and a bartender in New London (29). O'Neill is distinguished among American dramatists for the diversity of his characters throughout his canon. *The Emperor Jones* is surely one of the best examples of his ability to tackle universal psychological and philosophical issues through the unique lens of a racially or ethnically specific character, one from a background radically different from his own. For all the potentially stereotypical and superficial traits of Brutus Jones, he is clearly a strong protagonist through whom O'Neill raises profound and interesting questions about life and the human condition.

African American actors at the time had few choices of good roles to play in the theatre, and the first two who played this role in the 1920s, Charles Gilpin and Paul Robeson, gained recognition as a result of their association with this play. Although Gilpin eventually died in poverty never to play a major theatrical role again, his performance was critically acclaimed (33–34), and O'Neill himself later named him as the only actor "who carried out every notion of a character I had in mind" (37). Paul Robeson went on to be one of the major African American stage and screen actors of the early twentieth century, appearing in the film version of *The Emperor Jones* and perhaps best known for his performance in the 1936 film of the musical *Show Boat*.

### Setting and Plot Development

There are several indications in the stage directions for *The Emperor Jones* that the setting is not realistic. First of all, in a note beneath the character list, O'Neill explains, "The action of the play takes place on an island in the West Indies as yet not self-determined by White Marines. The form of native government is, for the time being, an Empire" (*CP 1913–1920* 1030). Not only is this place far away from U.S. soil, but the ironic tone of O'Neill's statement suggests that such a place does not exist; it is not a real empire on a real island. The scene locales that follow reinforce this impression: scenes 2 through 7 are set at the edge of, or within, the "Great Forest" (1030), not a real forest located on a map of the West Indies, but rather a generic and symbolic forest.

The only scene not set in or at the edge of the forest is the first one, which takes place in the audience chamber of the emperor's palace. This setting is the most realistic in the play, described as "*a spacious, high-ceilinged room with bare, white-washed walls*" (1031). With its archways, porticos, pillars, and throne, it is an identifiable place. The size of the throne and its bright color ("*a dazzling, eye-smiting scarlet*"), as well as the bright colors of the cushions and the floor matting, however, give the palace a somewhat unreal quality. Not a space regularly inhabited by most audience members, the palace has a scale and splendor that establish the grandeur of the central figure in the drama, the Emperor Jones.

Once Jones leaves the palace and embarks on his journey through the forest, the setting becomes increasingly expressionistic. In scene 2, the forest is "*a wall of darkness dividing the world*," the individual tree trunks "*enormous pillars of deeper blackness*," and the wind "*a somber monotone. . .lost in the leaves [that] moans in the air* (1044). In each subsequent scene, as Jones delves farther into the forest, it is described in similar terms, emphasizing its darkness and its denseness, from which various images emerge to haunt Jones. The forest thus has the familiar unreality of dream images. This dreamlike quality is enhanced by the sound effect of the tom-tom, beating like a human heart, regularly and at a faster pace from scene to scene. The descriptive language of the stage directions gives directors and scenic designers considerable leeway to depict the forest nonrealistically, emphasizing its blackness as a barrier that obstructs Jones's journey, as well as his sight, while strangely also, as dreams do, providing insight.

The story of *The Emperor Jones* is simple. Brutus Jones, an escaped convict from the United States, has made his way to this West Indian island, and in two years has gained enough money, influence, and power to become emperor. In the process, he has taken advantage of the superstitious beliefs of the island natives when an attempt on his life failed, and he has convinced them that only a silver bullet can kill him, thus preempting any further attempts on his life. He now rules with impunity and financially exploits his subjects. When the drama begins, the people have fled the palace and have gathered in the hills to plan their revolt against the emperor. Smithers, a sly businessman who originally hired Jones when Jones first arrived on the island and who now reluctantly serves Jones, warns him, and Jones leaves the palace to begin his escape from the island through the forest. He has planned for this eventuality, burying food at the edge of the forest that he will take with him for sustenance through the forest until he arrives at the coast. There, he will board a French boat to Martinique, where his money awaits him in savings. As he leaves the palace, armed with five lead bullets—and one silver one—in his revolver, the sound of the tom-tom is heard in the distance, signaling the efforts of the natives to stop him.

Jones's escape plan is immediately in jeopardy when he confronts the darkness of the forest at its edge and cannot locate the food he buried there. The play then takes a sharp turn away from realism when the "Little Formless Fears" appear, suggesting that Jones's fear is leading him to hallucinate and may be a further impediment to his trip through the dark forest. In a panic, he discharges the first of his lead bullets in a futile attempt to destroy the formless fears, signaling his whereabouts to the natives and lowering his defenses against them at the same time. In the next five scenes, Jones appears at an indistinct point in the forest where, in each case, he confronts an image from his personal or racial past that frightens him. First, he thinks he sees Jeff, the gambler he killed back in the United States. Next, he envisions the chain gang he worked on and the prison guard he killed before escaping. Then, a vision of a slave auction and another of a slave ship appear to him, followed by the image of a witch doctor and menacing crocodile. In fear, he fires all five of the remaining bullets, including the silver one, leaving him unarmed and lost in the dark forest. At the end of each scene, he is seen or heard running off; but at the end of scene 7, he lies on the ground "*whimpering with fear*" (1059).

Jones does not appear in the final scene of the play until the native soldiers carry his dead body out of the forest. In this scene, which takes place at the precise spot where Jones entered the forest, Lem, the tribal chief who has led the revolt against Jones, assures Smithers that they will "cotch" Jones, and much to Smithers's disbelief, they squat in a semicircle and wait. Sure enough, within a few minutes, a sound is heard in the forest, and it soon becomes clear that Jones has been wandering in circles, never moving very far from where he began. The soldiers shoot and kill him, using silver bullets, which they have spent the night molding from melted silver coins (this is ironic, as all night Jones has feared that they were chasing him through the forest). Lem and his soldiers believe that they have overcome a "charm" and killed the Emperor Jones, while the audience has observed not just the disrobing of an emperor, but the physical and psychological disintegration of a man named Brutus Jones.

### Character Development

*The Emperor Jones* is a one-character play; in fact, it is a character study. Jones's journey through the forest is really an internal journey into the recesses of his own mind and soul, and the characters he meets there—such as Jeff and the Prison Guard—are merely images in his own mind, more interesting for what they signify about Jones himself than for their own independent qualities. Two other characters who speak in the play—an old native woman and Lem—represent Jones's island subjects; they are simple, uneducated, and superstitious. The Old Woman appears at the beginning of the play to establish the fear that the people feel toward Jones. Smithers fears him, too, but Smithers also knows that Jones is a fraud, whereas the Old Woman believes in Jones's power. Lem appears at the end of the play, representing the simple will of the people to free themselves from the oppression of the Emperor Jones. Both the Old Woman and Lem serve as foils to Smithers, who chooses to remain subjected to the rule and influence of Jones as long as he sees a profit in it, and as foils to Jones himself, who, as an African American, has transcended the tribal mentality of the island people, but at the same time has succumbed to the corruption of the American capitalist system.

Smithers is an early example of O'Neill's ability to create appealing comic characters. This opportunistic cockney businessman has somehow made his way to this West Indian island, where he has made money by trading with the natives (a thinly veiled symbol of British imperialism), only to be usurped in that role by a wily American wheeler dealer (a somewhat less thinly veiled symbol of American imperialism). Smithers tries to strike a balance between serving Jones, in a racial reversal of the master/slave relationship, and serving Jones up to the natives. He warns Jones that the natives have fled to plot his downfall, and at the same time, he delights in the prospect of them catching him. He doubts that they can outsmart him, yet he is pleased when they do. He mocks Jones's pretensions when he is killed ("Where's yer 'igh an' mighty airs now, yer bloomin' Majesty?"), yet he pays tribute to his triumph of self-realization ("Silver bullets! Gawd blimey, but yer died in the 'eighth o' style, any'ow!") (1061). Reminiscent of some of George Bernard Shaw's cockney rascals such as Alfred Doolittle, Smithers is a bundle of ambivalence about race, class, and power, simultaneously repulsed and pleased by Jones's exploitation of his own people.

*The Emperor Jones* is all about Brutus Jones. In the first scene, he appears in full emperor's regalia, and through his interaction with Smithers, he establishes his authority. Although his background as a conman and a murderer has landed him in jail in America, he is strong, smart, and crafty enough to have beaten Smithers at his own game in a very short time and has risen to the Emperor's throne. Jones exudes self-confidence, to an extent that borders on hubris: "Ain't I de Emperor? De laws don't go for him" (1035). Even when confronted with the prospect of the revolt of his people, he responds with cool-headed assurance: "Den de revolution is at de post. And de Emperor better git his feet smokin' up de trail" (1039). He boasts that he can "outguess, outrun, outfight, an' outplay de whole lot o' dem all ovah de board any time o' de day er night!" (1041). If it were not for Smithers, the audience might be convinced by Jones's swagger, but Smithers keeps reminding him of the natives' superstitions and the role that "luck" has played in Jones's ascension to emperor. This is reminiscent, of course, of the reminders to the doomed heroes in Greek tragedies who fall from greatness when they defy fate and the gods. Jones is powerful and clever, but there is a chink in his armor. As Jones attempts to find his way in the forest in the subsequent scenes, the extreme confidence of scene 1 soon reveals itself to be the overcompensation of a man wracked by guilt and insecurities.

With each scene, Jones experiences a heightened degree of terror, signified throughout the rest of the play by the accelerating rate of the beating of the tom-tom (1041). That terror, however, is not driven solely by his physical disorientation and fear for his life, but also by the demons within his psyche with which he is confronted in each successive scene. Initially identified vaguely in scene 2 as the "Little Formless Fears," his demons take on more concrete shape in scenes 3 and 4, when he is haunted by the images of both of the men he has killed, Jeff the gambler and the prison guard, surely a manifestation of his guilty conscience. In scenes 5 and 6, he sees visions of a slave auction and a slave ship, respectively, images from his racial past that pointedly call into question his own exploitation of the island natives. Finally, in scene 7, he meets a Congo witch doctor being pursued by devils and demanding the sacrifice of Jones to appease some kind of primitive deity that takes the form of a huge crocodile with green eyes. Jones, who has left his "Jesus on de shelf" (1042) while in pursuit of material wealth, prays for mercy, "*beats his forehead abjectly to the ground*" (1058) in much the same way as he had laughed at the superstitious island natives for doing in his presence. This act signals his true identity as a mortal human being, riddled with guilt and sin, and at the mercy of some higher force.

His bravado in the first scene, or as Smithers calls it, "yer 'igh an' mighty airs" (1061), is revealed in the end for what it is—an act; it is a role he plays to hide his insecurities and uncertainties about his values and actions. Although Jones is an individual character with a very specific background, he is, in essence, a kind of Everyman through whom O'Neill explores the psychological struggles inherent in the human condition.

## THE HAIRY APE (1921)

Within two years of completing *The Emperor Jones*, O'Neill returned to the same expressionistic format to focus on another male character on the fringes of society. This time it was Yank, a stoker who sweats out a life for himself below deck in the stokehole of an ocean liner in *The Hairy Ape*. O'Neill claimed to have written *The Emperor Jones* and *The Hairy Ape* each in 10 days. The Gelbs quote a 1945 letter in which O'Neill calls both plays "easy": "They just came to me" (466). It is perhaps not coincidental that O'Neill so readily conceived both of these dreamlike dramas about outcasts in search of belonging during the years when both of his parents died, highlighting a preexisting sense of rootlessness for him and focusing his attention on his brother, who was hit especially hard by his mother's death in 1922. Years later, he would say of his brother, Jamie, who died in

1923: "He had never found his place. He had never belonged. I hope like my 'Hairy Ape' he does now" (Sheaffer 88).

### Setting and Plot Development

The Hairy Ape has multiple settings, indicative of the plight of its central character. Yank is a man without a place in the world, and during the course of the play, he wanders in search of one. He begins in a space that has felt like his "home" for some time, first in the fireman's forecastle of an ocean liner, where he rests, and then in the stokehole of the ship, where he works. In between these two scenes is a scene on the promenade deck, where the passengers relax and enjoy the cruise, oblivious to the dark, oppressive environment below. The scene on deck is described as "*beautiful*" and "*vivid*" with "*sunshine. . .in a great flood, the fresh sea wind blowing across it*" (CP 1920–1931 130), whereas the stokehole is characterized as dimly lit, with "*murky air laden with coal dust*" (135). The stage directions clearly indicate that none of the settings is meant to be realistic, beginning with the opening scene: "*The effect sought after is a cramped space in the bowels of a ship, imprisoned by white steel. The lines of bunks, the uprights supporting them, cross each other like the steel framework of a cage*" (121). This effect foreshadows the setting of the last scene, which is literally the gorilla's cage at the zoo. In between cages, Yank visits Fifth Avenue in New York City, a prison on Blackwells Island (very much like another cage), and I.W.W. local headquarters on the waterfront, all real places with just a touch of the surreal, usually conveyed through the lighting.

The story of The Hairy Ape is simple. Yank's position at the bottom of the social ladder and his opposition to those at the top are established in the first four scenes; in each subsequent scene, he attempts to find a place for himself in society. Unable to fit in anywhere, he ends up in the gorilla's cage at the zoo, where he dies alone.

Yank is the strong, respected leader of the stokers aboard a transatlantic liner sailing from New York City. Scene 1 sets the scene below deck in the firemen's forecastle, where the stokers drink, sing, and pass the time when they are not working. Arguments break out about their lot in life, with Yank resisting Long's calls for a revolt against the capitalists above deck, declaring the natural superiority of him and his mates, who "run de whole woiks," over "de rich guys dat tink dey're somep'n" (129). Convinced that he "belongs," Yank's worldview is shattered when a young, aristocratic woman, named Mildred, who is introduced in scene 2 on board as the daughter of the ship's owner traveling with her aunt, almost faints at the sight of him stoking coal in the stokehole. She calls him a "filthy beast" in scene 3. In one fell swoop, Yank falls from the top of the evolutionary ladder—"de whole ting is us!" (129)—to the bottom—a "great hairy ape" (141), and, egged on by his shipmates in scene 4, he is determined to regain his rightful place at the top—"I'll show her who's a ape!" (143).

In scene 5, Yank, accompanied by Long, seeks out Mildred and her ilk on Fifth Avenue on a Sunday morning. As the "Ladies and Gentlemen" emerge from church to walk along the avenue like automatons, they ignore Yank, avoiding eye contact and staring without affect, no matter how much Yank rails at or provokes them. Finally, Yank is besieged by a group of policemen who beat him down and arrest him. Alienated from the elitists on Fifth Avenue, Yank next attempts to connect with fellow human beings in prison in scene 6, in which the prisoners are represented as disembodied voices that taunt and provoke him. When he mentions the name of Mildred's millionaire father, one of these voices suggests that he join the Wobblies, the Industrial Workers of the World, or I.W.W., a labor organization actively, and nonviolently, opposed to big business. The I.W.W. recorded its highest membership and greatest influence in the early 1920s, when it also became the target of government repression. The inmate's Voice reads excerpts from a news article of a speech by a right-wing senator opposed to the Wobblies, who accuses its members of being a violent threat to the very fabric of democracy. In his frustration, Yank responds positively to the volatile language with which the senator describes the Wobblies and wants to join their cause, to "blow up tings" and "turn tings round" (154). Then, worked up into a rage, he bends the steel bars of his cell to make his escape. The guard turns the hose on him, but as the curtain falls, the sound of the water against the steel of his cell indicates that Yank escapes.

Scene 7 takes place about a month later, when Yank goes to the I.W.W. local headquarters and attempts to join the union. The stage directions suggest that this is a meeting room where members freely and openly congregate: *"The whole is decidedly cheap, banal, commonplace and unmysterious as a room could well be"* (155). Wrongly assuming that it is a "secret society," wary of police and other officials because of its antigovernment activities, Yank arouses the suspicions of the Secretary with his expectations of secret handshakes and passwords. When he explains that he wants to help their cause by blowing up Mildred's father's steelworks, they suspect that he is a spy sent by the government to entrap them, and they literally kick him out of the building (tellingly calling him a "brainless ape" [159]). Discouraged that even the Wobblies are not committed to the kind of meaningful action that he seeks against his perceived oppressors and therefore, not belonging there either, he is confused as to where to turn next.

Finally, scene 8 finds Yank at the monkey house at the zoo. A gorilla is in plain sight in a cage, while a "chattering" noise (reminiscent of the noises at the prison) suggests that others are nearby. From outside the cage, Yank compares his plight to that of the gorilla and decides that they are both "members of de same club—de Hairy Apes" (161). In an attempt to cement the bond between them and have the gorilla join his cause, Yank frees the gorilla from his cage, only to have the gorilla hug him so hard that he cracks Yank's ribs and kills him. The gorilla escapes and throws Yank in his cage, where Yank dies. The stage directions provide the playwright's intended meaning for the concluding tableau: "And, perhaps, the Hairy Ape at last belongs" (163).

### Character Development

Although there are more names listed as characters in *The Hairy Ape* than in *The Emperor Jones*, like its predecessor, this play is essentially a one-character drama, truly a character study of Robert Smith, better known in the play as Yank. Although they are depicted in a similarly dreamlike, expressionistic style, the other characters in *The Hairy Ape* are not so much manifestations of Yank's inner demons, as in *Jones*, but rather, manifestations of the oppressive forces surrounding Yank. *Jones* emphasizes the internal forces that shape a man's character; *Ape* emphasizes the external forces.

First, there are the stokers, a group of men who "*resemble those pictures in which the appearance of Neanderthal Man is guessed at…All the civilized white races are represented, but except for the slight differentiation in color of hair, skin, eyes, all these men are alike*" (121). Described as a group, and not as individuals, the stokers act like a chorus, responding to what Yank says as "Voices" speaking lines that are meant to sound spontaneous, sometimes sequentially and sometimes simultaneously. At one point, they chant in unison a "*refrain, stamping on the floor, pounding on the benches with fists*": "Drink, don't think!" (124). The only two characters who emerge as individuals from this group are Long and Paddy, and even they are depicted as "types."

Long, who is drunk in scene 1, is the spokesman for social revolution. He picks up on Yank's comment that home is hell to urge the men on to revolt against the capitalists who have made their working-class lives aboard ship a living hell. All the others shout him down, and Yank himself mocks his "Salvation Army-Socialist bull" (125), so this interaction makes it clear early on that Yank is not politically connected or motivated. Later, when Yank seeks revenge on Mildred, Long brings him to Fifth Avenue to confront the capitalist enemy. Yet, when Yank begins to challenge physically the men and women on the avenue, Long objects, fearful of being arrested. He flees, a clear indication that he is unwilling to support his words with action. Unlike Yank, Long lacks the passion for his mission; for Yank, it becomes very personal.

Paddy is an "*old, wizened Irishman*" (123) who recalls with longing the more romantic days of the clipper ships, when seafaring men could breathe the fresh air and experience the feeling of freedom on the wide open sea: "'Twas them days men belonged to ships, not now. 'Twas them days a ship was part of the sea, and a man was part of a ship, and the sea joined all together and made it one" (127). In contrast, Yank celebrates the power of the stoker, sweating in the dark bowels of the ocean liners, making them run. To Yank, the modern coal-driven and steel-reinforced era has given men like himself more power, and he does not even consider what may have been sacrificed for that power. Paddy represents a lost time, a time of innocence and purity, when man could experience a "oneness" with nature, a feeling denied to men at sea in the new machine age. Paddy represents what has been lost to the modern Everyman, represented by Yank.

Beside the stokers, there are other characters who function in groups, lacking any distinguishing individual characteristics and representing generic segments of society. In scene 5, the ladies and gentlemen on Fifth Avenue lack emotion and personality. They look and sound like robots, unaffected by anything Yank says or does, thus increasing his frustration and sense of isolation. In scene 6, the prisoners on Blackwells Island are merely disembodied voices, not characters, taunting Yank and egging him on to seek vengeance for his perceived wrongs. The Guard in this scene serves only a functional role as the expected figure of authority at the prison from whom Yank must escape. In scene 7, the Secretary at the I.W.W. headquarters merely represents the group in his dialogue with Yank, fearful of government intervention, cautious in his dealings with strangers, while the other men, defined only by their occupations—"*longshoremen, iron workers, and the like*" (155)—do not speak, but support the Secretary with physical action against Yank.

O'Neill explicitly describes Mildred and her aunt as "types," in the Aunt's case, "*even to the point of a double chin and lorgnettes*" (130). These two figures are caricatures of upper-class pomposity and pretentiousness, intended by O'Neill to have a deadening influence on the invigorating atmosphere at sea:

these two incongruous artificial figures, inert and disharmonious, the elder like a gray lump of dough touched up with rouge, the younger looking as if the vitality of her stock had been sapped before she was conceived, so that she is the expression not of its life energy but merely of the artificialities that energy had won for itself in the spending. (130)

Whereas the elder personage is perfectly content to remain in her pleasant, sun-drenched world, ignoring those less fortunate than she who have been denied wealth and comfort, her college-educated niece condescends with "groping sincerity" to "discover how the other half lives" (131). Mildred does not object to getting her white dress dirty in her descent to the stokehole, but that is because she has 50 white dresses and can just throw the dirty one overboard (133–134).

When actually face-to-face with the enraged Yank in the stokehole in scene 3, Mildred is horrified, revealing the superficiality of her social consciousness: "*her whole personality crushed, beaten in, collapsed, by the terrific impact of this unknown, abysmal brutality, naked and shameless*" (137). The reality of the stokers' brutal existence and Yank's anger are too much for Mildred, who is incapable of seeing the humanity within the "filthy beast" in front of her. Her denunciation brands and isolates Yank as the "hairy ape" and is the catalyst for his mission to seek retribution from the capitalists and find his place in the company of humankind.

According to Sheaffer, O'Neill once denied that he had been influenced by the European practitioners of expressionism in writing *The Hairy Ape*, in spite of its many dramaturgical characteristics that are typical of that style. It is in the character of Yank that O'Neill stakes his primary claim of distinction from expressionism:

> "I personally do not believe," O'Neill has said of Expressionism, "that an idea can be readily put over to an audience except through characters. When it sees 'A Man' and 'A Woman'—just abstractions, it loses the human contact by which it identifies itself with the protagonist. . .the character of Yank remains a man and everyone recognizes him as such." (76)

Perhaps it was O'Neill's facility with creating complex human characters, based so largely on his experiences with real people, that prevented him from ever adhering to expressionism wholeheartedly. Like Brutus Jones, Yank is a kind of Everyman, but he is a very particular Everyman. He is a full-blooded character with genuine feelings surrounded by stock cardboard figures, a realistic character among surrealistic caricatures.

From the beginning of Scene One, Yank stands out among his peers. Although he shares with them the "*appearance of Neanderthal Man*," he is the "*most highly developed*" among them. This means that he is not only stronger, more aggressive, and more vocal than the others, but also smarter and more emotional. In particular, he is angrier. In the first scene, he expresses contempt for the noise that the others make, the beer that they drink, and the songs that they sing; he condemns home, women, religion, and politics. He glories in the raw power of coal and steel, and in his role as the generator of that power, and he rejects Paddy's nostalgia for the cleaner, healthier, and as he sees it, weaker, old days of sailing vessels. He speaks with excessive pride in his role as the self-perceived source of energy for all human movement and action. He lives and works among others, but he is a loner: "Care for nobody, dat's de dope! To hell wit 'em all! And nix on nobody else carin'. I kin care for myself, get me!" (CP 1920–1931 129). His words echo the self-reliant rhetoric of the American hero, but his diction ironically confirms his status as the most ordinary of Americans. In the subsequent series of scenes, O'Neill builds on this paradox; Yank finds himself an unlikely hero, increasingly at odds with the world in which he lives.

In scene 3, the stokers appear to be merely cogs in a machine, a hot and dusty black machine in the bowels of the ship, far from the glorified picture of power described by Yank in scene 1. Again, Yank stands out from the group, this time railing against the unseen engineer above who blows the whistle demanding more fuel. Reduced to a *"gorilla-like"* state, he comes face-to-face with the true power brokers at the top of the socioeconomic ladder, represented by the daughter of the ship's owner, Mildred, who is horrified by Yank's appearance and fearful of his anger. Yank is hurt by her reaction—*"His mouth falls open, his eyes grow bewildered"*—but she faints at the sight of him and calls him a "filthy beast" (137), denying his humanity. Determined to regain his dignity, Yank then directs his anger toward the pedestrians on Fifth Avenue, gaining sympathy merely because his adversaries are so dehumanized. In terms of audience identification and sympathy, an ape trumps a machine.

In scene 6, Yank sustains his anger in the face of the ridicule of the prisoners, from whom he is distinguished from the outset when he is depicted in the pose of Rodin's "The Thinker" (150). In his uneducated simple-mindedness, he mistakenly takes the overblown antiunion rhetoric of a conservative politician to be the truth about the I.W.W. and mistakenly sees in that organization a channel for his rage against the forces of capitalism. When he puts this plan into action, however, he is rebuffed again, this time for threatening to take more action than those cooler heads in the union who share his antipathy for the lords of business are willing to risk. Again, Yank's rage seems uncontainable within any socially acceptable framework—which leads him to the zoo.

At the monkey house at the zoo, he discovers a caged gorilla in the pose of "The Thinker" (160). The gorilla is not identified in the character list that precedes the play text, perhaps because he is a reflection of what Yank would be like if he were merely an animal. Presumably played by an actor in a gorilla suit, the primate does not think or speak, as Yank does; he only acts. In his confrontation with the ape, Yank recognizes the difference between them:

> I kin make a bluff at talkin' and tinkin'—a'most git away wit it—a'most!—and dat's where de joker comes in.... I ain't on oith and I ain't in heaven, get me? I'm in de middle tryin' to separate 'em, takin' all de woist punches from bot' of 'em. Maybe dat's what dey call hell, huh? But you, yuh're at de bottom. You belong! Sure! Yuh're de on'y one in de woild dat does, yuh lucky stiff! (162)

When Yank breaks the lock on the cage and frees the gorilla, the difference between them becomes painfully clear. Yank extends his hand in a thoughtful gesture of brotherhood with the ape, and the gorilla responds instinctively with a *"murderous hug"* (163) that breaks Yank's ribs and kills him. In the end, Yank proves that he is not an ape; he is a human being. Like Jones, he is a kind of Everyman, desperately searching throughout the play for his place, his purpose, but lost and alone in the end, and maybe finally at peace in death.

## THE EMPEROR JONES AND THE HAIRY APE

### Thematic Issues

In both *The Emperor Jones* and *The Hairy Ape*, a single character is the central focus of the drama, to the exclusion of any significant secondary characters. In each play, the supporting cast is only important in relation to the central character. Both dramas use the focus on a single character to raise issues about the individual in relation to society. In *Jones*, the eponymous character begins at the top of his adopted society, as Emperor, having escaped from the bottom of American society, as prisoner. In *Ape*, Yank begins at the bottom of his society, aboard ship in the stokehole, but he asserts that his position there places him at the top of society, as he provides the energy that drives everything. Ostensibly, Jones is brought down by the revolt of his subjects, although in reality, he is brought down by his own guilt and insecurities. Ostensibly, Yank is brought down by his own limitations, although in reality, he is brought down by the indifference of the society in which he lives.

In both plays, the worlds in which the central characters find themselves are highly ritualized and oppressive to the expression of self. Jones has experienced two different worlds, one that imprisoned him and one that made him emperor, yet in both worlds, he is ultimately oppressed by the roles he must play. Although that oppression is related to his identity as an African American man, it is also more universally related to his identity as a human being. Human beings are forced to play specific roles by society, and these roles are sometimes counterintuitive and counterproductive (e.g., Brutus Jones, an escaped convict as emperor of the people on an island in the West Indies). Similarly, Yank experiences different worlds in the course of the play, from the stokehole of a ship to the union meeting hall; in each situation, he, too, is oppressed by the role he is forced to play, in this case, by virtue of his class. Yank seems to be yearning for something more than a stoker's dirty existence, yet he is unable to feel "at home" anywhere else. His attempts to relate to the ladies and gentlemen on Fifth Avenue or the union workers at the I.W.W. are also counterintuitive and counterproductive.

Both plays suggest that human beings are alone in the modern world. Neither Jones nor Yank finds much comfort in religious faith; Jones explicitly admits that he has left "Jesus on de shelf," and Yank mocks "dat Salvation Army-Socialist bull." Although Jones, terrified in the end, does cry out for God's mercy, it is unlikely that his call is answered. Both men journey alone through their respective worlds. Jones has Smithers to talk to in the beginning, but he leaves him behind; Yank initially sets off with Long, but Long soon abandons him. Both men find their journeys frustrating and frightening, and the people they meet or imagine are oddly unresponsive. Both men find peace in death at the end of their respective plays, but in neither case is it the peace of religious faith. Rather, it is the peace of death, of the end, nothing more and nothing less. In *Jones*, that peace is signified by the cessation of the beating of the tom-tom; in *Ape*, it is signified by the final stage direction, which explicitly suggests that "*perhaps, the Hairy Ape at last belongs.*" Both plays thus raise philosophical questions about the purpose and meaning of human existence.

Because the central figure is a black man, *The Emperor Jones* inevitably raises issues about race and racism in America. That an African American character is the protagonist of a theatrical work in the early 1920s is remarkable in itself. Furthermore, this protagonist is not just an ordinary man living an ordinary life, but he is an emperor, the ruler of an island empire. It can be said that O'Neill was being historically accurate by not placing Jones in a position of power within the United States, but Jones's ability to rise to power, even on a faraway island, presents the possibility and asks, why not? He clearly outsmarts the only white man around, and, as a successful capitalist, presents himself as a viable candidate for office back home. At the same time, however, O'Neill endows him with an extreme arrogance that inevitably leads to his downfall, and perhaps this characteristic is indicative of a white man's (biased) perception of what an African American man like Jones would be like if granted any power. Surely, his dialect and superstitious nature seem derived from long-held stereotypes.

In *The Hairy Ape*, there are issues of prejudice and stereotypes, but these are based more on issues of class than race. O'Neill stipulates that, among the stokers, "*all the civilized white races are represented, but except for the slight differentiation in color of hair, skin, eyes, all these men are alike*" (121). The varying dialects used in the dialogue spoken by the "voices" of the stokers suggest some ethnic diversity, but when O'Neill indicates that they are "alike," he groups them together as members of the same socio-economic class, self-identified with the group as "stokers." When Yank attempts to assert his individuality by making forays into higher levels of society, society resists and repels him. From the moment when Mildred recoils in horror at the "filthy beast," it is apparent that America is not a classless society.

Both plays cast capitalism in a negative light. In *Jones*, it is capitalism that corrupts Jones; his greed for money leads him to exploit the island natives, although they are, racially, his brothers and sisters. Of course, they are also his human brothers and sisters, and O'Neill certainly suggests that the corruption of capitalism is a human problem, not just a racial one. In the plight of Brutus Jones, the audience observes a graphic portrait of what a man sacrifices, morally and spiritually, in the pursuit of material wealth. In *Ape*, Yank rails against the capitalists, in particular, against the steel baron who owns the ship on which he labors. Capitalism keeps men like Yank down, cages them in and imprisons them in the cotton fields, in factories, and aboard ship. In the plight of Robert Smith ("Yank"), the audience observes the dehumanizing effects that the pigeonholing capitalist system can have on people.

When studied in the context of O'Neill's entire canon, these two plays share another notable commonality—the virtual absence of family matters and a striking irrelevance of intoxication and alcoholism. The central character in each play is a loner who makes virtually no mention of his family. The only reference is in *Ape* when Yank recalls that he ran away from his family to escape the "lickings" (124). Although the stokers in *The Hairy Ape*, including Yank, do get drunk in the first scene, their intoxication is not a central concern or factor in the drama, and once Yank sets out on his quest to belong, he remains strikingly sober. Likewise, when Jones journeys through the forest, he is under the influence only of his own inner demons and anxiety, not chemical substances.

### Stylistic and Literary Devices

Whether or not O'Neill was directly influenced by any of the expressionistic dramatists in Europe at the time, and his denials notwithstanding, both *The Emperor Jones* and *The Hairy Ape* are firmly rooted in the dramaturgical style of expressionism. This style emphasizes subjective feelings rather than objective reality; it is an attempt to depict reality beyond the superficial surfaces of realism. To accomplish this goal, expressionistic drama uses the technological devices available in the modern theatre to distort and/or exaggerate what is being depicted. Plot and character are less important than atmosphere and aroused feelings. Expressionistic drama does not have a plot with a discrete beginning, middle, and end; rather, it uses an episodic form, a series of relatively short scenes that move a central character through a variety of experiences. In expressionistic drama, characters are "types," often identified by a role or position in society, rather than by a name.

In his discussion of *The Emperor Jones* and *The Hairy Ape*, Sheaffer identifies the following as characteristic features of expressionism used by O'Neill in these plays: "masks or masklike faces; distorted settings that suggest a claustrophobic world in which everything is askew; depersonalized characters confined to their own orbits and unable to make contact with anyone else" (76). Sheaffer argues that O'Neill made more use of these devices in the later of these two plays, but there is clear evidence of them in both works.

In *Ape*, the masklike faces are most explicitly used in the Fifth Avenue scene: "*A procession of gaudy marionettes, yet with something of the relentless horror of Frankensteins in their detached, mechanical unawareness*" (CP 1920–1931 147). In the prison scene, the dramatist uses disembodied voices with similar depersonalizing effect. In *Jones*, although there is nothing quite as explicitly masklike, each of the apparitions that appears to Jones in his journey through the forest is described as expressionless, or with a single, unchanging expression. In the slave auction, for instance, the auctioneer is "*authoritative*," the spectators "*curious*," and their movements are described as "*marionettish*" (CP 1913–1920 1053). In the next scene, the slaves aboard the slave ship sit in "*crumpled, despairing attitudes*" (1055). Finally, the witch doctor is costumed with horns, beads, and bone ornaments on and around his face and head (1057), rendering his face "masklike" in appearance.

Both plays use "distorted settings that suggest a claustrophobic world in which everything is askew." In *Jones*, for example, when Jones first arrives at the edge of the Great Forest, it is described as "*a wall of darkness dividing the world*" (1044), and later as "*massed blackness. . .like an encompassing barrier*" (1047). In scene 7, which takes place somewhere in the forest, the setting is described as follows:

> The foot of a gigantic tree by the edge of a great river. A rough structure of boulders, like an altar, is by the tree. The raised river bank is in the nearer background. Beyond this the surface of the river spreads out, brilliant and unruffled in the moonlight, blotted out and merged into a veil of bluish mist in the distance. (1057)

This is no ordinary forest.

As Sheaffer points out, in *Ape*, O'Neill is even more clear about his intentions from the opening stage directions of the firemen's forecastle aboard ship (CP 1920–1931 121) and in his description of the stokehole in scene 3:

> A line of men, stripped to the waist, is before the furnace doors. They bend over, looking neither to right nor left, handling their shovels as if they were part of their bodies, with a strange, awkward, swinging rhythm. They use the shovels to throw open the furnace doors. Then from these fiery round holes in the black a flood of terrific light and heat pours full upon the men who are outlined in silhouette in the crouching, inhuman attitudes of chained gorillas. The men shovel with a rhythmic motion, swinging as on a pivot from the coal which lies in heaps on the floor behind to hurl it into the flaming mouths before them. (134–135)

This is no ordinary stokehole.

As for the "depersonalized characters confined to their own orbits and unable to make contact with anyone else," the secondary characters in both plays readily meet this requirement. Character analyses of Jones and Yank adequately demonstrate how both also fit this description in terms of their self-absorption and isolation, but in both cases, there is also sufficient evidence to support O'Neill's claim that his main characters in these two plays actually defy the expressionists' demand for depersonalization. Sheaffer explains that O'Neill drew this distinction in particular with reference to Yank: "Yank meant so much to O'Neill personally—he realized later that the play was 'unconscious autobiography'—that he resented Yank's being grouped with the dehumanized, rather faceless principals common to Expressionism" (76–77).

One other device that contributes to the expressionistic effect of both plays is the use of sound effects. One of the most memorable effects of *The Emperor Jones* is the use of the sound of the tom-tom to accompany Jones's journey through the forest. Starting in scene 1 at a rate of 72 beats per minute to mimic a normal heartbeat, it accelerates gradually through the rest of the play, as Jones becomes increasingly frightened and panicked. Although the beat literally emanates from the activity of the natives as they prepare to overtake and overthrow Jones by shooting him with the silver bullets they manufacture, it symbolically represents the inner anguish of Jones as he runs not only from them, but from his own demons. The tom-tom takes the audience inside the head of the Emperor Jones.

The sound effects in *The Hairy Ape* are not quite as focused and sustained, but O'Neill does invest real sounds, such as the rattling of the steel bars of the prison cells and the chattering of the unseen monkeys at the zoo, with the emotional weight of the respective moments for Yank, as he frantically attempts to break out of the confines of his socially defined and stifling identity. The sound effects in the stokehole are also quite striking:

> There is a tumult of noise—the brazen clang of the furnace doors as they are flung open or slammed shut, the grating, teeth-gritting grind of steel against steel, of crunching coal. This clash of sounds stuns one's ears with its rending dissonance. But there is order in it, rhythm, a mechanical regulated recurrence, a tempo. And rising above all, making the air hum with the quiver of liberated energy, the roar of leaping flames in the furnaces, the monotonous throbbing beat of the engines. (*CP 1920–1931* 135)

O'Neill achieves two effects here: one is the "rending dissonance," which defines Yank's experience throughout the play as he runs up against barrier after barrier; the other is the "monotonous...beat of the engines," which conveys the oppressive environment from which Yank yearns to escape, and of course, recalls the effect of the tom-tom in *Jones*.

One final effect that is unavoidable in a discussion of these two plays is the use of an animal on stage. In *Jones*, the large head of a crocodile with green eyes appears in the penultimate scene of the play, and in *Ape*, of course, a gorilla is a central figure in the final scene. In both cases, these nonhuman characters defy the age-old theatrical dictum to avoid casting animals and young children in plays, largely because they are difficult, if not impossible, to control. Each of these creatures must be controlled in production, because O'Neill is very specific in his stage directions about their actions. Because these are not realistic plays, however, the creatures do not have to be real. By using makeup, costumes, and lighting effects, directors and designers can present both the crocodile and the gorilla consistently with the style of these plays, that is, as distortions of reality. In each of O'Neill's two expressionistic dramas, the appearance of each creature is entirely logical within the illogical dream worlds of Jones and Yank, respectively. In each case, the animal represents a primitive instinct in the central character and therefore in human beings. In each case, the appearance of this primitive animal brings the hero face to face with the essence of his humanity.

### Alternate Perspective: A Mythic Reading

Mythic criticism examines how an artistic work tells old familiar stories in new and relevant ways. Myths are stories that reflect universal behaviors, ideas, and values within a particular culture, and in some cases, across cultures. Archetypes are the specific patterns of images, character types, and plot elements within these stories that evoke deep common responses from audiences across time and space. If dreams reveal an individual's unconscious, then myths and archetypes reveal what Carl Jung called the "collective unconscious."

One such myth is "the hero's quest," the story of a person who embarks on a journey, either to discover or save something of value or to gain redemption for some individual or collective transgression. Along the way, this person usually must meet both mental and physical challenges and overcome life-threatening obstacles. The most familiar example of this myth in early Western culture is the story of Odysseus in Homer's *The Odyssey*.

Both Jones in *The Emperor Jones* and Yank in *The Hairy Ape* embark on episodic journeys of redemption and discovery. Both men face a series of emotional and physical challenges as they proceed. Both men ultimately die with greater understanding of themselves, which brings each of them a kind of redemption. When the myth of the hero's quest culminates in death, it becomes an archetype for life itself: for all human beings, life is a quest that ends in death.

Jones's quest in *The Emperor Jones* begins as an escape and becomes a journey of self-discovery. It is also a spiritual pilgrimage of sorts, another manifestation of the myth of the quest. Early on, Jones admits that he has laid his "Jesus on de shelf" (CP 1913–1920 1042); he has abandoned his religious faith in the pursuit of wealth. Since his arrival on the island, he has capitalized on the superstitious beliefs of the natives in convincing them that he can be killed only by a silver bullet, and in making a silver bullet for himself, he reveals his own superstitious belief. On his journey through the forest, he sees a number of apparitions, which he suspects are ghosts, yet he cannot dismiss them as such; rather, he acts against them in fear, as if they were real. Each apparition heightens his anxiety and his sense of guilt, starting with Jeff, the man he killed over a pair of dice, and the guard he killed to escape from prison, and on to the slaves, from whom he is descended and whose legacy he has now betrayed in his corrupt performance as emperor. Finally, he arrives at the witch doctor's altar, which represents the most primal human instincts, and he demands human sacrifice to some higher power, strangely symbolized by a huge crocodile, and prompting Jones finally to call out for Jesus. Like the medieval Everyman, Jones is called to judgment on his day of reckoning, but the only answer the modern Everyman receives to his prayer is the impulse to use his last bullet—the silver bullet—against his vision in the darkness. Each confrontation with sin deprives Jones of another bullet, and in the end, without his bullets, he is defenseless. This Everyman's pilgrimage ends in betrayal, not in the peace of religious salvation, but at least in the peace that comes with death in a world devoid of faith.

Another interpretation of Jones's quest, more consistent with Jungian psychology, is that it is an inner quest, the unconscious, both personal and collective, represented symbolically by the dark, black forest. In this forest, Jones confronts his own particular guilt about the men he has killed, his cultural collective guilt about betraying his racial heritage, and finally his universal collective guilt about betraying his humanity. By the time he is killed by the natives' silver bullets, he has shot and destroyed all the negative images in his subconscious, and in this way, has painfully confronted and processed his guilt so that he is able to die with a clear conscience. Through his quest, and his suffering, Jones has gained psychological and perhaps spiritual (if not religious) redemption.

In *The Hairy Ape*, Yank sets out on a quest for revenge, which leads to self-discovery and redemption. After Mildred recoils from him in horror and calls him a "filthy beast" (*CP 1920–1931* 137), he is determined to "show her who's a ape!" (143). Unlike Jones's journey, Yank's does not suggest an internal quest. Rather, his remains external, a journey across society, as he seeks a way to get even with Mildred by proving not only that he is not a lesser being than she is, but, in fact, that he is greater.

His first challenge is to overcome the disarming aloofness of the upper class when he meets them on Fifth Avenue. As he strikes out against them, they merely disregard him, rendering him invisible. His anger lands him in jail, where he next finds himself isolated from, and at odds with, the other prisoners. They are content to rattle their cell bars and complain, but Yank needs to escape and take action. The next scene takes him to the union headquarters, where he hopes to find comrades in arms, but again he discovers that society has no pigeonhole that can contain his rage. The final leg of his journey brings him to the gorilla's cage at the zoo.

As in *The Emperor Jones*, O'Neill taps into the Jungian unconscious by using a creature that symbolizes primitive urges and impulses in human beings. In *Jones* it is a crocodile; in *Ape* it is a gorilla. Yank recognizes himself in the ape, but at the same time, he realizes that they are different. As the ape destroys Yank with a mighty hug, Yank accepts his death with equanimity and seems to be at peace. His quest does not bring him revenge on the upper class. Instead it brings him recognition of the status quo, and of his inability and unwillingness to accept his preordained place in the social order as defined by the capitalist system. There is no place in a rigid society like the one depicted in *The Hairy Ape* for a character with Yank's spirit for life. Yank's quest brings him self-discovery, redemption, and peace. Perhaps O'Neill suggests the need for the same kind of self-examination for American society itself.

## WORKS CITED

Gelb, Arthur and Barbara. *O'Neill: Life with Monte Cristo*. New York: Applause Books, 2000.

O'Neill, Eugene. *Complete Plays 1913–1920*. Ed. Travis Bogard. New York: Library of America, 1988.

———. *Complete Plays 1920–1931*. Ed. Travis Bogard. New York: Library of America, 1988.

Sheaffer, Louis. *O'Neill: Son and Artist*. Boston: Little, Brown, & Co., 1973.

# 5

## Desire Under the Elms (1924)

In 1924, after the deaths of his father, mother, and brother between the years 1920 and 1923, O'Neill wrote *Desire Under the Elms,* a play about a family in which three sons harbor intense hatred toward a hard and unforgiving father; and one of the sons, who is intensely loyal to his dead mother, falls in love with his father's new young wife, and she with him. In the end, to prove her love for the young man, the stepmother kills the baby they have had together. With all the biographical revelations of *Long Day's Journey Into Night,* supported by the fruits of all the subsequent research done by biographers like the Gelbs, Sheaffer, Black, and others, it is now easy enough to see, in the infanticidal, patricidal, and incestuous feelings and behavior of the characters in *Desire Under the Elms,* evidence of the tortured conscience of a man in mourning for his most intimate relatives. In fact, O'Neill claimed that the play came to him in a dream (Sheaffer 126). All of that aside, however, *Desire Under the Elms* is a work of intense passion that draws heavily on the earliest Western tradition of tragedy, Greek drama.

Written at the beginning of what has come to be known as O'Neill's middle, experimental period, *Desire* represents the first of O'Neill's explicit attempts to write an "American" tragedy using the basic plots of ancient Greek tragedy. In *Desire,* the dramatist "borrows" from the stories of three well-known Greek heroes: Oedipus (the man who hates—kills—his father, and loves—marries—his mother); Phaedra (the woman who lusts for her stepson); and Medea (the mother who kills her own children). Although these storylines move the play away from the more familiar terrain of most of O'Neill's naturalistic early dramas, the recognizable American character "types," nineteenth-century New England farmers, keep it firmly rooted in realism. By depicting ordinary American characters in the throes of extraordinary passions, O'Neill probes into mysteries beneath the surface of mundane naturalism. Whereas the human characters in Greek drama are clearly driven by the Gods, it is not clear what drives the human characters in *Desire Under the Elms,* thus raising twentieth-century questions about the essence of the human condition.

## SETTING AND PLOT DEVELOPMENT

The setting of *Desire Under the Elms* is an 1850 New England farmhouse. O'Neill is typically specific in the stage directions, and the characters frequently refer to aspects of the terrain that provide additional clues about what it should all look like. Two features of the setting stand out. One is the stone wall that separates the inhabitants of the harsh farm from the "softer" world beyond. Stones become a motif in the play, as Cabot and his sons reiterate throughout how harsh, dry, and unforgiving the land is, just like the old man who sustains it. In contrast to this physical attribute of the setting is the second important feature, on which O'Neill elaborates, at some poetic length, in the stage directions:

> Two enormous elms are on each side of the house. They bend their trailing branches down over the roof. They appear to protect and at the same time subdue. There is a sinister maternity in their aspect, a crushing, jealous absorption. They have developed from their intimate contact with the life of man in the house an appalling humaneness. They brood oppressively over the house. They are like exhausted women resting their sagging breasts and hands and hair on its roof, and when it rains their tears trickle down monotonously and rot on the shingles. (318)

A constant presence in the play, the soft maternal elms offset the harsh paternal force of the rocky terrain, capturing in visual scenic terms several of the central conflicts of the drama: life versus death, fertility versus sterility, mother versus father, easy or soft versus hard. The elms, as described in the stage directions, also obviously capture the contradictory feelings toward the mother figure in the play, as they "appear to protect and at the same time subdue" (318).

Theatrically, the concept behind the setting of *Desire* is important. Designed by Robert Edmond Jones, the farmhouse is constructed with removable walls facing the audience, so that the audience can see the action in the individual rooms, as well as outside the farmhouse, simultaneously. This feature of the set contributes to the realism of the play in that the audience can observe different interactions that are happening at the same time in real time. It also enables O'Neill to present evocative visual juxtapositions, thus adding to the nonrealistic, poetic, and even mythic quality of the drama. For example, in part 3, scene 1, downstairs in the kitchen, the townspeople celebrate with Cabot the birth of the baby he believes to be his son, while Eben sits brooding in his bedroom upstairs, and the baby he knows to be his lies silently in the cradle in the other upstairs bedroom. Later in the scene, Eben and Abbie meet in the bedroom where the baby is, and they embrace while standing over the cradle. The audience observes what is happening at this time in the house, not just in one room, but in multiple rooms; this device inevitably reminds the audience of the deception being perpetrated on Cabot, the love that binds Abbie to Eben, the distance that lies between both of them and Cabot, and especially the important sense of irony that underlies the action of this drama.

The play begins with the three Cabot brothers—Peter, Simeon, and Eben—awaiting the return of their father, Ephraim Cabot. Two of the brothers dream of escaping to find their fortune in the gold rush out West, while one of them—Eben—is scheming to gain control of the farm, which he believes his father has stolen from his mother. Eben, in particular, resents his father for allegedly working his mother to death while she was married to Cabot. When the three men learn that their father is about to return home with a new young wife on his arm, Eben helps his two brothers pursue their dream of traveling west to find gold by buying their shares of the farm with money his father has hidden in the floorboards. After waiting just long enough to meet their new "maw," and throw their freedom in Cabot's face, Peter and Simeon go off, singing and dancing, to find their "easy" fortune in "Californi-a," leaving Eben as the sole heir to the Cabot farm—that is, until Abbie stakes her claim to it.

Abbie Putnam is much younger than her new husband, Ephraim Cabot, and as she reveals some information about her past, it becomes clear that she sees him and his farm as her way out of a harsh and hopeless life. What she is not expecting is to find herself attracted to her husband's son, a man much closer to her in age and vitality: "*There is. . .about her whole personality the same unsettled, untamed, desperate quality which is so apparent in Eben*" (335). Although at first they both try to deny their natural instincts and speak disdainfully to each other, it is clear that they are both drawn to each other. Part 1 ends with Eben, the sole remaining son, squaring off against his father in a battle over the farm, while Abbie stakes her claim to the farm and to Eben.

At the beginning of part 2, when Cabot tells Abbie that he would rather burn the farm down than leave it to Eben, but that he will only leave the farm to a male heir, she recognizes her opportunity. Vowing to Cabot that she will bear him a son, she sets out to seduce Eben. In a sequence of two sexually suggestive scenes, she succeeds. Eben ultimately succumbs to her advances in the front parlor, the one unoccupied room of the farmhouse, where Eben's mother had been waked, and which has become sacred to Eben ever since her death. Abbie succeeds in seducing Eben by promising to give him the love and forgiveness he seeks from his mother. Eben finally justifies sleeping with Abbie to exact vengeance on his father for his mother. Scene 3 ends with a "fierce, bruising kiss," as Eben confesses, "An' I love yew, Abbie!—now I kin say it! I been dyin' fur want o' ye—every hour since ye come! I love ye!" (355). Part 2 then concludes with scene 4, in which Abbie and Eben declare their true love for each other (their lust having been transformed to love), and Eben confidently asserts his advantage over Cabot. ("I'm the prize rooster o' this roost.") Meanwhile Cabot remains blissfully unaware of the betrayal that has just been perpetrated by his wife and son.

At the beginning of part 3, the townspeople have come to celebrate with Ephraim Cabot the birth of his son, whom they all know to be Eben's, which makes the celebration highly ironic. The townspeople laugh behind Cabot's back, as he gets drunk and brags about his procreative strength and potency. Meanwhile, Abbie wanders around the room distractedly, looking for Eben, who sits brooding in one bedroom upstairs while the baby sleeps in a cradle in the other bedroom (the audience observing all of this simultaneously, as a result of the structure of the set, conceptualized by O'Neill and designed by Robert Edmond Jones, as noted previously). At the end of this scene, Eben walks into the baby's room, and when Abbie joins him there, they embrace, visually emphasizing the ironic nature of the celebration occurring downstairs. Eben then expresses his resentment at having to keep his paternity secret, and Abbie reassures him that she loves him, and that "Somethin's bound t'happen" (363). Although Cabot does not see the couple embracing upstairs, he voices his suspicion that something unnatural is happening in his house: "Even the music can't drive it out—somethin'. Ye kin feel it droppin' off the elums, climbin' up the roof, sneakin' down the chimney, pokin' in the corners!" (363).

While the celebration continues inside the house in scene 2, Eben meets Cabot outside, and Cabot advises him to go inside to the party because he should be thinking about marrying one of the "purty gals" in there to gain a share of another farm. When Eben then stakes his claim to the Cabot farm, his father derides him for his ignorance in not understanding that the farm will be passed on to the new son born to him and Abbie. In fact, he reveals to Eben that from the very start, Abbie's goal has been to acquire the farm for her own, and it is through her son that she will do so. Eben immediately reacts with rage at the idea that he has been used by Abbie, and his impulse is to kill her; Cabot steps in his way, though, and the two men wrestle, with Cabot emerging triumphant, just as Abbie enters. As Abbie then tries to comfort Eben, he turns on her; in spite of their previously declared love for each other, he accuses her of deceiving him in order to steal the farm, and he vows to leave her and the farm behind. When he suggests that the birth of their son has changed everything, Abbie contrives to win his love back by removing the one obstacle that she understands has now come between them.

Scene 3 begins with Abbie standing over the baby's cradle, "*her face full of terror yet with an undercurrent of desperate triumph*" (369). When she descends to the kitchen and runs to embrace Eben, saying "I done it, Eben!" (369), he at first thinks she has killed Cabot, and the implication is that this might have been a good idea that would allow them to be together (and, with the death of the father, adhering more closely to the Oedipus storyline). When Eben learns that she has murdered their son, however, he reacts with horror and continuing distrust of the woman he had previously claimed to love, suspecting first that Abbie intends to pin the murder on him and then that she selfishly did it to hurt him ("Ye killed him fur bein' mine!" [371]). As Eben vows revenge and races off to get the sheriff to arrest her, Abbie collapses in grief over losing Eben's love.

At the beginning of scene 4, Cabot learns that Abbie has murdered the baby, and that Eben, and not he, is the father. Furious that she has killed the baby and dazed by the reality of what has transpired between his wife and his son, he resigns himself to his lonesomeness. At first, he vows to destroy the farm and leave to seek his fortune with his other two sons in California, but when he learns that the money he has saved is gone (exchanged by Eben for his brothers' shares of the farm), he resigns himself to follow the hand of God and remain on the farm alone until he dies. Meanwhile, Eben returns from the sheriff's having had a change of heart. He throws himself at Abbie's knees, asks for her forgiveness, declares his love for her, and vows to share in her punishment whatever that may be ("prison 'r death 'r hell 'r anythin'!" [375]). As the sheriff escorts them off to their punishment, Abbie and Eben admire the "purty" sunrise and declare their undying love for each other. The sheriff gets the last words in the play, which reinforce the deep sense of irony at the heart of the drama: "It's a jim-dandy farm, no denyin'. Wished I owned it!" (378).

## CHARACTER DEVELOPMENT

All the significant characters in this play, and especially the three main characters—Cabot, Eben, and Abbie—are driven by *desire*, and specifically by the desire to possess something, whether it is the gold in the hills of California or the rocky farm in New England. In his or her quest to possess, each is guided by a different force: for Cabot, it is faith; for Eben, it is revenge; for Abbie, it is greed. Eben and Abbie feel lust for each other from the moment they meet, but at first, their desire for the farm keeps them apart. In the end, it is their desire and love for each other that leads them into each other's arms and away from the farm. Cabot remains true to his desire, and to his God, until the end, when he remains alone in possession of the farm.

Using a device that he had previously used with great effect in *Anna Christie* and that would eventually become a trademark of his dramaturgy, O'Neill delays Cabot's entrance through the first three-and-a-half scenes, during which the audience sees him through the eyes of his three sons, who all hate him. When he finally enters, accompanied by his new, young wife, Abbie, the audience expects him to be a cold, harsh, and even abusive, man, which he is. Through the course of the play, however, the audience discovers his "softer" side, symbolized by his preference for sleeping with the cows in the barn, and also learns the reason for his harshness ("God hain't easy" [348]). In his long, confessional monologue in part 2, scene 2, Cabot explains that he is driven by the hand of God to work hard, and not to take the easy road to comfort and fortune. Cabot is the archetypal New England Puritan, self-righteously defined by the Puritan work ethic that makes him hard on himself, as well as on others. It is only at the very end of the play, when he feels beaten by the shameful behavior of his wife and son, that he drops his guard momentarily, and considers leaving the farm behind for the gold in California, but his belief in God brings him back, determined to live out his final days alone on his farm. In the end, Cabot seems transformed by the events of the drama, in that he no longer feels restless in his loneliness. Rather, he seems content with it.

It is their love for each other that ultimately transforms the two other main characters, Abbie and Eben. Eben is a confused and conflicted young man. At first, he appears bitter and resentful toward his father, who, in his eyes, has abused and exploited his mother, working her to death and then stealing her farm. Eben seeks vengeance for his mother against his father.

His brothers play right into his hands when their hatred of the old man drives them to abandon the farm to seek their fortune in California, leaving Eben as the sole apparent heir. Using his father's hidden savings to pay the brothers off is but a small act of revenge in Eben's larger scheme.

Eben's behavior is motivated equally by hatred of his father and love and devotion to his deceased mother. When Cabot returns with his new bride, therefore, Eben resents her as a surrogate mother. The more he finds himself attracted to her, the more he tries to deny it, because to be attracted in any way to the woman who has replaced his mother feels disloyal to him, and to be sexually attracted to her is repellent. Nevertheless, he is drawn to her, and, with Abbie's seductive encouragement, he eventually convinces himself that having sex with his father's wife is the ultimate act of revenge that he can take against his father in the name of his mother; thus disloyalty becomes loyalty and repulsion succumbs to seduction.

After consummating their physical relationship at the end of part 2, scene 3, Eben seems like a different man in scene 4, as his brooding, distrustful demeanor changes to one of cocky self-satisfaction and contentment. Eben and Abbie have fallen in love. Eben's happiness is short-lived, however, primarily as a result of his innately suspicious nature, especially toward women. It takes only the slightest suggestion that Abbie has been motivated by greed, and not love, in seducing him to cause him to revert to his original venomous posture toward Abbie. For all his love and devotion to his mother, it seems likely that Eben also feels abandoned by her, thus causing an innate fear of betrayal, especially by women. He lashes out at Abbie, calling her a lying whore, and when she kills the baby, he calls her a murderer and a thief, temporarily forgetting about his goal of revenge against his father, and now seeking revenge against Abbie by turning her over to the sheriff (perhaps by doing this, he achieves revenge against his mother, and also, perhaps, against himself for betraying his mother by sleeping with Abbie). In the end, Eben resolves his inner turmoil as his love for Abbie triumphs over his desire for the farm or for revenge on his father. He returns to the farm determined to share with Abbie the punishment for the murder of their son (and implicitly for their adulterous behavior) and declares his love for her. In the end, Eben finds love and seems like a richer person for it (even without the farm), although ironically, the implication is that it has cost him his freedom, if not his life.

In many ways, Abbie is the most interesting and problematic character in the play. From the outset, she is clearly a strong woman who has suffered but is determined to better herself, using whatever means are available to her, even if that violates traditional moral precepts. So she marries Cabot to stake her claim to his farm, and then she contrives to seduce his son to secure that claim by producing a male heir for Cabot. When she then falls in love with Eben, she remains true to her nature, as she continues to take whatever action is necessary, in spite of its moral implications, to attain her goal, which is now Eben's love rather than the farm. Abbie is not an admirable character from a moral perspective; she is an adulterer and a murderer, and she commits a kind of incest in seducing her husband's son. In the end, however, she accepts her punishment for her crime. It is interesting that O'Neill makes the central female character in the play so strong. She is certainly more sure of herself than Eben, and at least as determined as Cabot. Like Eben, she seems to grow during the course of the play, as her lust for Eben transforms into love, and ultimately, she chooses that love over the farm. At the end of the play, she exits arm-in-arm with Eben, but she is also escorted by the sheriff. As with Eben, love comes at the expense of her freedom, if not her life.

The only other characters of any note in the play are the two brothers, Simeon and Peter. Their roles are primarily to serve as foils to Eben. Like Eben, they hate and resent their father, but unlike their younger brother, they have no strong attachment to a mother figure, and they seek their independence and fortune by abandoning the farm and their father, rather than remaining there to work on and inherit the farm. They are one-dimensional characters who represent the opposing American value to Cabot's New England Puritanism. They represent that strain of the American dream that promises fortune and wealth to anyone, no matter where a person starts on the socioeconomic ladder; if a person is in the right place at the right time, he or she can strike it rich. Their exultant celebration at the prospect of gaining their freedom is a paean to American opportunity, as well as a testament to how oppressive their father's home is. Their simple exultation stands witness to the complex paradoxical nature of Eben's struggle to transcend that oppression through love and ultimately death.

## THEMATIC ISSUES

*Desire Under the Elms* raises questions of moral relativism. Whereas Cabot's references to God and scripture assume a traditional Judeo-Christian value system, the behavior of Eben and Abbie challenges that system. The December–May marriage of Cabot to Abbie appears unnatural, which is emphasized when Abbie and Eben are immediately "naturally" attracted to each other, more so than are Abbie and Cabot, as indicated in the stage directions and dialogue. Yet Cabot frequently refers to something "oneasy," or unnatural, "pokin' about" in the house, suggesting that it is the adulterous and incestuous relationship between Abbie and Eben that is "unnatural" in a moral sense. Still, as Abbie and Eben consummate their sexual relationship and fall in love in part 2, it does seem "natural," and the question is whether two people should deny their true, inner "natural" feelings for each other because of an external code of conduct and ethics that says that acting on those feelings is "wrong."

These moral questions are raised again when Abbie murders her baby to prove her love for Eben. In this case, with the murder of a baby, O'Neill seems to stack the deck. It is difficult to justify this action with any argument of moral relativism. Is the taking of a human life, especially that of a helpless infant, justified because it is done to save a relationship? It seems not, according to the law. As the sheriff enters to arrest Abbie for murder, he asks no questions about motive, and she seems determined to accept her punishment. Eben, who has not had a direct hand in the murder, makes a case against himself, as he vows to share in Abbie's punishment equally, guilty, he says, by association, for putting the idea of murdering the baby in Abbie's mind. Of course, when he accepts punishment along with Abbie, it is implicitly for the other sins he has committed. In the end, however, although punished, Abbie and Eben have each other. The conclusion of the play seems to suggest that crimes (and sins) will be punished, but at the same time, that "love triumphs" over all. Although they admit their guilt and accept their punishment, both Abbie and Eben seem content, indeed exultant, in their love for each other. Human beings are sometimes driven by innate (natural) forces stronger than their learned ideas about right and wrong or what, according to society, is "natural." O'Neill's drama does not resolve these complex moral conundrums; it only raises them for the audience's consideration of what it means to be human.

One key word in the title, *elms*, suggests an important theme of the play when understood in the context of O'Neill's symbolic use of the elm trees in the scenic design. As described in the stage directions, these trees "protect" and "subdue"; their "sinister maternity" suggests an ambivalent attitude about motherhood, and by extension, about family. As a child develops and matures, the family is obviously a source of protection from the outside world, but at the same time, it can overprotect a child to the point of oppression, in which case the maturing child begins to feel confined and even stifled as an individual. Through his description of the elms, O'Neill seems to place the burden for this paradoxical effect on the mother, an emphasis that is reinforced throughout the play in Eben's relationship with both his deceased mother and his new stepmother.

Ironically, in promising to protect him, as his mother would, Abbie seduces him, which releases him from his "subdued" role as son, and allows him to become her lover. The seduction concludes and the sexual consummation takes place in the very room—the dark and abandoned front parlor, where the mother was waked—that has become associated with the stifling effect the mother has had on her son. After their tryst in the parlor, Abbie throws open the window to let in the light, symbolically indicating Eben's transformation from son to lover.

The seduction of Eben suggests another major theme of this play that is also found in its title—desire. Each character wants to possess something, or someone. Peter and Simeon desire wealth, and they leave the farm to seek their fortune out West. The three main characters—Cabot, Eben, and Abbie—all desire to own the farm, and they become locked in an intense struggle for possession of it. Desires of the flesh also drive both Eben and Abbie, and their lust for each other becomes confused with their desire for the farm. When that lust turns to love, the desire of their hearts overcomes their desire for the farm. When driven by desire, human beings behave irrationally and sometimes immorally. Because O'Neill is so specific in depicting these characters as New Englanders, he also suggests that Americans, in particular, driven by the desire to attain the American dream—whether in the gold in the hills of California or in the forbidding soil of a Connecticut farm—risk becoming corrupted by that dream at the expense of their souls. This is what makes the final line of the play so ironic: "It's a jim-dandy farm, no denyin'. Wished I owned it!" The Sheriff, another ordinary American, covets the farm, without any knowledge of, or concern for, the cost.

Finally, the heavy use of irony in the play enriches its thematic suggestiveness. Theatrical irony occurs when the audience is aware of something about which one or more of the characters in the play are unaware. For instance, Cabot's celebration of the baby's birth in part 3, scene 1, is ironic because the audience knows what Cabot does not know—that the baby is Eben's and not his. Similarly, the final line of the play, spoken by the sheriff and quoted previously, is ironic because the audience knows what the sheriff does not—that possession of this farm ("Wished I owned it!") has come at a severe and unforgiving price. The recurrence of so many incidents of characters' lack of awareness suggests a blindness that is characteristic of human existence. Through his use of irony, O'Neill suggests that there is an unknown, and perhaps unknowable, force that drives human experience. As much as humans believe that they control their own destiny, the evidence of life, ironically, suggests otherwise.

## STYLISTIC AND LITERARY DEVICES

A discussion of Desire Under the Elms would not be complete without some consideration of the dialect. In the tradition of the Irish naturalistic dramatist, J. M. Synge, whose works he admired, O'Neill captured in his dialogue the everyday speech of real people, written phonetically, so that actors would know exactly what each word should sound like. Much of the text is almost unidentifiable as the English language. For example:

> Yew must've cared a lot fur yewr Maw, didn't ye? My Maw died afore I'd growed. I don't remember her none. (*a pause*) But yew won't hate me long, Eben. I'm not the wust in the world—an' yew an' me've got a lot in common. I kin tell that by lookin' at ye. (338)

Much of the spelling is unrecognizable as English, and the grammar and syntax are strained, to say the least. When read aloud, however, the words begin to make sense, because they *sound* right, and soon enough, even an untrained reader begins to sound like a New England farmer.

Because it can be difficult to learn and to sustain, directors are sometimes tempted to eliminate the dialect and to have the actors speak the words with traditional pronunciations, often arguing that eliminating the dialect universalizes the characters. The point is, however, that the dialect itself has a universalizing effect. Even ordinary people, common farmers in mid-nineteenth-century New England, act on deep passions and are capable of profound love, as well as hatred. Because O'Neill uses the ancient Greek archetypes, the contrast between the mythic expectations suggested by those archetypes and the reality of O'Neill's everyday people makes the drama that much more profound.

Although highly naturalistic in character and dialogue, *Desire Under the Elms* reaches lyrical heights through its use of imagery and symbolism. The maternal elms and the dry, cold stones constitute the primary image patterns in the drama; and they work together to convey a sense of the mysterious, powerful forces that control human lives. The "natural" world of the play becomes one with the human world in a way that is poetic and mysterious, stylistically capturing the feeling of awe inspired by the action of the drama.

## ALTERNATE PERSPECTIVE: A FREUDIAN READING

In Freudian (or psychoanalytic) literary criticism, the reader considers the text as if it were a dream and finds in the symbolic content of the dream/text suggestive insights into the psyche of the dreamer/author. O'Neill claimed to Kenneth MacGowan, in 1924, that the play that was to become *Desire Under the Elms* had come to him in a dream (Sheaffer 126), so it is particularly fitting to apply Sigmund Freud's theories of the unconscious and dream interpretation to an analysis of this play. In this case, considered as the "dream work" of a man who has recently experienced the loss of his father, mother, and brother, *Desire Under the Elms* reveals a great deal about the tormented subconscious of the dramatist at this time. (See Stephen Black's psychoanalytic biography, *Eugene O'Neill: Beyond Mourning and Tragedy* for an extended application of psychoanalytic theory to this play and others in the context of O'Neill's life.)

Although O'Neill obviously draws on the Greek story of Oedipus in attempting to write an American tragedy, there is also some evidence that he may have derived the plot of *Desire* from a psychoanalytic case study (Black 311). Nevertheless, in 1924 and afterwards, the use of the Oedipus story inevitably associates the play with Freud's oedipal theory (itself based on the Sophocles drama), which posits that all young boys subconsciously desire to supplant their fathers in their mothers' affections. Most boys naturally grow out of this stage of development, but sometimes, these subconscious wishes may linger into adolescence and beyond, creating difficulties for the affected individuals in forging mature relationships, especially with members of the opposite sex. It is not uncommon for men who are "stuck" at the oedipal stage to become involved with women who are "unavailable" to them. When considered from a psychoanalytic perspective, the basic situation of *Desire Under the Elms,* in which a young man clearly lusts for his father's wife, strongly suggests not only that the 25-year-old character (Eben) suffers from an Oedipus complex, but also that the 36-year-old author (O'Neill) might be so diagnosed. In *Eugene O'Neill: Beyond Mourning and Tragedy*, Black suggests that Eben is "an expression of Eugene's identification with his brother, particularly his identification with Jamie's oedipal war with their father," and then adds, "he [O'Neill] substituted his brother for himself, yet he could hardly have escaped scot-free" (310–312).

From the outset of the play, the maternal influence is apparent, at first, symbolically, through the description of the elm trees. According to Black, "the famous description of the elms expresses a sense that a maternal presence watches over the farm, inescapable and overpowering" (307). O'Neill further describes the house and its surroundings in some detail:

> The action of the entire play takes place in, and immediately outside of, the Cabot farmhouse in New England, in the year 1850. The south end of the house faces front to a stone wall with a wooden gate at center opening on a country road. . . . There is a path running from the gate around the right corner of the house to the front door. . . . The end wall facing us has two windows in its upper story, two larger ones on the floor below. (318)

In Freudian dream interpretation, a house represents the human form, and when a wall of a house has breaks in it (e.g., balconies, windows), it represents a female form. Even more specifically, doors, gates, and windows signify the female genital opening (Freud 139). Robert Edmond Jones's innovative scenic design allows the house's façade, with four windows and a door, as well as a centrally placed gate to be visible to the audience throughout the course of the drama. In Freudian terms, then, in conjunction with the maternal, breastlike elm trees, this house establishes a setting that is not only a farmhouse in New England, but also the manifestation of a subconscious focused sexually on the female, and specifically, on the maternal.

As the play begins, three men enter into this symbolically female world and according to Freud, the number three symbolizes male genitalia (137). The only environmental element that is obviously associated with males are the stones, which, in the play, are synonymous with rocks (141), and the way in which the Cabot brothers speak about the stones reinforces their masculine association: "Here—it's stones atop o'the ground—stones atop o' stones—makin' stone walls—year atop o' year—" (O'Neill 320). In Freudian interpretation, elongation imagery is always phallic (Freud 138). Furthermore, the first scene of part 1 concludes with Peter and Simeon joining Eben in the kitchen, entering the house through the door (representing the female genital opening). Previously in the scene, the brothers reveal that their father has been away from home for two months, and in Freudian terms, a journey often signifies death (144). Thus by the end of the first scene of the play, O'Neill has presented a symbolic scenario of a son (three males who identify with stones) who has replaced the dead father (away on a journey) sexually (the stone wall grows bigger; they enter the house through the door) in relation to the mother (the house, the doors, windows, gate, and elm trees).

Freudian implications continue to be all too obvious in O'Neill's blatant use of symbolism, which can sometimes become rather complex. The elms, for example, not only have a "sinister maternity" about them, but Abbie gives them seemingly contradictory phallic significance when, in part 2, scene 1, as she begins to seduce Eben, she compares his "natural" attraction to her to the natural growth of the elm trees: "an'[Nature] makes you grow bigger—like a tree—like them elums—" (O'Neill 342). These symbolically seductive lines are spoken by a young woman who is *not* Eben's mother, but rather, his stepmother. Although, as in a dream, the sexual attraction toward the mother is displaced onto a "safer" figure, yet, as his stepmother, she would still be considered "off-limits" by society.

Abbie continues to be symbolically associated with Eben's (and O'Neill's) own mother as she seduces Eben and lures him into the front parlor, the room where his mother was waked and that has been closed and dark since her death. Again, if rooms are symbols for female genitalia, and doors and windows "represent the genital opening" (Freud 138), then in part 2, scene 3, this room that is associated with Eben's mother, which has been closed but is now opened, becomes more specifically associated with sexual intimacy with the mother. Although Eben is *not* literally having sexual relations with his own mother, the heavy Freudian symbolism suggests that when he consummates his lust for Abbie in "Maw's" front parlor (352–355), and when Abbie pushes open the shutters of the parlor window (355), these actions symbolize Eben's wish to sleep with his mother, which by psychoanalytic extension, can also suggest the playwright's wish for maternal intimacy.

Once the sexual relationship is consummated and the baby is born, the consequences suggest a guilty conscience at work. Eben is, in effect, punished for his illicit act when Abbie kills the baby in a misguided effort to prove her true love for Eben. Black has suggested that the death of the baby has interesting subconscious implications for the playwright in terms of his "reluctance to be a father and his (and [his second wife] Agnes's) sometime ambivalence toward [their son] Shane's intrusion on their intimacy" (Black 313). The baby's death also may suggest O'Neill's own death wish. There is considerable evidence that O'Neill had a death wish, including at least one suicide attempt, and it is not unusual in a dream for the wish to be "displaced" onto a different person (this death wish is even more explicitly suggested in *Long Day's Journey Into Night*, in which the dead baby is named Eugene).

O'Neill was disappointed in his mother for her failure, in his eyes, to provide the kind of nurturing intimacy he needed as a child. Indeed, Black suggests that he "resented to the point of hatred her inability to care for him in infancy or care for him when he was sick" (281–282). There is also substantial evidence (in *Long Day's Journey*, as well as in the biographical research) that O'Neill felt guilty about the role his own birth played in his mother's addiction to morphine, which, in part, disabled her from providing the maternal love he needed. When she died in 1922, her son must have experienced overwhelmingly mixed emotions, many of which—grief, guilt, anger, hatred, love, desire—are revealed in the play *Desire Under the Elms*, which came to him in a dream two years later.

## WORKS CITED

Black, Stephen A. *Eugene O'Neill: Beyond Mourning and Tragedy*. New Haven: Yale University Press, 1999.

Freud, Sigmund. *A General Introduction to Psychoanalysis*. Trans. Joan Riviere. New York: Simon and Schuster, 1969.

O'Neill, Eugene. *Complete Plays 1920–1931*. Ed. Travis Bogard. New York: Library of America, 1988.

Sheaffer, Louis. *O'Neill: Son and Artist*. Boston: Little, Brown, & Co., 1973.

# 6

# *Ah, Wilderness!* (1932)

Like *Desire Under the Elms, Ah, Wilderness!* came to O'Neill in his sleep one night (Sheaffer 404). Unlike *Desire,* and every other play he wrote, though, *Ah, Wilderness!* is a comedy. Set in New England in 1906, this domestic comedy is O'Neill's nostalgic look back at a time of innocence in America, an innocence that he himself had never experienced, certainly not within his family. O'Neill called this play "a sort of wishing out loud," and said, "That's the way I would have *liked* my boyhood to have been" (404). Before he embarked on the serious autobiographical works that have become commonly regarded as his greatest dramas, he wrote a comedy in which he looked at many of the same issues and family dynamics through a much more brightly colored lens. It is no coincidence that his late dramas include finely tuned comedic elements unlike anything in his earlier dramas, which is undoubtedly a factor in their claim to greatness.

As a comedy, *Ah, Wilderness!* has a dark underside that reflects many of the serious themes of O'Neill's other plays: for example, the debilitating effects of alcohol, the "enabling" behavior of families, the evasiveness of lasting happiness, the pains of adolescent yearning for independence, the disappointments of love and romance. It is commonly considered the "flip side" of *Long Day's Journey Into Night,* written later about the boyhood O'Neill actually *did* have. That reality lies behind the slamming doors of *Ah, Wilderness!* O'Neill was very fond of the play, and was obviously aware of its double-edge: "For me it has the sweet charm of a dream of lost youth, a wistfulness of regret, a poignantly melancholy memory of dead things and people—but a smiling memory as of those who still live" (406).

## SETTING AND PLOT DEVELOPMENT

The setting of *Ah, Wilderness!* is the "*sitting room of the Miller home in a large small-town in Connecticut*" on July 4, 1906. O'Neill's biographers have readily confirmed that the "large small-town in Connecticut" is New London, where O'Neill spent the summers of his boyhood with his family in the only "home" they ever knew, and that most of the characters in the play are based on people O'Neill knew there. The detailed description of the sitting room matches in structure, arrangement, and even decorative style (in both, for example, the floor is covered with an "inoffensive" rug), that of the Tyrones' living room in *Long Day's Journey Into Night*, and both sets are obviously modeled on the layout of the Monte Cristo Cottage, O'Neill's boyhood home on Pequot Avenue in New London, Connecticut (now a registered national landmark).

A comparison of the two opening scenic descriptions reveals differences in the kinds of books in the bookcases ("*boys' and girls' books and the best-selling novels of many past years*" [O'Neill 5] versus Shakespeare, Nietzsche, Swinburne, et al. [717]), in a few of the furnishings (e.g., five chairs around the center table rather than four), and in little else. The Miller house is "*furnished with scrupulous medium-priced tastelessness of the period*" (5), which is consistent with the way in which the Tyrones speak of their house. In act 1, the Miller home is described as "*homely looking and cheerful in the morning sunlight* (5), and "*sunshine comes through the windows*" (717) of the Tyrone home (although, for the most part, that bright cheerfulness remains dominant in the Miller household throughout the play, whereas in the Tyrones', it soon disappears behind the thickening, ominous fog as the long day progresses into night).

The setting of the play includes the date, about which O'Neill is very specific. It can hardly be a coincidence that O'Neill sets the action on July 4, Independence Day in the United States, as this will be a day during which Richard Miller will struggle to declare his independence from his family. Furthermore, the observance of Independence Day suggests a patriotic, nationalistic spirit and a sense of innocence, the loss of which O'Neill mourned when he wrote the play in 1932:

And do you like Pa & Ma and all the rest? Fine people, all of them, to me. Lovable! I hope they will seem so to others, and it's the truth. There were innumerable such people in these U.S. There still are, except life has carried us out of their orbit, we no longer see or know them.... But if America ever pulls out of its present mess and back to something approaching its old integrity and uniqueness, I think it will be owing to the fundamental simple homely decency of such folk.... I mean I believe it's still there as a basis to build a new American faith upon. (Sheaffer 407)

So O'Neill returns to July 4, 1906, to capture that spirit of purity and hope, which was difficult to muster in the 1930s. Also, the holiday celebration brings the family together in a way that enables O'Neill to suggest some of the tensions underlying family dynamics that, on the surface, appear quite calm and comforting.

Furthermore, in 1906, O'Neill himself was 18 years old; it was the summer before his departure for Princeton, a summer in which his parents traveled abroad, leaving Eugene alone in New London under the influence of his brother Jamie, who, according to Stephen Black, "spent the summer drinking and whoring" (88). O'Neill, then, was not nearly as naïve as Richard, especially when it came to liquor and prostitutes; but, like Richard, he was still finding his way, and finding his voice. According to Black, O'Neill "was...reading his seditious authors, who now included Nietzsche. Nietzsche led him to Wagner, the Greeks, and tragedy" (88). Apparently, O'Neill considered attending Yale, where most graduates of his prep school went, but instead, chose Princeton, perhaps because "at Princeton he might be able to develop further his own interests, regardless of whether they coincided with the curriculum" (88). During that year at Princeton (1906–1907) O'Neill first read works by a number of authors on Richard's reading list, such as Oscar Wilde, and in the spring semester, O'Neill first saw a production of Ibsen's *Hedda Gabler*, reference to which figures prominently (and very humorously) in the scene of Richard's drunken return to the Miller household in act 3, scene 2 of *Ah, Wilderness!*

Act 1 opens just as the family is finishing breakfast. The youngest son, Tommy, is setting off firecrackers, providing a regular aural reminder of the holiday, and the others all announce their plans for the day. The older son, Arthur, is going to see his girlfriend, and Mildred, the daughter, is going to a friend's house on the beach. The adults—Nat and Essie Miller, Nat's sister Lily, and Essie's brother Sid—plan an automobile ride around town before the men attend the annual Sachem Club picnic, where they usually get drunk, although Miller, and especially Sid, are admonished not to do so this year. This warning, directed especially at Sid, suggests early on that Sid's drinking is the cause of considerable tension between Lily and him. The only character not immediately accounted for is Richard, the middle son, who has remained in the dining room reading a book. His siblings make fun of his studiousness and his mother questions his choice of authors, but his father defends and to some extent identifies with both of these attributes. When asked his plans for the day, Richard speaks out against what he perceives as the false values of the holiday, establishing himself as the "young rebel" in the family.

Richard's girlfriend is Muriel McComber, whose father, Dave Mc-Comber, a businessman who advertises in Nat Miller's newspaper, stops by to complain that Richard has been sending what McComber considers blasphemous writings (from the books Richard has been reading) to Muriel, thereby attempting to corrupt his daughter's morals (O'Neill 19). When he demands that Miller punish Richard, Miller defends his son, tells McComber to mind his own business, and asks him to leave; but before leaving, McComber delivers a letter from Muriel to Richard informing him that she is breaking off their relationship. After McComber leaves, when Richard reads the letter from Muriel, he calls her a "coward," and resolves to get revenge. The first act ends with everyone heading out for their July 4 activities, except for Richard, who remains home alone, feeling alienated from the family, his girlfriend, and the patriotic celebrations around him: "Darn the Fourth of July, anyway! I wish we still belonged to England! (*He strides off in an indignant fury of misery through the front parlor*)" (26).

Act 2 begins with Mrs. Miller and Lily making preparations for the holiday dinner, with the assistance of Norah, the maid. Their dialogue reveals two important plot elements: one, a source of underlying tension in the play, is that Lily has been in love with Sid since she broke off her engagement to him 16 years ago because of his drinking, which is the reason that she still will not consider marrying him; and the other, a source of humor in the dinner scene to come, is that, for years, Mrs. Miller has been telling her husband that he has been eating weakfish, when she has been serving him bluefish, which he says contains a "certain oil" that poisons him. A third plot element introduced in this scene, a source of both tension and humor later in the play, is Richard's plan to help out a friend of his older brother's by joining him on a "date" with two prostitutes at a bar. Still feeling angry at Muriel, and at odds with his family and the July 4 festivities, Richard welcomes this opportunity to do something prohibited to "get even" with everyone.

Finally, the family sits down to dinner, as Miller and Sid return from their picnic, noticeably drunk, especially Sid. Miller enters and sits first, preparing the way for Sid's entrance, urging the others to pretend not to notice. They try, but as Sid talks to his spoon, discards it, and drinks his soup directly from the bowl, they break down and begin to laugh, which leads the way to an extended comic scene, the centerpiece of which is Miller's discovery that he has been eating bluefish for years, in spite of his protests that it poisons him. The dinner concludes with Sid self-mockingly asking Lily to marry him, knowing full well that she will reject the offer. After Sid leaves to go to bed, Lily gently berates the others and herself for encouraging Sid with their laughter. After she leaves the room, Richard declares that Lily is to blame for Sid's problems, "like all women love to ruin men's lives" (49), seeing in Sid's debilitation justification for his own debauchery planned for that evening.

Two scenes in the play take place outside the Miller home and show Richard's encounters with women. The first of these scenes is in the back room of a bar where Richard meets Belle, a prostitute. As Richard tries to appear experienced with cigarettes, liquor, and women, his lack of experience becomes increasingly apparent, much to Belle's frustration at first, but much to her amusement after he pays her five dollars *not* to go upstairs. He claims he has "sworn off" (sex with other women, presumably), and that he will "remain faithful" (57) to his girlfriend, a sentiment that Belle cynically debunks. While priming him for seduction, Belle encourages Richard to order more drinks and urges the bartender to make them stronger. By the time a salesman enters the back room and presents Belle with the opportunity for some real business, Richard has become intoxicated. When the Salesman warns the Bartender that he is liable for serving someone who is clearly a minor, the Bartender kicks Richard out, sending him into the streets to return home.

In act 3, scene 2, which takes place at just about the time scene 1 ends, the family passes an ordinary July 4 evening at home, except that the absence of Richard causes a high level of anxiety, especially for Mrs. Miller. Miller does his best to maintain a routine sense of calm, engaging in conversation about Mildred's handwriting and encouraging Arthur, after he returns from an evening with his girlfriend's family, to sing, all in the interest of distracting Mrs. Miller from watching the clock and worrying about Richard. As Arthur sings a popular sentimental song of the period, Sid and Lily play out what is clearly a ritual of (Sid's) self-denigration and (Lily's) forgiveness. After a while, all of this activity is interrupted by a noise from the piazza announcing Richard's return. When he enters, obviously intoxicated, looking disheveled and drunkenly quoting poetry, he evokes anger from his father, fear and concern from his mother, and knowing sympathy from his Uncle Sid. Sid takes him upstairs to "fix" him up, while his mother imagines the terrible things he has done, especially with a "bad woman" named Hedda, not realizing that he has been quoting from Ibsen's play, *Hedda Gabler*.

Act 4, scene 1 takes place at 1 P.M. on the next day, enough time for Richard to have slept off the effects of the previous night's adventure. Miller comes home from work at lunchtime to punish Richard, only to find that Mrs. Miller has allowed him to stay in bed all morning, indicative of her mixed impulses both to punish and protect her son. She promises that he will get his real punishment when his father returns in the evening, yet she also beseeches Miller not to be too harsh with him. When Mrs. Miller tells Miller that she does not have the heart to wake up their son, he returns to work, after which Richard emerges from his bedroom and announces that he will not drink again because "it wasn't any fun.... It only made me sadder—and sick—so I don't see any sense in it" (82). This revelation satisfies his mother that he is sufficiently repentant (although he insists that it has nothing to do with morals), and as she exits, she instructs him to stay in the house for the day as punishment. When his sister Mildred returns home with a letter from Muriel, however, in which Muriel states that her father had forced her to write the previous letter, she did not mean a word of it, and she plans to sneak out of her house that night to meet him, his love for her is immediately revived. He takes the opportunity to sneak away while nobody else is home, instructing Mildred to tell his parents later where he has gone, so that they do not worry as they had the night before.

Act 4, scene 2 is the second of the two scenes set outside of the Miller house. Here Richard is waiting on the beach for Muriel. When she arrives, at first he tries to hide his excitement about seeing her again, acting nonchalant as a way to pay her back for his suffering; but when she threatens to leave, he reveals his true happiness. As they then sit together in the moonlight, each one describes the risks they have taken to be together. Richard tells Muriel about his escapades at the bar with Belle the night before, exaggerating some of the details for romantic effect. Muriel is angered at the revelation that Belle kissed him, but when Richard swears to her that he does not love Belle, but only her, she forgives him, and declares her love for him. This exchange leads to a much anticipated kiss in the moonlight, with Richard quoting romantic poetry and promising a honeymoon "on the road to Mandalay!" (97).

Act 4, scene 3 takes place back at the Miller house at 10 o'clock that night, just a little while after Muriel and Richard have presumably parted at the beach. This scene directly parallels act 3, scene 2, in which Richard returns home from his rendezvous with Belle. In this scene, however, Mr. and Mrs. Miller more calmly await Richard's return from his rendezvous with Muriel. After some discussion about Richard's punishment and speculation about the significance for Richard of his relationship with Muriel.

Richard enters, this time under the influence of love, not liquor. Mrs. Miller quickly excuses herself so that Miller can have a talk with Richard. After strongly reinforcing Richard's feelings of self-disgust for getting drunk, Miller inquires about Richard's involvement with the prostitute at the bar, and Richard reassures him that he did not go to bed with her. Nevertheless, this leads Miller into the obligatory, and humorously awkward, father/son talk about the natural sexual desires of young men. After Miller advises Richard not to fulfill those desires by having relations with prostitutes, Richard confesses his true love for Muriel and his intention to marry her, which brings Miller's lecture to an abrupt end, much to his own relief. When Richard then asks about his punishment and his father tells him that his punishment is that he will not be going to Yale, Richard happily welcomes this sentence as a means to marry Muriel sooner, which leads his father to reverse his decision and punish him by sending him to Yale!

At this point Mrs. Miller returns, and Richard kisses his parents good-night before going out on the piazza to watch the moon set, inspiring his father to quote from "The Rubaiyat of Omar Khayyam," one of the literary works in Richard's collection: "Yet Ah, that Spring should vanish with the Rose!/That Youth's sweet-scented manuscript should close!" (107). While acknowledging the transitory nature of spring and youth, the play concludes with an affirmation of the enduring nature of love, when Miller adds his own commentary on his quote from "The Rubaiyat": "Well, Spring isn't everything, is it, Essie? There's a lot to be said for Autumn. That's got beauty, too. And Winter—if you're together" (107). The play ends as the Miller parents exit together through the back parlor to their bedroom, while Richard remains alone and content in the moonlight, capturing in one final tableau both the hope and disappointment of youth, as well as the power of enduring love.

## CHARACTER DEVELOPMENT

Given that *Ah, Wilderness!* is a depiction of the kind of family life O'Neill wished he had had as a young boy, it is not surprising that some of the family figures are rather idealized. The large cast of *Ah, Wilderness!* is built around conventional stereotypes such as the anxiously overprotective mother, the gossipy younger sister, and the stern and Puritanical New England businessman. Yet many of the characters who are based on stereotypes such as Lily, Sid, Muriel, Belle, and Richard sometimes behave, or speak, in surprising ways.

Mrs. Miller (Essie) is a stereotypically overprotective and nurturing mother and a forgiving and supportive wife, very much the opposite of

O'Neill's own mother (and, therefore, of Mary Tyrone, his fictionalized depiction of her in *Long Day's Journey Into Night*). From her first words in the play, with which she corrects Tommy's grammar, to her last words (which are *the* last words of the play), with which she affirms her husband's optimistic sentiments, Mrs. Miller never swerves from her traditional role as the matriarch of this successful New England family. She conforms to the gender role stereotype of her time, taking charge of all things domestic, including meals and the early education of her children, while turning to her husband to be the enforcer. At the same time, she comically reinforces the ironic truth of this stereotype—that the man is *not* ultimately in control—when she orchestrates the domestic routine to protect Richard from any severe punishment her husband might inflict (which she superficially encourages him to do). Mrs. Miller is a bundle of humorous contradictions: she expresses shock and outrage at her son Richard's choice of reading material, yet she cites that material as evidence of his intelligence; she objects to the morals of some of the writers whose works Richard reads (although she has never read these works), yet she lies to her husband every time she serves him blue fish. Of course, in the comic spirit of the play, these contradictions are depicted as symptomatic of a harmless, normal human foible, and not the source of intrafamilial tension and strife, as such foibles and their symptoms are in so many other of O'Neill's family dramas, and especially in *Long Day's Journey Into Night*.

Miller's behavior and personality remain constant throughout the play. Although he plays the role of "head of the household," defending and protecting his family from outside threats (e.g., Dave McComber, the ills associated with liquor and prostitutes), he is also a kindly and understanding father, who goes along with his wife's soft approach to punishment, and is sympathetic to his son's "radical" taste in literature. Unlike O'Neill's own father (and therefore unlike James Tyrone in *Long Day's Journey Into Night*), he does not take himself too seriously, as evidenced by his bumbling, yet endearing attempt to lecture Richard about sex, as well as by his self-deprecating reaction to the loving abuse he takes when the blue fish deception is revealed.

Richard's three siblings (Arthur, Mildred, and Tommy) are secondary characters, to be sure, and they play off traditional American family stereotypes. The mischievous Tommy (the youngest) sets off firecrackers on July 4, even though he has been warned against doing so, and he finagles his way into staying up late on this special occasion. His sister Mildred gossips about and teases her brothers incessantly. Arthur is the conceited older brother, trying to appear too mature for the antics of his younger siblings.

Other stereotypical secondary characters are McComber, Wint, the Bartender, the Salesman, Norah, and Muriel. McComber is the close-minded, self-righteous, small-town New England businessman, a composite of the New London elite who felt threatened by unconventional attitudes and behaviors and who, in those turn-of-the-century summers, protected their daughters from the likes of Eugene O'Neill and especially his brother Jamie. Although Richard is rebellious, his rebellion is played out in the books he reads and quotes, rather than in actions. In fact, when presented with the opportunity to behave immorally, he resists, unlike Wint, Arthur's college friend, who is described as *"a typical, good-looking college boy of the period. . .the hell-raising sport type"* (34). It is Wint who lures Richard to the Pleasant Beach House, and while Richard struggles with his conscience downstairs at the bar with Belle, Wint is upstairs with Edith, another prostitute. Although Wint appears only in one short scene, he represents the temptation of women and drink that waits outside the door, ready to corrupt the values of the young American male as he leaves the comfort of his home.

The Bartender and the Salesman are purely functional characters, defined by their professions. They help dramatize Belle's identity as a hooker, and with her, they add a sufficiently threatening dose of seediness to the barroom scene in the third act to repel Richard from that corrupting world of temptation back to his idyllic and safe home and girlfriend. The Bartender and Belle anticipate the bartenders and prostitutes of *The Iceman Cometh*, and in the Salesman, O'Neill creates a simple initial sketch of Hickey.

Norah, the "Second Girl," is also a simple character. Her mere presence as a servant in this relatively modest middle-class household suggests the pretensions of the American middle class, and the subservience of the Irish immigrants (from whom O'Neill was descended) at this time. Norah provides several comic moments in the second act, as she clumsily serves the family, perhaps suggesting the incongruity of household servants in a supposedly classless American society. Norah also adds an important note to the chorus of voices that enable Sid to continue drinking: "Ah, Miss Lily, don't mind him. He's only under the influence. Sure, there's no harm in him at all" (42). It is this "peasant Irish" notion, that drinking is "a good man's failing," which is firmly embedded in O'Neill's father's ethnic and economic heritage, that encouraged continuing alcoholic consumption in O'Neill's own family.

Richard's girlfriend Muriel appears in only one scene, but she is a constant offstage presence, as much of Richard's behavior throughout the play is reactive to her. She is the romanticized star-crossed girlfriend, naïve by

Richard's pretentious standards, but bold enough to sneak out of her house even though she has been forbidden by her father from seeing Richard. In the scene with Richard at the beach, at first she seems shy and nervous about being seen there together; yet she not only sits in the moonlight with Richard, but she eventually encourages him to kiss her. From initiating their romantic rendezvous to inquiring about their honeymoon plans, Muriel seems very much in control of this young relationship, much as Richard's mother is very much in control of her more mature marital relationship. Muriel takes practical action whereas Richard mostly merely muses and reacts.

Although it might appear that Belle is a stereotypical prostitute of the period—brash, forward, and provocative—she also shows a softer, more vulnerable side. As Richard begins to feel comfortable with her, and to grow fond of her (he is also feeling quite drunk, of course), he wonders why she (a "nice girl") is a prostitute, and he advises her to reform. Her reply is telling: "You can do a lot with me for five dollars—but you can't reform me, see"; her demeanor changes and she speaks "*sharply*" and "*with an ugly sneer*" (57–58), suggesting deeper emotions than a merely superficial characterization would indicate. Sheaffer considers Belle to be O'Neill's "most realistic prostitute to date" (404), her words recalling Anna Christie's angry turn to prostitution, and anticipating the prostitutes in *The Iceman Cometh*, who grapple with the distinction between pipe dreams and reality.

Lily is Nat Miller's sister, an unmarried schoolteacher who lives with her brother and his rather large family. Over the years, she has become very fond of her sister-in-law's brother, Sid, who also lives in the Miller house when he returns to town, which is apparently quite often. Sid is not successful at holding down jobs in other places, whereas his brother-in-law Nat will always give him work on his newspaper. He has difficulty keeping jobs because he is an alcoholic, which is also the reason that Lily will never marry him. Although Sid's mock proposal and Lily's mock rejection are part of the comic ritual performed when Sid gets drunk, it is a refrain in the play that has sad undertones for both characters, and naturally anticipates the much more serious, even tragic, repetitive patterns of blame and denial in the Tyrone family in *Long Day's Journey Into Night*. Immediately after the comic dinner scene in act 2, Lily berates the family, including herself, for laughing at Sid and encouraging his antics, and his drinking. She insists that she will never marry him, yet she is always there to forgive him when he is drunk and lost. Ironically, as long as she keeps forgiving him, he will continue drinking, which means that, with her forgiveness, she helps to ensure that they will never marry.

This is an interesting, comically ironic twist on a recurring, and mostly sad, character dynamic in O'Neill's drama—the incorrigible alcoholic and the all-forgiving woman (Hickey/Evelyn in *Iceman*, Tyrone/Josie in *Moon for the Misbegotten*, and to some extent, Tyrone/Jamie/Mary in *Long Day's Journey Into Night*). Sid is a more stereotypically comic drunk than virtually any other O'Neill character. The dinner scene is the comic centerpiece of the play, with Miller's self-deprecating humor providing the subtle and tender domestic comic undertones while Sid's antics (talking to his spoon, eating the lobster shells) provide the belly laughs. Yet beneath the comic and stereotypical surface lies the sad story of a man bent on self-destruction. Unable to keep a job and unable to find any meaningful purpose for his life, Sid drinks, and the more he drinks, the more he alienates the one person who could offer him salvation through love. The never-ending cycle of transgression, forgiveness, and reconciliation in his relationship with Lily makes the funniest character in the play—Sid—also one of the two saddest (the other, of course, being Lily).

Finally, Richard Miller is the central character in the play, and as a developing, somewhat confused, adolescent, he is certainly the most complex. At first, he appears to be a young rebel. His romantic quotes and exclamations, although mostly humored by his conservative New England family, are of some concern to his parents, especially to his mother. Richard represents American idealism when he rants against the evils of capitalism: "Home of the slave is what they ought to call it—the wage slave ground under the heel of the capitalist class, starving, crying for bread for his children, and all he gets is a stone!" (O'Neill 13). He admiringly quotes poetry intended to sweep his beloved off her feet: "You have my being between the hands of you! You are my love, mine own soul's heart, more dear than mine own soul, more beautiful than God!" (97). Of course, these sentiments border on treason, on the one hand, and blasphemy, on the other. Yet in the mouth of an impressionable adolescent like Richard, they convey hope.

Richard's rebelliousness is tempered by his father's tolerance for, and even sympathy with, the views expressed by his son's favorite authors. After stepping to the edge of the dark side in his rendezvous with Belle, Richard retreats to the comfort and reassurance of his conservative home. Even in his experience with alcohol, Richard recoils from the ill effects that define his uncle's existence and returns to the safer world of his girlfriend, siblings, mother, and father. In the end, as Richard recognizes that his parents were once the same young, idealistic lovers as he and Muriel now are, he reaches a level of maturity that allows him to see beyond himself and his own yearnings, as he acknowledges his place in life's endless cycle: "Yes, I'll bet those must have been wonderful nights, too. You sort of forget the moon was the same way back then—and everything" (105). *Ah, Wilderness!* is the story of Richard's coming of age. At the end of the play, he stands ready to face the world on his own, as a mature, responsible young man. This image of Richard is quite different from that of O'Neill himself and his brother at the same age, who, as depicted in *Long Day's Journey*, remained locked in a self-destructive familial prison well into their adult years.

## THEMATIC ISSUES

As commentators and scholars have observed, in *Ah, Wilderness!* O'Neill developed many of the same themes of his serious drama—such as family ties, alcohol dependency, the hopes and disappointments of love, and the essential aloneness of the individual—but from a more lighthearted angle. Sheaffer affirms the play's stature in O'Neill's canon: "Rather than an anomaly among his works, the comedy is based on his obsession with family life and his own past, the twin foundation stones of his finest writings" (405). What Sheaffer says of the characters in *Ah, Wilderness!* may also be said of its themes: they are "familiar," but "now limned with fond humor" (404).

The Miller family is tight-knit, in the best sense of the word. Parents care about their children; children respect their parents; siblings torment each other, but in a crisis, they support each other; members of the extended family are welcome to stay. Although the Miller children have their separate romantic engagements, and the adult males their men-only picnic, the Fourth of July is a time to be with family, and the cornerstone of the family celebration is the holiday dinner. The biggest threat to the family's cohesiveness comes from Richard, who, in his adolescent struggle to find an identity separate from the one he has within his family, seems to reject their values. Twice he literally leaves the confines of the family home to venture out on his own. In each case, Richard experiments with a new voice—one drunk with liquor, the other with romance—and in both cases, he returns home to fine-tune those voices within the family context.

In act 4, scene 1, the morning after his drunken flirtation with Belle, Richard assures his mother that he will never get drunk again, but he is careful to emphasize that it is for reasons of his own:

> I won't do it again...But that's not because I think it was wicked or any such old-fogy moral notion, but because it wasn't any fun. It didn't make me happy and funny like it does Uncle Sid...It only made me sadder—and sick—so I don't see any sense in it. (O'Neill 82)

Similarly, in act 4, scene 3, when he returns from his romantic date on the beach with Muriel, he pleasantly surprises his father with his reasons for not having sex with a prostitute:

> But I didn't! ...She wanted me to—but I wouldn't. I gave her the five dollars just so she'd let me out of it. Honest, Pa, I didn't! She made everything seem rotten and dirty—and—I didn't want to do a thing like that to Muriel—no matter how bad I thought she'd treated me—even after I felt drunk, I didn't. Honest! (103)

In both cases, although his actions are consistent with the values of his family, the reasons for his actions are his own. He seems to have discovered a sense of himself that is a clear indication of an emerging maturity that can occur only when a child is no longer dependent on his family for his self-identity; yet his self-identity is not entirely independent of his family, especially of its values. This is why it is such a remarkable moment when Richard kisses his father toward the end of the play:

> First time he's done that in years. I don't believe in kissing between fathers and sons after a certain age—seems mushy and silly—but that meant something! And I don't think we'll ever have to worry about his being safe—from himself—again. And I guess no matter what life will do to him, he can take care of it now. (106)

In this coming-of-age comedy, O'Neill suggests that children can attain independence from family ties without completely becoming untied from the family, something that, in his own family, he and his brother were never quite able to do.

Alcoholism plagues many characters in O'Neill's plays, and *Ah, Wilderness!* is no exception. Although the symptoms of alcohol dependency are played for laughs more than in any of O'Neill's other dramas, underlying the humor is the sad desperation of a self-destructive man. When Sid seeks forgiveness from Lily, he reveals a low level of self-esteem that inevitably keeps him dependent on alcohol:

> You're right, Lily!—right not to forgive me!—I'm no good and never will be!—I'm a no-good drunken bum!—you shouldn't even wipe your feet on me!—I'm a dirty, rotten drunk!—no good to myself or anybody else!—if I had any guts I'd kill myself, and good riddance!—but I haven't!—I'm yellow, too!—a yellow, drunken bum! (*He hides his face in his hands and begins to sob like a sick little boy.*) (70–71)

When Lily forgives him, she enables him to drink again, ensuring that he will always consider himself unworthy of her, and therefore, he will be unworthy of her. Beneath Sid's comic actions, which lead Richard to believe that his uncle is "happy and funny" (82), lies the distressing and painful truth about alcohol dependency, which is that it makes people sad and pitiable.

Richard's dalliance with drinking also contributes to the demytholo-gizing of intoxication that is characteristic of O'Neill's depiction of the effects of alcoholism in most of his later plays. Thus although Richard precociously quotes literature that glorifies drinking and intoxication in terms of Dionysian transcendence ("Eilert Lovborg will come—with vine leaves in his hair!" [60]), his actual experience with drunkenness is much more prosaic ("Ma! I feel—rotten!" [74]). In Sid's case, the negative conse-quences of his drinking are far more severe than feeling physically "rotten." Yet Richard's introduction to the effects of alcohol, as well as Sid's antics at the dinner table, are primarily humorous largely because they are played out in the safe domestic environment of the Miller home.

Just as the play depicts two sides of drinking and alcoholism, it also depicts two sides of love and romance. On the one hand, the Millers are happily married, and their relationship is enduring. On the other hand, Sid and Lily are never able to find constancy in their commitment to each other and so remain forever disappointed and frustrated. The oldest Miller offspring, Arthur, seems well on his way toward his parents' comfortable level of love and commitment in his relationship with Elsie Rand; but the next in line, Richard, seeks something more passionate and romantic, something more risky, in his relationship with Muriel. By the end of the play, though, he seems to recognize the beauty of his parents' long-lasting love affair and even to recognize the potential in it for romance and pas-sion. When Miller takes account of his family at the end of the day in act 4, scene 3, he proudly proclaims that love has triumphed: "Then, from all reports, we seem to be completely surrounded by love!" (101). Although it is evident that Sid and Lily are never going to know the complete satis-faction of a truly committed love relationship, Miller's account includes a report that Sid and Lily have gone down to the beach to listen to the band. Their "problems" are pushed aside, so that even they are included in the circle of love.

Miller reminds his wife of the possibility of enduring love and compan-ionship with another person at the end of Ah, Wilderness!: "Well, Spring isn't everything, is it, Essie? There's a lot to be said for Autumn. That's got beauty, too. And Winter—if you're together" (107). Although the conclu-sion of the play affirms this sentiment, with so many of the characters in couples, there are, nevertheless, intimations of the existential aloneness of human beings, consistent with O'Neill's vision in his darker plays. For one thing, as indicated previously, there is Sid, whose alcoholism alienates him from the one person whose companionship might make him feel whole. And Lily, the unmarried schoolteacher aunt, intensifies her isolation from others in her refusal to marry Sid. Most significantly, in existential terms, Richard, in his rebelliousness, stakes his claim to independence, which also entails standing alone (as he does, literally, at the end of the play) and taking responsibility for his own actions. Finally, even as Mr. and Mrs. Miller have the last optimistic words in the play, affirming love, they exit *"out of the moonlight, back into the darkness of the front parlor"* (107), the very room that leads into O'Neill's much darker vision of his youth as depicted in *Long Day's Journey Into Night*. Implicit in this darker vision is the ultimate isolation of the individual, even within the context of a loving family.

## STYLISTIC AND LITERARY DEVICES

O'Neill used music and sound effects to establish mood in his earliest naturalistic plays, such as the boisterous singing and dancing in "Moon of the Caribees" and the mournful steamers' whistles in *Anna Christie*, and in an expressionistic drama like *The Emperor Jones*, the beating of the tom-tom takes on powerful psychological significance. The more mature dramatist continued to use music and sound in his later plays not only to achieve similar effects but also sometimes to provide ironic commentary on the action. In *Ah, Wilderness!* the music and sound effects provide a meaningful counterpoint to the comic surface of the drama.

Early in the play, when the youngest Miller child, Tommy, runs off after breakfast, his mother warns him to set off firecrackers far away from the house. Significantly, however, a few moments later, just as Sid expresses his gratitude for his sister's hospitality with a well-known cliché—"there's no place like home" (8)—the sound of Tommy's firecrackers nearby suggests that things may not be quite as peaceful and idyllic as that cliché implies: *"As if to punctuate this remark, there begins a series of bangs from just beyond the porch outside as Tommy inaugurates his celebration by setting off a package of firecrackers. The assembled family jump in their chairs"* (8). Most immediately, it is apparent that Tommy does not necessarily follow his mother's instructions or adhere to her wishes. Beyond that, though, the sound effect at that moment strongly suggests that Sid may neither find nor bring peace to this "home sweet home." O'Neill emphasizes this effect, and extends it to the whole family, in the stage directions after

Mrs. Miller returns from having warned Tommy again, saying "Now we'll have a little peace":

> *As if to contradict this, the bang of firecrackers and torpedoes begins from the rear of the house, left, and continues at intervals throughout the scene, not nearly so loud as the first explosion, but sufficiently emphatic to form a disturbing punctuation to the conversation.* (8)

Like the beating of the tom-tom in the earlier *The Emperor Jones*, and like the foghorn in act 4 of the later *Long Day's Journey Into Night*, the firecrackers become a constant reminder of subtext, in this case, that there are disturbances (e.g., Sid's alcoholism, Sid and Lily's doomed relationship, Richard's rebellious questioning of the status quo) lying just beneath the surface of this seemingly peaceful family. The sound of the slamming door, especially in acts 1 and 2, has a similar effect.

O'Neill's use of music also helps set the mood and tone of his drama, and the source of the music lies within the drama itself, for example, in act 3, scene 2, when Arthur and Mildred play and sing songs to help distract their mother from her worries about Richard's whereabouts. The impact of these songs, however, is anything but cheering, as the stage directions indicate when he begins to sing an "old sentimental favorite" called "Then You'll Remember Me":

> *The effect on his audience is instant. Miller gazes before him with a ruminating melancholy, his face seeming to become gently sorrowful and old. Mrs. Miller stares before her, her expression becoming more and more doleful. Lily forgets to pretend to read her book but looks over it, her face growing tragically sad. As for Sid, he is moved to his remorseful, guilt-stricken depths. His mouth pulls down at the corners and he seems about to cry.* (69)

Arthur and Mildred's concert then becomes the melancholy background accompaniment to Sid and Lily's sad ritual of apologies, forgiveness, reconciliation, and resigned acceptance. The second song, "Dearie," has the same effect as the first, only "*intensified*" (70), leading Mrs. Miller to comment "*dolefully*," "I wish he wouldn't sing such sad songs" (70). When the more upbeat "Waiting at the Church" finally breaks the somber mood, all except Mrs. Miller, who remains "*dolefully preoccupied*" (71), either laugh or smile, but even this song provides an ironically bittersweet undertone to the scene. The lyrics refer jokingly to the inability of a man to marry his girlfriend because his wife will not allow him to do so, but a simple substitution of "the booze" for "my wife" seriously describes the situation between Sid and Lily: "Can't get away to marry you today, My wife [the booze] won't let me!" (71). This musical moment is followed soon after by an awkward separation of Sid and Lily, as well as the continuing interruption of the attempts at uplifting music: "*Mildred keeps starting to run over popular tunes but always gets stuck and turns to another*" (72). So the music has not only failed to comfort Mrs. Miller, but it has also implicitly called attention to the sad reality of the relationship between Sid and Lily.

O'Neill uses music and sound effects to intensify and comment on the underlying feelings of his characters. The sad and ironic songs Arthur sings, as well as the firecrackers going off and the doors slamming, all punctuate the play with either sadness, tension, or both. If this were just a happy family with no problems, the music would be different and the sound effects less jolting; the play would be superficial, the comedy pure sentimentality. This, however, is a family that *seems* happy, one that functions *in spite of* its problems, and the music and sound effects provide reminders of that reality.

## ALTERNATE PERSPECTIVE: GENRE ANALYSIS

Genre analysis considers how a particular literary work meets, violates, modifies, or redefines the requirements imposed by the conventions of specific literary genres. So, a critic might, for example, analyze how a novelist uses narrative techniques to tell his or her story, how a poet uses the sonnet form to convey an emotion, or what makes a work tragic, melodramatic, or comic. *Ah, Wilderness!* is regarded as O'Neill's only comedy, so it is especially interesting to consider how this otherwise serious, even somber, dramatist retuned his dramaturgy to strike a comic note.

John Gassner once described *Ah, Wilderness!* as "one of the most attractive of American domestic comedies, nothing less and nothing more" (Gassner 34–35), but in fact it is more than that. O'Neill himself said of *Ah, Wilderness!*:

> Yes, it *is* a comedy—and not in a satiric vein like *Marco M.*—and not deliberately spoofing at the period (like most modern comedies of other days) to which we now in our hopeless befuddlement and disintegration and stupidity feel so idiotically superior, but laughing at its absurdities while at the same time appreciating and emphasizing its lost spiritual & ethical values.
>
> But, hell, that doesn't say what I mean. It's in the mood of the play, as you'll see when you read it.... it is purely a play of nostalgia for youth.... A play about people, simple people of another day but real American people....*And* a comedy! It's damned funny (at least to me!). But it makes me weep a few tears too! (Bogard & Bryer, 409, 412)

*Ah, Wilderness!* is funny, with physical, verbal, and situational humor throughout, and it is also resoundingly comic.

There are moments of physical humor, as in act 1, when the sound of firecrackers makes everyone jump after Mrs. Miller has explicitly instructed Tommy not to set them off close to the house, yet he does so anyway, and in act 2, when the servant Norah slams the pantry door, after Mrs. Miller has explicitly instructed her not to do so, also causing others onstage to jump in their places in surprise. Then, of course, there are Sid's drunken antics in the dinner scene in act 2, when he struggles to eat his soup with a spoon, and later, when he eats the claw of a lobster, "shells and all" (O'Neill 46).

There is also verbal humor in the play, most examples also occurring in the dinner scene, in Sid's intoxicated musings, as when Mrs. Miller scolds him for drinking his soup directly from the bowl without a spoon:

> Are you—publicly rebuking me before assembled—? Isn't soup liquid? Aren't liquids drunk? (*Then considering this to himself*) What if they are drunk? It's a good man's failing. (40)

And again, a few moments later, when Miller expresses his concerns about eating bluefish, Sid fuels his brother-in-law's suspicions with his linguistically playful speculation: "Aha! Nat, I suspect—plot! This fish looks blue to me—very blue—in fact despondent, desperate, and—" (42).

Pratfalls and puns are funny, but much of the humor of *Ah, Wilderness!* derives from the awkward situations in which O'Neill places his characters that puts them at cross-purposes. When Richard interacts with the prostitute Belle at the bar in his quest to get even with his family and girlfriend by showing them how mature and unbound by convention he is, the humor lies in the contrast between his romantic naïveté and her earthy worldliness. In this scene, O'Neill captures the gentle humor implicit in the common situation of a young person trying to appear to be someone he or she is not and in the end, being true to him or herself.

Another humorous situation arises in act 4, scene 3, when Miller awkwardly attempts to advise his son on the dangers of consorting with prostitutes, unaware of just how unpleasant Richard's experience with Belle has been. Again, the humor lies in the familiar scene of a parent striving to fulfill his perceived duty to teach his child something the child already knows. Miller struggles to find the right words, when in fact, no words are necessary. O'Neill mines this situation for more laughs when Miller tells Richard that his punishment is not to go to Yale, but Richard has already decided for himself that he does not want to go to Yale so that he can remain at home and marry Muriel sooner. When he reveals this to his father,

Miller reverses himself and punishes Richard by promising to send him to Yale (some punishment!).

The most extensive and effective comic situation in the play is the dinner scene in act 2. Although Sid's intoxication is the source of much of the humor in this scene, the bluefish trick is truly the centerpiece. Beyond the humor inherent in the revelation of the harmless deception of Miller by his good and loving wife, which is acknowledged by all the other characters involved, Miller's willingness to laugh at himself along with the others extends the comic repercussions of the scene. As he tells the story of saving the life of Red Sisk, the others at the table exchange glances, indicating that he has told this story many times before. This leads Sid, in his drunkenness, to mock Miller, both for repeating and embellishing his story over the years. When Sid finally taunts him by complaining about the "peculiar oil" in lobsters and clams that poisons him, recalling Miller's own refrain about bluefish, Miller accepts the teasing "*good-naturedly*": "You seem to be getting a lot of fun kidding me. Go ahead, then. I don't mind" (46). This tolerance for good-natured kidding is quite different from the attitude expressed by fathers (and mothers, for that matter) in virtually all of O'Neill's other family dramas written previously, and it establishes the essentially comic mood of the play. In a publicly patriarchal system, if the patriarch is genuinely benevolent, that spirit generally pervades the entire system, in this case, the Miller family.

As O'Neill himself remarked, however, the humor in the play is tinged with a sad nostalgia suggested by its "mood," by the mundane details of everyday life not found in the more patently serious plays O'Neill wrote up until this time. Small moments of domestic relations throughout the play reinforce the mood established by the domestic details in the opening scene: the son displaying good manners in saying "excuse me" to leave the breakfast table, the mother correcting his grammar ("May I?" not "Can I?"), the sister teasing her older brother about his romantic affairs, the children engaging in some "roughhousing." For example, as the sister trips the younger brother, he pushes her back and tickles her, and the older brother cheerfully eggs on the other two. Moments such as these contribute to an atmosphere of domestic comfort unknown to O'Neill in his own family and perhaps less familiar to many American families in the 1930s (thus the "lost spiritual and ethical values" O'Neill refers to in his remarks on the play). In difficult times, Americans tend to recall the "good old days." Whether these days are real or idealized, that seems to be what O'Neill had in mind here, and what led him to "weep a few tears."

In addition, there are sources of tension and sadness in the play, such as Richard's alienation, Sid's alcoholism, and especially, Sid and Lily's mutual romantic disappointment, which underlie, and to some degree, undercut the humor. Early in the second act, when Richard is alone with Aunt Lily, they engage in a kind of philosophical debate, with Richard the voice of pessimism and Lily, ironically, making the case for optimism:

> RICHARD— Nothing matters.
>
> LILY— (*puts her arm around him sympathetically*) You really mustn't let yourself take it so seriously. You know, something happens and things like that [Richard's "breakup" with Muriel] come up, and we think there's no hope...But then—if we really, *really* love—why, then something else is bound to happen soon that changes everything again, and it's all as it was before the misunderstanding, and everything works out all right in the end. That's the way it is with life.
>
> RICHARD— (*with a tragic sneer*) Life! Life is a joke! And everything comes out all wrong in the end! (31–32)

It is not ultimately Richard's pessimism, but what he calls Lily's "silly optimism," that wins out in the end. Everything working out "all right" for Lily actually means settling for something less than what an individual really wants from life, which is clearly her situation with Sid. Although the Millers may strike the audience as a little sad because of what they suggest people settle for in life, they still provide comfort because of how they suggest people actually get on in life.

The comic spirit affirms life. Shakespearean comedy typically ends in marriage, often multiple marriages, signifying the hope that lies in union and procreation. In the final words of Ah Wilderness! Nat and Essie Miller affirm life:

> MILLER— Well, Spring isn't everything, is it, Essie? There's a lot to be said for Autumn. That's got beauty, too. And Winter—if you're together.
>
> MRS. MILLER— (*simply*) Yes, Nat. (She kisses him and they move quietly out of the moonlight, back into the darkness of the front parlor.) (107)

They are together at the end, as are Richard and Muriel (although he stands alone in the moonlight only thinking about her, "like a statue of Love's Young Dream" (107), they have been reconciled on stage in the previous scene), as well as (although offstage) Arthur and Elsie, Muriel and her latest beau, and even Sid and Lily. Although perhaps foreshadowing in the stage directions (in the darkness of the front parlor) the playwright's return to metaphysical darkness in his later plays, the ending of *Ah, Wilderness!* is comic in the spirit of Shakespearean comedy. The play is ultimately a comedy of affirmation and hope.

## WORKS CITED

Black, Stephen A. *Eugene O'Neill: Beyond Mourning and Tragedy.* New Haven: Yale University Press, 1999.

Bogard, Travis and Jackson R. Bryer, eds. *Selected Letters of Eugene O'Neill.* New Haven: Yale University Press, 1988.

Gassner, John. *Eugene O'Neill.* Minneapolis: University of Minnesota Press, 1965.

O'Neill, Eugene. *Complete Plays 1932–1943.* Ed. Travis Bogard. New York: Library of America, 1988.

Sheaffer, Louis. *O'Neill: Son and Artist.* Boston: Little, Brown, & Co., 1973.

# 7

# *The Iceman Cometh* (1939)

During his years at Tao House (1937–1944), O'Neill interrupted his work on the ambitious historical cycle of plays he had begun ("A Tale of Possessors Self-Dispossessed") to turn his attention to more personal material. Of the four important plays he developed from that material, two (*Long Day's Journey Into Night* and *A Moon for the Misbegotten*) are based on his troubled family of origin and two (*The Iceman Cometh* and the one-act *Hughie*) are based on his life and acquaintances when he lived "on the skids" as a young man in New York City around the time when he had attempted to end his life. In the former two, O'Neill made his own tortured family a microcosm of the mad loneliness of modern existence. In the latter two, he does the same with the sparse and dismal lives of down-and-outers living on the edge of society in New York City. In all of these plays, O'Neill drew even more explicitly than he had done previously on his own experiences to depict the "hopeless hope" that had come to define his life vision, as quoted by the Gelbs: "'Only through the unattainable does man achieve a hope worth living and dying for—and so attain himself. He with the spiritual guerdon of a hope in hopelessness is nearest to the stars and the rainbow's foot'" (*O'Neill: Life* 423).

By the time O'Neill had completed *The Iceman Cometh* in 1939, he had not had a new play of his produced on Broadway in almost six years. But due to poor health and his despair over the state of the world (Gelbs, *O'Neill* 835), he could not face the stress of a production at that time. Once the United States had entered World War II in 1941, he believed that a production of his play would have to wait until well beyond the end of the hostilities: "the pessimism of the play would run counter to public optimism and would result in a bad reception by the audience." He expected that within a year of the war's end, however, "there would be considerable disillusionment, and...the public would then be more inclined to listen to what he had to say in this play" (855). When the play was finally produced on Broadway, in October 1946, it had been 12 years since a work of his had been mounted on the Great White Way. O'Neill's was no longer the household name it had become in theatre circles and beyond in the 1920s and 1930s, and this new production failed to arouse the critical acclaim his works had received in those years.

Many reviewers found the production lacking, particularly the performance of James Barton in the lead role of Hickey, and they were mixed in their appraisal of the play itself. Many criticized it for its length and repetitiousness, but several observers saw these qualities as essential elements of O'Neill's dramaturgy. His friend and associate Lawrence Langner once suggested that the play should be cut, to which the dramatist replied, "The hell with your cuts!" (875). On another occasion O'Neill explained that, "If there are repetitions...they'll have to remain in, because I feel they are absolutely necessary to what I am trying to get over" (870). His intentions were not to be realized on stage for another 10 years, when José Quintero directed the landmark 1956 Circle-in-the-Square production with noted sensitivity to the musical nature of the piece: "It resembles a complex musical form, with themes repeating themselves with slight variations, as melodies do in a symphony" (Quintero 28). One commentator on that successful production explained: "The truth is, about *The Iceman Cometh*, all kinds of things are happening all the time, but you have to listen and watch, and you hear repetition because that is the way O'Neill planned it, so that you cannot miss his meaning, and the emotions generated by his drama" (Gelbs, *O'Neill* 877).

From the time he completed *Iceman* in 1939, O'Neill believed that it was a special achievement, as quoted by the Gelbs from a correspondence with Lawrence Langner:

> "I have a confident hunch that this play, as drama, is one of the best things I've ever done. In some ways, perhaps *the* best. What I mean is, there are moments in it that suddenly strip the secret soul of man stark naked, not in cruelty or moral superiority, but with an understanding compassion which sees him as a victim of the ironies of life and of himself. Those moments are for me the depth of tragedy, with nothing more that can possibly be said." (837)

*The Iceman Cometh* is one of O'Neill's most dramaturgically complex and interesting works. With its large and rich cast of characters, many of whom remain on stage together throughout much of the drama, and its paradoxically profound combination of philosophical discourse and drunken barroom banter, it has become one of the signature plays of the twentieth century about the plight of modern human beings.

## SETTING AND PLOT DEVELOPMENT

The setting of *The Iceman Cometh* is generally viewed as a composite of three of the seedy bar/hotels in New York City that O'Neill frequented in his young vagabond years, including a place called the "Hell Hole" (Sheaffer 490). O'Neill describes the space in great detail, including the precise numbers of tables and chairs, and the positions of the occupants of these chairs. The precision of his stage directions suggests that each detail is drawn from his memory, from the sign on the toilet door to the "*dirty black curtain*" that separates the "back room" from the barroom.

Harry Hope's saloon is not an appealing place in which to spend time, let alone in which to live. The opening scene of *The Iceman Cometh* is quite extraordinary. The curtain rises on a stage crowded with tables, chairs, and 10 people, all of whom, except for one, are asleep. It is not surprising that several characters who later enter label it a morgue; the atmosphere is deadening, and the inhabitants seem dead. It is dirty, dreary, and worn down. Although "*the back room is crammed with round tables and chairs*" (O'Neill 565), and it is occupied by a large group of people, it seems an inhospitable, even lonely place. The windows are "*so glazed with grime one cannot see through them*" (565), and most of the action takes place during the night or early in the morning, so that there is little more than "*gray subdued light*" (565) coming through the few dirty windows. All four acts take place on this one set, although the audience hears about events that take place outside, such as Harry Hope's excursion across the street. The audience is also repeatedly reminded of the rooms upstairs, to which the patrons of Harry Hope's sometimes retreat and for which these patrons owe rent to Hope. The saloon is a world unto itself, protecting its inhabitants from the perils of reality outside and providing escape from the loneliness of the rooms upstairs.

Aside from the highly naturalistic detail with which the setting is described, it also takes on symbolic significance, as explicitly captured by Larry early in act 1, in response to Parritt's inquiry: "What kind of joint is it, anyway?"

It's the No Chance Saloon. It's Bedrock Bar, The End of the Line Café. The Bottom of the Sea Rathskeller! Don't you notice the beautiful calm in the atmosphere? That's because it's the last harbor. No one here has to worry about where they're going next, because there is no farther they can go. It's a great comfort to them. Although even here they keep up the appearances of life with a few harmless pipe dreams about their yesterdays and tomorrows, as you'll see if you're here long. (577–578)

Larry's vision of Harry Hope's extends its domain beyond the walls, windows, and doors on stage, just as the diverse gathering of human beings who reside within this space also expands its population to include all people. In fact, one of the factors cited as an asset of the 1956 Circle-in-the-Square production, aside from Quintero's sensitive direction and Jason Robards Jr.'s career-making performance, is the "arena staging in a one-time nightclub," which had just this effect on the audience. According to one reviewer, it was "as if you were sitting right in Harry Hope's bar, along with all the other lovely bums" (Sheaffer 585).

There is no single plot with a beginning, middle, and end in *The Iceman Cometh*. In some ways, it is comparable to a Greek tragedy in that the time that passes on stage is not much more than a single day, yet the information that is revealed tells a story that encompasses a lifetime, in fact, several lifetimes. The play depicts approximately two days in the lives of a large group of characters, and although there is something special about what happens during this particular period, there is also something quite mundane about the passing of this time. There are as many stories as there are characters in the play, although it is helpful to identify three different, though related, strands. All of them begin before the opening of the play. Two of them more or less conclude at the end of the play, whereas the third extends beyond the final curtain. The first two stories are Hickey's and Parritt's, and the third is the communal story of all the other inhabitants of Harry Hope's. Each act will build to a climax around an anticipated event, and each act will end with a surprise revelation from Hickey and a plea for happiness.

The first act provides the exposition for all three of these storylines, although Hickey's is intentionally vague, as his story is meant to be something of a mystery. The first storyline to be introduced is the communal one. Much of the large cast of characters is first seen asleep on stage, and Larry plays the narrator's role, introducing each character to Parritt, who has never met any of them before, and at the same time, to the audience. As each character awakens during the course of the long opening act, each one reveals a little bit more about his persona. Eventually, it becomes clear that all of these characters (including the ones who enter later, that is, Margie, Pearl, Cora, and Chuck) are in the same basic situation. Each is passing the time at Harry Hope's while avoiding more meaningful activities, either those in which he or she had previously been involved (i.e., Hope, Mosher, McGloin, Willie, Joe, Wetjoen, Lewis, Hugo, and Jimmy) or to which he or she newly claims to aspire (i.e., Chuck, Cora, and Larry). A variation on this scenario is illustrated by those characters who strain to assert a self-identity that is in stark contrast to the reality of their circumstances (i.e., Rocky, Margie, and Pearl). All of these characters survive from day to day by believing in what O'Neill calls "pipe dreams." Into their blissful self-deluded world enters the much anticipated Hickey, who usually brings them relief by treating them all to unlimited alcoholic beverages. This time, however, he arrives with a vow to reform them, not of their dependence on alcohol, but rather, of their dependence on pipe dreams.

The one stranger is Parritt, a younger man than the others, who has come in search of Larry. His character serves the play's structure well, because, as a newcomer, he knows nobody at Harry Hope's and nothing about them, so his curiosity (which mirrors that of the audience) prods Larry and the others into revealing information about themselves. Parritt, however, does more than provide realistic exposition. He also plays a specific role in breaking through Larry's resilient wall of denial, drawing him out of the grandstand and on to the playing field of pipe dreams. Furthermore, he has his own story to tell that parallels (or "parrots") that of Hickey and helps O'Neill emphasize some of the key themes of the play.

In act 1, Parritt reveals that his mother, with whom Larry had at one time had a relationship, is one of the Movement's leaders and is now in prison, allegedly having been betrayed by someone within the Movement itself. Parritt claims to be on the run from the authorities, who may associate him with his mother, and at the same time, to have left the Movement, disillusioned with its failure to enact revolutionary change. He hopes to find a sympathetic ally in Larry, who repeatedly expresses disenchantment with the Movement, and it soon becomes apparent that Parritt also seeks a father figure in Larry, the only man in his mother's life who ever expressed interest in and concern for him. Larry tries not to show much of that concern now, but does so, in spite of himself, all the while regarding Parritt with suspicion. Parritt's extremely defensive response to Hugo's innocently drunken attack on him as a stool pigeon reinforces Larry's unspoken suspicions. So at the end of act 1, it is apparent that Parritt is running from something and that he feels guilty about something involving his mother.

The main event of act 1 is the arrival of Hickey. Within moments of the start of the first conversation between Larry and Rocky, Rocky explains that the men in the back room of the bar do not go upstairs to sleep in the beds that they rent because they do not want to miss Hickey's arrival, which will certainly be accompanied by free drinks. Larry then adds another incentive for them to wait in the back room: "Hickey's a great one to make a joke of everything and cheer you up" (O'Neill 571). Throughout the following scene in which the individual characters and their pipe dreams are revealed, several of the characters make references to Hickey's arrival, their expectation of free booze, and their anticipation of Hickey's uplifting sense of humor. In what is surely one of the longest delayed entrances in all of dramatic literature, O'Neill masterfully orchestrates the introduction of an array of characters, sows the seeds of several stories, a number of which are shrouded in a vague sense of mystery, and builds an intense feeling of anticipation for the arrival of a new character. When Hickey finally does enter, approximately 45 minutes into the drama, he both fulfills and upsets the communal expectations of both the characters on stage and the audience. Although he initially brings both good cheer—"Hello, Gang!"—and free drinks—"Do your duty, Brother Rocky. Bring on the rat poison!" (607)—he surprises them when he himself does not drink along with them, claiming to have found peace in freedom from pipe dreams. When he suggests that he has come to save them, not from alcohol, but from their pipe dreams, he arouses their fears and anxieties.

During act 2, which takes place close to midnight on the same day, amid the bustle of preparing for Hope's birthday party, several of the characters complain about Hickey's interference in their lives, while the others remain in their rooms upstairs trying to avoid Hickey's intrusions. The characters have become quite testy with each other, as they have been prodded by Hickey to challenge each other's pipe dreams. For instance, when Cora announces that she and Chuck are getting married the next day, and Pearl reminds her that her past behavior is hardly a recommendation for monogamous married life, Cora calls Pearl a whore, reminding her of the truth about herself, which leads to a sequence of events in which Rocky slaps Pearl and Margie, thus casting himself as their pimp in spite of his protests to the contrary. The reality of their lives without their pipe dreams is frightening to them because it disrupts the peaceful coexistence they have manufactured at the expense of the truth. Similarly, Lewis and Wetjoen have moved beyond their usual name calling and come to blows (637–638), and Mosher and McGloin threaten to do the same (639–640). As Larry observes, Hickey's quest for truth is a "movement that'll blow up the world!" (622).

As the group becomes anxious and edgy, the other two storylines also move ahead. Parritt reveals more evidence to Larry that he has betrayed his mother, and continues to appeal for Larry's sympathy. At this point, he claims to have done it from a sense of patriotic duty that was offended by the un-American flavor of the Movement. Meanwhile, Larry tries desperately to remain in the "grandstand," in spite of his natural inclination to feel what Hickey tells him is his "old kind of pity" (628–629) for Parritt, the kind that enables pipe dreams, in this case by forgiving Parritt. Larry clearly struggles with the truth about what Parritt has done that he senses in the guilt and anxiety beneath the young man's words.

The main event of the second act is Hope's birthday party. The furniture has been rearranged to accommodate the entire group at one long table and presents and a cake are displayed on a side table. Hickey unveils a gift of quarts of champagne with which to mark the special occasion, and he prevails on Cora to provide musical accompaniment for the festivities. All of the preparation reaches its ironic climax as Hickey orchestrates the entrance of Hope precisely at the stroke of midnight, and he enters to a "*spiritless chorus*" of "Happy Birthday, Harry!" from the group and Cora's rather unpolished piano-playing and singing (640–641). Hope's acknowledgment of his friends' efforts is less than gracious, as he angrily lashes out at them in misplaced self-defense against the interference of Hickey. When Hickey generously proposes a toast to Hope, but includes in it his proposal of a new life of peace without pipe dreams, Hope struggles with his conflicted feelings of friendly gratitude and guilty fear. Larry, again displaying pity in spite of himself, supports Hope by attacking Hickey, wondering if the salesman is behaving so strangely because his wife has been unfaithful to him. This leads Hickey to make the revelation that ends act 2, which is that his wife Evelyn has died. As Hickey claims to be happy that she is finally rid of him and at peace, the others are struck dumb with "*bewildered, incredulous confusion*" (650) as the curtain falls.

Act 3 takes place on the morning of the next day, Harry Hope's birthday. The only characters on stage at the beginning are Joe, Rocky, Larry, Hugo, and Parritt. The others have retreated to their rooms to hide from Hickey, who is still preaching to all of them to put their pipe dreams into action. There is still a great deal of agitation in the air, because in their hearts, none of them really believes that his or her pipe dream is possible to realize. Everyone behaves self-defensively against Hickey's attacks, because underlying each person's anxiety is the fear of failure, the knowledge that the pipe dream is just that—only a dream. Self-defensiveness leads to hostilities projected outward toward others rather than inward toward the self. For example, Rocky tells of ongoing bickering between him and his "stable" about their inability to own up to their true occupations, and soon after, he and Chuck almost come to blows because Chuck's self-deceptive aspiration toward respectability through marriage threatens Rocky's identity as a bartender and not a pimp. Similarly, hostilities emerge between Joe and the two bartenders, as Joe identifies the racism that underlies their acceptance of him as one of them, and hints at the self-hatred that underlies his own willingness to be accepted as white.

Toward the beginning of the act, before the other characters enter, Parritt reveals more explicitly to Larry that he is the one who has turned his mother in to the authorities, and now he reveals that he did not do it out of patriotism, but rather out of greed for the money to spend on a prostitute. Parritt feels threatened by the vague connection and familiarity that Hickey claims to feel with him, especially now that Hickey has revealed that his wife is dead. Larry still tries to avoid the truth about Parritt.

Most of the other characters eventually enter, cleaned up and struggling to maintain a sober appearance, each on his way out of Harry Hope's to pursue a more meaningful existence in the outside world. Both Wetjoen and Lewis are planning to get jobs to earn money to pay for their passages home. Mosher is off to regain a position at the circus, and McGloin hopes to be reinstated with the police department. Willie seeks employment at the D.A.'s office, and Joe is going to open his own gambling house. Chuck and Cora are off to get married and move to a farm in New Jersey.

Chuck and Cora take off at the sound of Hickey approaching with Jimmy and Hope, but the others linger, still afraid to step outside. Once Hickey arrives, though, he shames them into leaving; one by one they make their departures, including Jimmy, who is off to get his old job back at the newspaper. That leaves Hope and sets up the darkly comic main event of act 3, Hope's stroll in the neighborhood. After a great deal of hesitation and rationalization, Hope finally embarks on his walk across the street, only to return to the bar within moments in a panic, complaining about an automobile that almost hit him, which nobody in the bar has seen. His retreat, of course, is symbolic of the experience that each of the other residents will have as he or she confronts life without a pipe dream. Hickey promises them peace, but on returning from the street, Hope is distressed and only wants to drink enough to pass out.

Hope's distress troubles Hickey, as it is not the peaceful contentment he had promised, and, as he tries to measure his own balance of distress and peace against Hope's, the third act arrives at its climactic moment. Larry suspects that Hickey drove his wife to suicide, and so, in defense of his friends, he presses the issue with the hope of embarrassing Hickey; but Hickey unexpectedly reveals, to the horror of those few still gathered at Harry Hope's, that Evelyn was murdered. Hickey remains troubled that Hope is not feeling happy after taking a walk in the neighborhood and divesting himself of his pipe dream by recognizing that he is never going to change his life, because Hope's experience suggests that Hickey himself may not be as content as he appears even after the death of his wife supposedly freed him from his pipe dreams.

In act 4, in what amounts to a long confessional monologue that is the centerpiece of the act, Hickey resolves the mystery of Evelyn's murder with revelations that resonate personally for all the other characters at Harry Hope's. His confession is punctuated, on the one hand, by a chorus of denial from most of the group who do not want to hear the truth and, on the other hand, by the parallel confession of Parritt, who desperately wants to face the truth, but needs Larry's approval to do so (thus bringing Larry out of the "grandstand" and into the action).

The act takes place early in the morning of the next day, not long after midnight, by which time most of the characters have returned to Harry Hope's. All of them have ventured out, at Hickey's insistence, to make the changes in their lives about which they have been dreaming, and each has returned, as Hope had, distraught over the recognition that his or her hoped-for change is, in truth, hopeless. Chuck and Cora have split up. Jimmy was found at the docks, contemplating drowning himself, but unable to do so. Joe borrowed a gun with which to rob someone, but could not go through with it. All in all, as Rocky observes, "dere ain't enough guts left in de whole gang to battle a mosquito!" (684). What is worse, the liquor they have consumed since returning is not having the desired effect. Most of them are unable to attain the drunken oblivion they seek to escape from the reality of their existences without their pipe dreams.

When Hickey returns, he seems perplexed by the distress he feels among his friends. His hope had been that they would have begun to celebrate their liberation from the burden of their pipe dreams, but because just the opposite has occurred, he feels compelled to confess to them that he has killed his wife. Then he tells them the whole story of his relationship with Evelyn, so that they will understand the peace he claims to have attained, and which he claims he has tried to bring to them. His long story is one of drunken binges and extramarital relationships that have betrayed Evelyn's love for him. Her love for him, however, brought only forgiveness and understanding, never anger or rebuke, which deepened Hickey's feelings of guilt to the point of intolerance. He claims that he loved Evelyn too much to kill himself or to leave her, because either of those actions would have left her distraught and she would have died believing that he did not love her, which he did. Then, as he stood by her bed while she slept, about to leave her again to go on his semi-annual binge at Harry Hope's, he decided that the best thing he could do for her, and for himself, was to kill her.

So he shot and killed her, hearing himself saying, "Well, you know what you can do with your pipe dream now, you damned bitch!" (700).

His immediate response to hearing these words spoken aloud again is to retract them. He cannot accept that he could express any sentiment resembling hatred to the woman he loved, so he attributes these words to insanity. His impulsive response that he would have had to be insane to say such a thing about Evelyn provides Hope with hope. He latches on to that excuse as an explanation for all of Hickey's behavior since he has appeared at the bar, and he rationalizes his own subsequent behavior, as well as that of all the others, as an attempt to humor his/their old friend Hickey. Hickey immediately sees that this excuse will enable them all to return to their pipe dreams, invalidating the philosophy he has been preaching to them, as well as his attempts to rationalize his own behavior. After an initial hesitation, Hickey agrees with Hope's assessment of the situation and surrenders his rationale about the peace that comes from living without pipe dreams. As the detectives, who have appeared midway through his confession, take him away, he accepts death as the alternative to living without pipe dreams, as he tells the detectives that he is ready for execution.

The second plot strand that is resolved in act 4 is Parritt's story. He responds viscerally to much of Hickey's confession, seeing his own plight in Hickey's. Although he has not killed his mother, as Hickey has killed his wife, he knows that his betrayal of her is tantamount to doing so. He echoes Hickey's condemnation of Evelyn's tormenting pipe dreams in his own of his mother's "freedom pipe dream" (704), but unlike Hickey, Parritt claims complete sanity, at which point Larry finally signs off on Parritt's self-execution: "Go! Get the hell out of life, God damn you, before I choke it out of you!.... Go, for the love of Christ, you mad tortured bastard, for your own sake!" (704–705). Parritt exits and moments later, as Larry sits silently waiting, the sound of something falling from above and landing on the ground outside denotes Parritt's suicide, an act that Larry has the inclination, but not the will, to do himself. Instead, he sits apart from the others and accepts his inability to remain in the grandstand: "I'll be a weak fool looking with pity at the two sides of everything till the day I die!" (710). In this acceptance, Larry finally does relinquish his pipe dream and becomes, as he says, "the only real convert to death Hickey made here" (710).

The play ends with all the other characters seizing on Hickey's alleged insanity to revert to their previous state of bliss, fueled by the renewed sense of hope provided by their restored pipe dreams. Significantly, along with hope, the "kick" returns to the liquor, and they all finally achieve the state of oblivious intoxication that they originally had hoped for in Hickey's arrival, as well as the kind of drunken merriment intended for Hope's birthday. As each character sings a chorus of a different song, a "*weird cacophony*" arises in celebration of their surprising camaraderie. It is the irrepressible Hugo, the washed-up anarchist, who unites them, first in opposition to his persistent repetition of the French Revolutionary song "The Carmagnole" (an ironic call to action from a character who does nothing throughout the play), and finally, in response to his denunciation of them as "Capitalist Svine." They join him in his declamation from the poem "Revolution," which out of context, becomes a fitting accompaniment to their return to the comfort of their illusions: "The days grow hot, O Babylon! (*They all take it up and shout in enthusiastic jeering chorus*) 'Tis cool beneath thy willow trees!" (711). The play thus ends with loud laughter and the ironic celebration of believing in pipe dreams as a revolutionary act. At the same time, Larry sits off to the side, staring silently in front of him, contemplating death.

## CHARACTER DEVELOPMENT

*The Iceman Cometh* is, rather remarkably, both a star vehicle and an ensemble piece at the same time. The drama focuses on the character of Hickey, yet its full effectiveness depends equally on the ensemble cast surrounding him. It is a large cast, and many of the characters, most of whom live at Harry Hope's, are on stage for most of the playing time, making it a rather complicated play to stage. Although the ensemble is comparable to a Greek chorus, often, and especially in act 4, responding as a group, O'Neill distinguishes each member of the ensemble with unique characteristics, reflecting an ethnically, racially, and to some extent even socioeconomically diverse group. Beyond that, although they all have pipe dreams to sustain them and they share a mutual investment in reinforcing each other's belief in pipe dreams, the specific nature of each pipe dream is unique to each character. Three characters who are part of the ensemble stand out as more rounded characters than the rest (although not quite on the level of Hickey): Hope, the proprietor; Larry, the "grandstand foolosopher"; and Parritt, the outsider. Finally, there are two minor characters who play only a functional role in the drama: Moran and Lieb are the two detectives who appear in the final moments of the play to arrest Hickey, ordinary-looking men who do their jobs by the book and follow the script that law enforcement officials have been reading on stage and screen as long as they have been called "cops": "Can it! I've had enough of your act. Save it for the jury" (702).

There are 10 male and 3 female characters who together form the main part of the ensemble. Each one has a pipe dream, a belief in something he or she is planning to do to change his or her current situation. Each one speaks of this plan, but never acts on it. Rather, each remains at Harry Hope's bar day after day, depending on the whims of Hope, and the semi-annual generosity of Hickey, for alcoholic sustenance. Some of them identify closely with one or two others, and a few are more or less loners.

Ed Mosher used to work at the circus box office, but he got fired for keeping too much of the shortchanged profits for himself. Pat McGloin is a former police officer who lost his badge for taking graft. Both believe they can be reinstated in their old positions. Willie Oban is a graduate of Harvard Law School who believes he can still take up the practice of law and offers his services to several of the residents of Harry Hope's. Joe Mott is an African American who once ran a gambling house for blacks, and he plans to do so again. Piet Wejoen was a Boer officer in the war against Britain, and Cecil Lewis was his adversary. Both were dishonorably discharged, yet each still hopes to return home to a hero's welcome. James Cameron (aka Jimmy Tomorrow) is a journalist who covered the Boer War, lost his position because he is an alcoholic, and now hopes to sober up enough to prevail upon his editor to give him another chance. Hugo Kalmar is an Anarchist who has left the Movement and now lives in his own sleepy world of anarchist rantings and revolutionary fervor. He not only never leaves Harry Hope's, but he can barely lift his head up off the table. Rocky Pioggi is one of the two bartenders at Harry Hope's establishment. He takes money from two prostitutes and mistreats them, but denies that he is a pimp and takes pride in his honest work as a bartender. Pearl and Margie are prostitutes who call themselves "tarts." They play the role of "good girls" as long as Rocky plays the role of bartender, but as soon as Rocky behaves like a pimp, they behave like hookers. Chuck Morello, the other bartender, plans to marry a third prostitute, Cora, and move to a farm in New Jersey, even though he knows nothing about farm life and he has no trust in the faithfulness of his fiancée. Cora shares Chuck's dream, as well as his ignorance about farm life, and she distrusts his ability to stop drinking. It is interesting to note that all the male characters are identified by their surnames (and the two detectives are identified by only surnames), but the prostitutes are identified only by first names.

Harry Hope is the proprietor, and as such, has a somewhat higher social status in the group. They owe him rent and money for drinks, and part of his pipe dream is that someday he will make them all pay up. He is, in many ways, what we would today call an "enabler": the longer he continues to provide free liquor, the longer they will continue to suffer the ill effects of alcoholism; the longer he allows the others to have a free ride at his establishment, the longer they will continue to postpone acting on their pipe dreams. He is an alcoholic himself, of course, and although he is able to feel superior to them by virtue of their dependence on him, he is just as dependent on alcohol as they are, and he is just as much an adherent of the "pipe dream philosophy of life" as they are. Hope's pipe dream is to take a walk around his neighborhood, symbolic for getting involved in life again, something he has not done in the 20 years since his wife Bessie died.

Each of these characters follows a similar trajectory in the course of the play. They are all in various stages of withdrawal on the morning when the play begins, waiting and hoping for Hickey's arrival to bring them relief. When Hickey does oblige, they are confronted with his new intention to free them of their pipe dreams. Hickey dogs each and every one of them, both in the on-stage action of the play and in reports of off-stage interactions, until most of them leave the bar and venture into the outside world, allegedly in an effort to act on their intentions. Hickey knows that each of them will fail—that is the nature of pipe dreams—and each of them returns having done so. Hope's adventure attempting to cross the street is the only one for which the audience is provided an eyewitness account (674–675). Hope's sadly comic exploit symbolizes the off-stage actions of all the other characters. Like Hope, each one ends up running back into the bar, having been overcome by the impossibility of taking meaningful action in the world: "But bejees, something ran over me! Must have been myself, I guess" (677). Upon returning to the bar, they all try to escape from the despair brought on by their experiences by drinking, but the liquor has lost its kick, which only returns after Hickey provides the bait of his insanity, which bails them out of accepting that their pipe dreams are false. They are then able to return to their original state of calm belief that tomorrow, or someday, things will be different. So each of these characters is forced to confront the reality behind his or her pipe dream and is then allowed to retreat behind the hope of the pipe dream again in the end.

The two characters, aside from Hickey, who do not follow this path are Parritt and Larry. As the outsider in the play, the one character who has never been at Harry Hope's before, Don Parritt elicits exposition from the others, especially Larry, as he inquires about the others and their surroundings. Parritt also adds another layer of mystery to the drama as his story of betrayal gradually emerges along with Hickey's. He plays a pivotal role in between Larry and Hickey. He has had a previous relationship with Larry that evokes vague, but emotional responses from Larry that belie his claims of disengagement from human affairs. He also seems to have a kind of spiritual connection with Hickey (whom he has never met before) that enables him to follow Hickey's lead and confess his shameful transgression. Larry is the biggest challenge to Hickey's crusade, and it is through Parritt that Hickey ultimately affects him.

From the outset, Parritt appears to be hiding something. He seems to be riddled with anxiety, and he is highly defensive. He is proof that living with pipe dreams is not a condition unique to the residents of Harry Hope's. As his story emerges, he desperately attempts to frame his behavior in terms that depict him in as tolerable a light as possible. Just like the women in the play who call themselves tarts instead of whores, Parritt claims to be a patriot rather than a stool pigeon. So just like all the other characters in the play, Parritt's life is built on pipe dreams. The difference between Parritt and the others is that he seems uncomfortable with himself. He does not experience what Larry identifies as the "beautiful calm" of the "End-of-the-Line Café" (577) at Harry Hope's. Because he is "on the wagon," he does not even call on the power of intoxication to calm his nerves. He is seeking relief for his guilty conscience from Larry, and he finds it, thanks to Hickey. As Hickey confesses that he murdered his wife Evelyn out of hatred, Parritt acknowledges the same offense in his own betrayal of his mother. Unable to face life without any illusion about what he has done, he takes his own life, with Larry's reluctant blessing, by jumping to his death off the fire escape in the alley. Parritt's action is barely noticed as the other characters return to the oblivion of alcohol and their pipe dreams, but it does represent a harsh alternative to the easier dishonesty of the group and, by extension, of most people.

One other alternative is represented by Larry Slade. Taking his place in the "grandstand," sometimes as a kind of narrator, he often comments on the words and behavior of the others, presenting a façade as the objective observer. He is more involved, though, than he lets on, and he cares more about his friends than he would admit. In the philosophical discourse of the drama, Larry does take sides; he stands up for the pipe dream in the face of Hickey's attack. From the beginning of the play, Larry rejects facing the truth as the key to living life: "As the history of the world proves, the truth has no bearing on anything. It's irrelevant and immaterial, as the lawyers say" (569–570).

At the same time, Larry excludes himself from this lot, claiming to have left his pipe dreams behind when he abandoned the Movement. It is Parritt's appearance on the scene that exposes Larry's hypocrisy, as the pity he feels for Parritt strongly suggests that although he may have physically abandoned the Movement, he has not done so emotionally. He still has feelings for Parritt and for Parritt's mother, which reveals that his stance of disengagement from life, without pipe dreams, is itself a pipe dream. In the end, he admits that he is incapable of not caring, and he implores Parritt to do what he is incapable of doing himself, ending life.

Hickey diagnoses Larry accurately, and with some foreshadowing, in act 2, when he predicts that after Larry admits that his detachment from life is a lie, "you'll say to yourself, I'm just an old man who is scared of life, but even more scared of dying. So I'm keeping drunk and hanging on to life at any price" (629). Even earlier in the play, in act 1, Larry provides insight into his own character when he offers Parritt the only answer he can give to the big question about life's meaning, which he finds in a poem to morphine by Heine:

"Lo, sleep is good; better is death; in sooth,
The best of all were never to be born." (582)

Of course, there is profound irony in the wish never to have been born written by someone for whom that is impossible. It is not a death wish, but it is a wish not to be alive. It effectively describes Larry's death-in-life position at the end of the play, when he sits lifeless on the stage, "the only real convert to death Hickey made" (710). He ultimately and ironically rejects the pipe dreams that enable the other characters to celebrate life riotously in the closing moments, yet he is also too cowardly to embrace the death to which Parritt plunges of his own volition. Instead, he simply sits condemned to wait life out until death arrives: "I'll be a weak fool looking with pity at the two sides of everything till the day I die!....May that day come soon!" (710).

Hickey is a complex and fascinating character. On a symbolic level, he can represent Christ, death, or truth, or even the American Everyman (his last name is *Hick*man). On a realistic level, he is a confused and tormented human being, tortured by feelings of guilt, seeking forgiveness for his perceived wrongdoings, and struggling with the angst that has come to define existence for many people in the modern era. His long delayed, and highly anticipated, entrance establishes him as the central figure in a masterfully crafted ensemble drama. Preacher, salesman, jokester, and master of ceremonies, he regularly provides the other characters with the comfort of drink, whereas he now confronts them with the discomfort of the truth. They love him for the former and despise him for the latter.

As they eagerly await his arrival, the others create an image of Hickey as a fun-loving, easy-going, and friendly guy, whose humor and good cheer bring life to the dreary environment of Harry Hope's saloon and hope to its denizens. His unusually delayed arrival is a cause for some concern, and when Cora announces his appearance in the neighborhood, joy is mixed with a new curiosity as she informs the group that Hickey seems to be "different, or somethin'" (606). Cora's impression is soon confirmed as Hickey enters, and although he still puts on a jovial front, he behaves in unexpected ways, most notably at first by not imbibing along with the others when he orders drinks all around. It is clear that Hickey is preoccupied and troubled by something, and over the course of the next three acts, the nature of his troubles is gradually revealed.

There is no question that Hickey is fond of the inhabitants of Harry Hope's. Except for Parritt, a visitor of whom he is suspicious, he has known all of the other characters for a long time, and they provide a semiannual respite for him from the routine of his life as a salesman. Unlike all of the other characters in the play, Hickey has a job that is considered socially respectable, even somewhat esteemed, at the time in which the play is set (circa 1912). Furthermore, given that he does *not* live at Harry Hope's, and that he has money to treat all the others when he visits, presumably he has been rather successful at this occupation. His persuasive gregariousness during the course of the play is surely the sign of a skillful salesman. Yet he is regularly drawn to Harry Hope's to spend time with this group of down-and-outers, perhaps because he is always aware that he could be one drink away from joining them permanently.

Until the time of the play, Hickey has been functioning as an "enabler," as he sympathizes with the characters' plights and reinforces their excuses to stay at Harry Hope's and to remain dependent on alcohol and pipe dreams. With his entrance on this day, he has changed his perspective on them and on himself. He now sees his role as their savior; he will save them from their misery by forcing them to acknowledge that their pipe dreams are false, as he claims to have done himself. He repeatedly assures them (and each of the first three acts ends with a version of his promise) that his only goal is to see them happy. His insistence throughout is excessive and seems defensive, and as they begin to return in act 3 from their confrontations with truth out in the world, showing only signs of despondency, he begins to question his own feelings. At the end of act 2, he reveals that his wife Evelyn is dead, at the end of act 3, that she has been murdered, and with each revelation, he claims to be at peace with himself. It soon becomes clear, however, that his behavior at Harry Hope's is symptomatic of anything but inner peace.

The long monologue in which he confesses to have killed Evelyn himself reveals the inner workings of a guilt-ridden alcoholic who has psychologically abused his wife and made a sham of his marriage by being repeatedly unfaithful, irresponsible, and unavailable. Her relentless forgiveness enables him to continue to behave reprehensibly until his guilt becomes overwhelming, and instead of condemning himself, he condemns her, literally, to death, as he shoots her in her sleep. Gradually suspecting that seeing this action as a positive step toward living life without illusions (and without alcohol) is a rationalization, and reinforced by the resistance of the others to facing the truth, Hickey must confront his own dishonesty and guilt. This leads him to accept the death sentence to which he expects to be condemned. In the end, however, he reserves his indictment for himself only, as he tacitly agrees to allow Harry Hope and the others to return to their pipe dreams by creating a new one, that he, Hickey, is insane. That is the only explanation for why he would curse Evelyn and kill her and, more important for the others, that is the only reason that they have gone along with his mission and tried to face the truth about their own pipe dreams. Hickey's acceptance of the truth leads to death. Although the play ends with the riotous return to the oblivion of pipe dreams, suggesting that this is the more comfortable approach to life, Hickey's confrontation with the truth, though painful and ultimately self-destructive, is also noble. In the most positive, classical sense of the term, it is tragic.

That Hickey is a tragic figure does not mean that his story is sad and depressing; rather, it is sad and uplifting. Hickey gains self-knowledge through the course of the play, and because of that self-knowledge, he ends up a more whole person than he was at the outset. It is not necessarily a condemnation of the choice of the lie of a pipe dream to say that it is still more noble to attempt to face reality as Hickey has done. Although it has led him to an awful act and a fatal end, he acquires a certain kind of dignity and heroism for his courage to face the truth, take bold action, and ultimately accept responsibility for its consequences. A common man in an egalitarian American society, whose existence seems quite ordinary and mundane, yet whose existential struggle is real, grand, and important, Hickey is a tragic figure for the modern world.

## THEMATIC ISSUES

*The Iceman Cometh* is not ostensibly one of O'Neill's family plays, yet family dynamics, most notably between husband and wife (Hickey-Evelyn) and son and mother (Parritt-Rosa), provide a lens through which O'Neill presents one of his important recurrent themes, that of guilt, betrayal, and responsibility. Of interest, in the case of both relationships, only the male figures appear on stage; the two female characters never appear in the play, but figure prominently in the characterization and behavior of both men. Parritt and Hickey begin the play in a state of denial about their responsibility for the fate of an important woman in each of their lives, in

Parritt's case, his mother, and in Hickey's case, his wife. Both characters are wracked by guilt for having betrayed these women whom they love, and in the end, both end their own lives in repentance for their transgressions. This development in each character's life suggests a common theme of responsibility of one human being for another, especially within a family. The breaking of this bond is both painful and shameful.

Another important theme in the play is dependency and co-dependency, symbolized by the addictive and/or enabling behavior of virtually every character in *The Iceman Cometh*. O'Neill discovered in alcoholism a metaphor for the torture of human relationships, the individual struggle to balance self-sufficiency with a natural instinct to coexist with other human beings. Virtually all of the characters in the play depend on alcohol, under the influence of which they remain well defended against the truth of their miserable lives. They primarily depend on Hope and Hickey to keep the liquor flowing. Hickey's intervention, however, demonstrates that they depend on each other's belief and validation more than on the alcohol. Hickey continues to provide the alcohol, but when he challenges their mutual belief and reinforcement of each other's pipe dreams, that is when the liquor loses its "kick." If these individuals cannot depend on each other to reinforce their belief in their pipe dreams, which defines each one's sense of self, then they cannot go on, which is what happens in acts 3 and 4. Just as alcoholics and those around them develop patterns of mutual dependency that reinforce the addictive behavior while ignoring the potential costs, so these characters develop patterns of mutual dependency that reinforce pipe dreams while ignoring the potential costs. It is thus in the return to these addictive and enabling patterns at the end of act 4 that the characters in *The Iceman Cometh* find what O'Neill calls "hopeless hope...because any victory we *may* win, is never the one we dreamed of winning. The point is that life in itself is nothing. It is the *dream* that keeps us fighting, willing—living!" (Gelbs, *O'Neill: Life* 422–423). The enabling pattern that forms the recurrent interpersonal dynamic in *Iceman* signifies the human need to offer and find hope in the face of despair.

Alcoholics continually seek escape from and transcendence over their troubles by drinking, in spite of their awareness that excessive drinking only artificially and temporarily masks their misery, while, in fact, it physiologically destroys their constitution. Yet they continue to drink. "Hopeless hope" means that human beings persevere by finding (artificial) ways to make life meaningful (i.e., pipe dreams) in the face of their awareness that there is no way to make life truly meaningful. Yet they continue to believe and to hope. In his late plays, and most especially in *The Iceman Cometh*, O'Neill abandoned the expressionistic devices of his middle period and discovered in one of the most real facts of his own life—alcoholism—the perfect naturalistic device through which to convey one of the central paradoxes of his tragic vision.

Religion plays an important role in this play, mostly on a figurative rather than a literal level. None of the characters is particularly religious (although Hickey's father was a preacher), nor does religious faith enter directly into the discourse on a meaningful life. Yet the religious symbolism in the play is unavoidable. First of all, like his father, Hickey is something of a preacher in the play, and he obviously has parlayed the elocutionary skills learned at his father's knee into success as a salesman. In the play, he preaches reform to the misfits at Harry Hope's, not religious reform, but still a kind of spiritual reform. Even more significantly, as noted in a 1958 article by Cyrus Day, the setting for Hope's birthday party in act 2 invokes da Vinci's famous painting "The Last Supper," as all the characters sit behind and at the two ends of the long table, facing the audience. There are 12 characters sitting at the table, representing the 12 disciples of Christ, including one—Parritt—who is a traitor, like Judas. Hickey is clearly the Christ figure who will sacrifice himself to save all the others. Day elaborates on other points of resemblance and based on this and other evidence, he detects an anti-Christian undertone in the play. Day contends that "Over and above their private illusions...stands Christianity, the collective illusion of what O'Neill thought of as our bankrupt Western civilization" (7).

*The Iceman Cometh* has a remarkable degree of thematic unity. It is among the most deliberately philosophical of all of O'Neill's plays, even establishing at its center a discourse between a cynically self-proclaimed philosopher (the "foolosopher" Larry) and a born-again preacher (the salesman Hickey). In a famous critique of the original production, Mary McCarthy criticized O'Neill for trying to "write a Platonic dialogue in the style of 'Casey at the Bat'" (Sheaffer 586). Yet part of the beauty of this play is just that, that even the most common of human beings is capable of deep self-assessment and profound contemplation. *The Iceman Cometh* is relentless in its insistence on philosophically challenging the audience to reflect on the meaning of life. Through the repeated use of the term *pipe dreams*, O'Neill keeps his eyes, as well as those of the audience, on the question of how to cope with reality, whether it is better to face the harsh truths of life or to hide behind comforting illusions.

There are no "bad guys" in this play. Even though they all may be drunks and outcasts, and each of them may be pitiable, none of the characters (with the possible exception of Parritt) is malicious or hateful. The audience members can easily see themselves represented in some way by at least one of the characters on stage, who represent a multicultural cross section of American society. Furthermore, if an observer is willing to view the play on a metaphorical level, then he or she can easily identify with any of the characters on stage as a member of the human family trying to get through each day of what is not always clearly a meaningful existence. The likeability of so many of the characters makes their choice to live life with illusions seem irreprehensible. Yet the persuasive rhetoric and winning personality of the central figure in the ensemble, Hickey the preacher/salesman, also gives one pause. On the face of it, most people would agree with Hickey that it is preferable to live life without illusions, to face reality and be honest with oneself and others. On the other hand, these characters are so much happier with their pipe dreams than without them.

Each character in the play has a dream, either a false sense of self or an unrealistic plan for the future, that allows him or her to while away the time at Harry Hope's, content with the perennial promise of "tomorrow." As Larry explains at the outset of the play, tomorrow is sacred to these characters:

> They all have a touching credulity concerning tomorrows.... It'll be a great day for them, tomorrow—the Feast of All Fools, with brass bands playing! Their ships will come in, loaded to the gunwales with cancelled regrets and promises fulfilled and clean slates and new leases! (O'Neill 569)

The play thus begins with the calm atmosphere of the "No-Chance Saloon," free of the anxiety of failure because nobody ever actually acts on his or her dreams. At the same time, the atmosphere is deadly, compared several times to a morgue, suggesting an emptiness to this kind of existence, one that is readily filled with drink. As long as they have hope in their pipe dreams, these characters are ripe for a transcendent kind of intoxication.

Hickey enters to represent the counterargument, that pipe dreams are deadening, and that the only way to find true peace is to face up to pipe dreams for what they are, to abandon the false sense of hope that they provide, and to accept the harsh truth about oneself and one's life. Through the sheer force of his personality, Hickey manipulates virtually every single character in the play to try on his philosophy, and it ends up backfiring on them and on Hickey himself. Instead of finding peace, each character becomes more despondent and stressed without his or her pipe dream than he or she was with it, suggesting that one is better off living with the illusion. In fact, as soon as the opportunity to do so presents itself, in the form of Hickey's insanity, they seize it. With renewed hope, the booze regains its kick, and they are all once again restored to a state of blissful self-deception. The three exceptions are Parritt, who commits suicide; Hickey himself, who is taken off by the police, presumably to execution or life imprisonment for murder; and Larry, who rejects all other purpose in life except to await his death. Thus O'Neill presents the dilemma of whether it is better to live life with or without illusion both philosophically, in so much of the lengthy and repetitive dialogue of the play, and visually, in the play's final tableau—general celebration onstage, with Larry "in his chair by the window...oblivious to their racket" (711). He does not, however, present a definitive answer. Presumably, he leaves that for each member of the audience to decide.

## STYLISTIC AND LITERARY DEVICES

In *The Iceman Cometh*, as in his other late plays, O'Neill returns to an essentially naturalistic style. Of all the late plays, *Iceman* (and to some extent, *Hughie*) most strongly resembles earlier naturalistic European drama of the turn of the century, obviously recalling Gorky's *The Lower Depths*, for instance, in its seedy setting and proletarian characters. In addition, as in his early sea plays, O'Neill represents a plethora of ethnicities and distinguishes one character from the others largely through the use of dialect. *The Iceman Cometh* is a virtual symphony of American voices, ranging from African American to Italian to Irish to WASP. Few of the characters are employed and those who are earn their livings as hookers and bartenders/pimps. The world of Harry Hope's seems to be what you would see if you peaked through the dirtied window of any saloon on or near the waterfront in New York City early in the second decade of the twentieth century.

One of the central characteristics of this world is the excessive consumption of alcohol. An alcoholic himself, and surrounded by alcoholics as a young man, both at and away from home, O'Neill used his own first-hand knowledge of the physical and psychological effects of alcoholic intoxication and dependency to add a layer of true detail to his play. The symptoms of late-stage alcoholism are apparent in the initial descriptions of a number of the characters who are discovered asleep when the curtain rises. Wetjoen, for instance, has "*sodden bloodshot blue eyes*" (567), and Willie's face is "*haggard*" and "*dissipated*" (568); "*time and whiskey have melted* [McGloin's face] *down into a good-humored parasite's characterlessness*" (567). Willie has the shakes and Hope's mood swings drastically from one moment, when he is friendly and understanding of the others' plights, to the next, when he is disdainful toward and demeaning of them. Indeed, all the characters experience low moments of despondency and high moments of elation. Hugo recurrently awakens in a childlike state with his repetitive accusatory prattle, only to retreat to the oblivion of sleep each time. Virtually all of the characters pass long periods of time silent on stage, either sleeping or in a daze, responding mechanically to physical stimuli in the environment, like familiar tunes, loud noises and voices, and words that carry unpleasant associations. They also respond positively to the promise of another drink. They repeat themselves, both verbally and behaviorally. Some critics have objected to the repetitiveness of the play, yet it is precisely this repetitiveness that is a sign of its naturalistic accuracy. Surely, the lives of addicts are nothing if not repetitive.

The effects of alcohol consumption vary. When the characters believe in their pipe dreams, alcohol has a "kick"; they feel better when they drink. In act 1, when Hickey arrives and treats them to drinks, the intoxicating effect is almost instantaneous (except for some temporary faltering caused by Hickey's unfamiliar new demeanor). When Hickey forces them to go out and try to realize their pipe dreams, and those dreams are exposed as false and unattainable, the characters become despondent and unable to get that "kick" no matter how much alcohol they consume. Finally, when Hickey is taken off by the police, and their belief in their pipe dreams is restored, the exhilarating effect is, once again, instantaneous. All of the characters in *The Iceman Cometh* depend on their pipe dreams to survive from day to day, and without their pipe dreams, even alcohol cannot protect them from the emptiness at the bottom of the bottle.

Even though O'Neill's late plays mark a return to a naturalistic style, these dramas are also heavily symbolic. In *The Iceman Cometh*, the primary symbolic entity is a figure that never appears on stage—the iceman—and its symbolic significance is richly ambiguous. Atop a long list of evocative titles in O'Neill's canon sits *The Iceman Cometh*, perhaps the most compelling of them all.

First of all, the title is linguistically contradictory. "The Iceman," although today obsolete, refers to an occupation common at the time of the play, that of the man who delivered ice for the iceboxes in people's homes before the days of the refrigerator. Yet, the biblical verb form—-eth—incongruently suggests an activity that is holy. Furthermore, because the verb itself means both to arrive and to reach a sexual climax, the title conveys something both sacred and profane. This incongruity is heightened when characters in the play refer to Hickey's oft-repeated suggestion that his wife is having extramarital sex with the iceman. Common jokes at the time involved lonely housewives who had been left home when their husbands were off at work and would seek companionship and sexual fulfillment in the arms of the iceman, a regular domestic visitor in those days. Specifically, as Day and others have observed, the title is an ironic allusion to a passage in the New Testament: "'While the bridegroom tarried, they all slumbered and slept. And at midnight there was a cry made, Behold the bridegroom cometh'—Matthew 25:5–6" (3). As Day points out, "In the symbolism of theology, the bridegroom is always Christ, giver of the eternal. Waiting for the bridegroom symbolizes man's hope of redemption.... Union with the bridegroom signifies victory over death and salvation in the world to come" (5). The iceman's coming signifies adulterous sex; the vulgar connotation demeans the biblical allusion.

Because the human body turns cold when it is lifeless, the iceman may also be a reference to death, the coldness of ice suggesting the absence of warmth, the absence of warm blood, the absence of life. If the iceman represents death, then the use of the biblical "cometh," seems more appropriate, suggesting a pronouncement of an eternal truth, that death comes to all human beings. Yet it still parodies the biblical allusion to the bridegroom, as the iceman does not bring the promise of salvation, but only a cold, lonely death, such as that of Evelyn (5). Evelyn does not have an affair with the iceman. Rather, Hickey kills her, so he is the iceman who brings death. Many of the characters in the play, in fact, complain that Hickey brings death to Harry Hope's when he compels them to destroy their pipe dreams. He brings death to their pipe dreams, death to their hopes, and therefore death to them, signified by the lack of "kick" in the liquor. O'Neill's play is about the uncertainty of living life in the face of the certainty of death, and this premise, which foreshadows existentialism, is captured in the paradoxical title of the drama and played out symbolically in the play itself through the many explicit and implicit allusions to the iceman.

## ALTERNATE PERSPECTIVE: A MARXIST APPROACH

Marxist criticism begins with the premise that economics reveals the values of a culture, and that within the economic system of a society lies its power structure. Marxist critics identify the ways in which an economic system affects the human condition, and often, in particular, the deleterious effects of capitalist ideology on the human spirit.

*The Iceman Cometh* is characterized by a strongly anticapitalist sentiment. Among the denizens of Harry Hope's, three of the men—Hugo, Larry, and Parritt—are explicitly identified with anticapitalist ideology. All three have been associated with "the Movement," a vague reference to the revolutionary Anarchist movement of the early twentieth century, although none of these characters ever delineates the specific tenets of Anarchist ideology, nor does their behavior advocate for the Movement as a viable alternative to capitalism. In fact, all three have abandoned the Movement (and in Hugo's case, been abandoned by it), and they have hardly discovered a more acceptable alternative. Parritt is on the run after having betrayed the Movement, and Larry and Hugo have both withdrawn into alcoholic oblivion behind the doors of Harry Hope's.

At the end, two of these three characters are removed from the center of the action—one to the sidelines and the other to his death in the alleyway—while the drunken outbursts of the third trivialize the Movement. The drunken Anarchist Hugo (whose family name, Kalmar, as noted by several observers, is an obvious ironic allusion to Karl Marx) rants and raves throughout the drama, spewing quasi-revolutionary slogans and deriding capitalism at every turn. It is hard to take Hugo seriously, but the repetition of his anticapitalist rhetoric is unavoidable. In the final scene, Hugo interrupts the raucous celebration to sing the revolutionary "La Carmagnole," only to be derisively shouted down by the others. He ridicules them in his habitual comic fashion as "Capitalist Svine!" and "Stupid bourgeois monkeys!" and resorts, defensively, to his usual revolutionary/ romantic refrain: "The days grow hot, O Babylon! 'Tis cool beneath thy willow trees!" (O'Neill 711). This time, however, the entire group mockingly takes up the second line of the refrain, and Hugo happily joins them in joyful self-mockery. Anarchy prevails at the end. The organized Anarchist movement may be rejected, and perhaps, as Winifred Frazer has suggested, "the dream of a better world through revolution is...discredited" (3), yet the discordant triumph of anarchy itself at the end of the play, led by the crazed Hugo, nevertheless strikes a jarring, if unfocused, blow against the prevailing capitalistic order.

In *The Iceman Cometh*, O'Neill gathers together at Harry Hope's a group of characters who represent the "have-nots" of a capitalist culture. All of them exist on the edge of society, without the means of subsistence, surviving only by exploiting the reluctant and self-serving generosity of Harry Hope, the proprietor. All of them have, in one way or another, failed within the norms of capitalism and have now become unproductive, forgotten outsiders, living on the fringe, surviving from day to day on whiskey and the transparent hopes of their pipe dreams.

Capitalism, especially the particular brand identified with the "American Dream," promises material success to all, yet grants it only to a relative few; the majority of the others while away their days only dreaming of it. Most of the residents of Harry Hope's dream of regaining their places within the system, getting their old jobs back and becoming "successful."

For example, Mosher seeks employment again at the circus and Jimmy at a newspaper, while Joe, the black entrepreneur, plans to open his own gambling establishment and Willie, the Harvard Law graduate, will join the District Attorney's staff. On some deep level, each character knows that his dream is a lie and that he will never realize it, but each relies on that lie for hope in the face of failure.

The only characters at Harry Hope's (besides Hope himself) who do actually earn a living are the three women and the two bartenders, but their identities are linked literally to one of the perceived evils of capitalism, exploitation, and figuratively to another, spiritual corruption. The two bartenders, Rocky and Chuck, earn their living, first of all, off of the alcohol dependency of other people. More significantly, however, as pimps, they earn money by exploiting the women who work for them. Chuck and Cora hide behind the façade of intended marriage, and Rocky, Margie, and Pearl, hide behind the façade of euphemisms (bartender versus pimp; tart versus whore). Yet the reality is that these women sell their bodies for money and the men profit from that degrading transaction. Of course, prostitution itself is a preferred metaphor for everything that is wrong with the capitalist system. All people who function within capitalism are prostitutes, selling their souls for money.

Then there is Harry Hope, the proprietor of the establishment where all the others spend their time. As the property owner, he would seem to have the power, yet he is powerless, as dependent on the penniless sycophants who live off of him as they are on him. The system has corrupted him, too, so that he has become what we would today call an enabler, always finding reasons to forgive the rent and provide free booze to the others who exploit his loneliness and his impotence for their own gain. None of them acts to effect change. Rather, they remain as drunk as possible, their good cheer founded on alcohol and lies.

Into this world of down-and-outers enters Hickey, the salesman/preacher who represents the lure of capitalism, always promising to buy happiness, in his case, with the purchase of rounds of drinks. The salesman is the middle man in an economic transaction. Neither the producer of goods nor the consumer, he lives or dies on the power of persuasion, and Hickey can be very persuasive, even to himself. The effect of the drinks he usually purchases for everyone is to lull them into a false sense of contentment, the only brand of happiness provided by capitalism. This time, however, Hickey arrives to sell the others a different bill of goods, happiness derived from facing up to their false pipe dreams, purging themselves of these dreams, and living with truth. Hickey reiterates in every act that he wants to see his friends "happy," but without their pipe dreams they have nothing, and in spite of Hickey's powers of persuasion, they only become more depressed, until Hickey himself has to acknowledge that his own happiness is itself an illusion. No less than the prostitutes, Hickey has sold his soul in the pursuit of success, lying to and cheating on his wife and never able to live up to her ideal. Within American capitalism, it is impossible to be success-ful and to be good, and although Hickey is the most financially successful character in the play, he is also the most troubled. In the end, it costs him his wife and his life. Money cannot buy happiness, as capitalism often seems to promise.

At the conclusion of *The Iceman Cometh*, both Larry and Parritt re-ject false hope and each chooses to face his own hopeless reality, leading Larry to give up on life in stoic isolation and Parritt to give up on life by suicide. The other characters dismiss Hickey as insane and return to their drunken revelry, suggesting that the only chance for happiness within the capitalist system lies in the false hope of a pipe dream. As Larry explains to Rocky early in the play, "The lie of a pipe dream is what gives life to the whole misbegotten mad lot of us, drunk or sober" (O'Neill 570). This may be the preferred mode of survival for these characters, but it is clearly a life based on and sustained by lies. From a Marxist perspective, that is the only kind of life possible under a capitalist system, and a life based on the false hope of capitalism may not be worth living.

## WORKS CITED

Day, Cyrus. "The Iceman and the Bridegroom: Some Observations on the Death of O'Neill's Salesman." *Modern Drama*, May 1958: 3–9.

Frazer, Winifred L. "Revolution in *The Iceman Cometh*." *Modern Drama* March 1979: 1–8.

Gelb, Arthur and Barbara. *O'Neill*. New York: Harper & Row, 1962.

———. *O'Neill: Life with Monte Cristo*. New York: Applause Books, 2000.

O'Neill, Eugene. *Complete Plays 1932–1943*. Ed. Travis Bogard. New York: Library of America, 1988.

Quintero, José. "Postscript to a Journey." *Theatre Arts*, April 1957: 27–29, 88.

Sheaffer, Louis. *O'Neill: Son and Artist*. Boston: Little, Brown, & Co., 1973.

# 8

## Long Day's Journey Into Night (1941)

An intensely personal drama, *Long Day's Journey Into Night* is, as many scholars have noted, the play that defines Eugene O'Neill, both as a person and as an artist. It can be said that virtually every play he wrote before was a draft for *Long Day's Journey*. In earlier plays, versions of his parents and his brother are embedded in the families that he depicts on stage; but in *Long Day's Journey Into Night,* they emerge as fully formed, fictional creations with the strongest possible literal resemblance to his own family members.

O'Neill wrote *Long Day's Journey Into Night* in the final years of his creative life, between 1939 and 1941. Perhaps he knew that if he did not get it done during those years, because of his physical deterioration, he might never get it done. His wife Carlotta described the extraordinary emotional impact that writing this play had on O'Neill: "He would come out of his study at the end of a day gaunt and sometimes weeping" (Berlin 148). The inscription he wrote to Carlotta, which appears in the published version of the play, reveals the depth of personal feeling that was associated with this play for the dramatist:

I give you the original script of this play of old sorrow, written in tears and blood. A sadly inappropriate gift, it would seem, for a day celebrating happiness. But you will understand. I mean it as a tribute to your love and tenderness which gave me the faith in love that enabled me to face my dead at last and write this play—write it with deep pity and understanding and forgiveness for all the four haunted Tyrones. (O'Neill 714)

When O'Neill penned these lines, he had no intention of the public knowing of the autobiographical truths that lay barely beneath the surface of this drama. He sent it to Bennett Cerf at Random House with explicit instructions that it not be published until 25 years after his death, and it was never to be produced. Because of Carlotta's decision to allow its publication and production only three years after his death, the public discovered the power of the drama much sooner than O'Neill intended, and O'Neill's own words in the dedication prompted speculation and research into its autobiographical revelations. *Long Day's Journey* earned O'Neill his fourth Pulitzer prize for drama (posthumously) and unequivocally established O'Neill in the pantheon of the world's greatest dramatists. Its power is due only in part to its autobiographical revelations. *Long Day's Journey Into Night* is one of the great works of drama primarily because of the characters, their story, the issues they raise, and the emotions they stir in the audience.

## SETTING AND PLOT DEVELOPMENT

*Long Day's Journey Into Night* takes place in one single summer day, but encompasses a lifetime, in fact, four lifetimes. The setting is the Tyrones' summer house, and O'Neill's typically detailed stage directions re-create the O'Neill's summer residence in New London, Connecticut, in its layout and furnishings, down to the titles of specific books in the bookcases. All of the "action" of the play occurs in the "living room," but O'Neill makes several other unseen spaces in the house key components of the play's setting because of what happens there before characters enter and after they leave the living room. Several times, and in different, telling configurations, the family enters from and exits to the dining room through the back parlor (although the audience never actually sees them having meals together). Jamie and Edmund make their respective drunken entrances in act 4 through the darkened front parlor (making the front parlor the conduit to and from the external world). Mary ascends the stairs to the "spare room" above several times during the play, where she takes morphine. She spends most of act 4 up there, as the men listen with dread for sounds of her moving above and descending the staircase, culminating in her piano playing in the front parlor before she enters the living room for the final scene. Although O'Neill makes the audience aware of all these other spaces in the house, at the same time, he cuts the living room off from the world outside with the wall of fog that gradually deepens right outside the windows, thus conveying both the isolation of the four Tyrones and their dependency on each other.

Strictly speaking, *Long Day's Journey* does not have a conventional plot; that is, like many of O'Neill's other plays, it does not tell a discrete story with a clear beginning, middle, and end. Rather, it depicts a day in the life of the Tyrone family, not an ordinary day by any means, but a day in which circumstances conspire to bring to a boil several of the tense conflicts that have been heating up in this family for years. It is a day on which the family will learn that Edmund, the younger son, has contracted tuberculosis (then called consumption and believed by many at the time to be fatal). They will also acknowledge and accept that Mary, the mother and wife, has resumed her addictive use of morphine, probably never again to escape its hold on her. These two developments provide the context for a series of confrontations among the four Tyrones that are characterized by a cyclical and repetitive pattern of guilt, denial, blame, and forgiveness.

The play begins in the morning as the parents, Mary and James Tyrone, emerge from breakfast into the living room in the middle of what appears to be a warm and loving exchange of pleasantries. The only indication of discord is Tyrone's concern that his sons are telling jokes at his expense, but even this seems to indicate no more than the harmless, often loving, mockery directed by adult children at their father. When the sons, Jamie and Edmund, follow their parents into the living room from the dining room, this joking continues. There are, however, increasing signs of underlying tension, especially between Tyrone and his older son, Jamie, as well as increasingly apparent efforts to protect Mary from any evidence that Edmund may not be well. When Mary exits to tend to the servants, the tension between Tyrone and Jamie erupts into outright conflict. They argue angrily over who is to blame for Edmund's ill health, Mary's vulnerability, and Jamie's disappointing station in life. The conflict, however, is tempered by moments of reconciliation, when they acknowledge a shared sense of hope about Mary's restored health and well-being.

When Mary returns, the two men quickly exit to trim the hedges outside, leaving Mary alone for only a moment as her younger son, Edmund, joins her. Their conversation parallels the previous one between Tyrone and Jamie in that, again, questions of guilt and blame arise amid concerns for Edmund's health and Mary's stability. In particular, Mary conveys a sense of paranoia about the degree of concern the three men are showing for her, so to reassure her, Edmund leaves her alone in the living room and exits outside.

Act 2, scene 1 brings the two siblings together in the living room without their parents for the first time. The maid, Cathleen, also appears at the beginning of this scene, bearing a bottle of bourbon, a crucial stage property that has been absent up to this time, but from this point forward, plays an important role in the family dynamics. One of the bottle's functions becomes apparent almost immediately; the two siblings establish a bond as they sneak a drink before their father returns. Their ensuing conversation echoes the previous ones between the parents and sons, as Jamie blames Edmund for allowing their mother to be alone upstairs, and Edmund denies that leaving her alone will be a problem. Jamie also offers more explicit evidence that something is chronically wrong with their mother. He indicates that "this game" has been ongoing since both brothers were quite young.

When Mary enters, the stage directions indicate that "*she appears to be less nervous . . . her eyes are brighter, and there is a peculiar detachment in her voice and manner, as if she were a little withdrawn from her words and actions*" (747). O'Neill also stipulates that "*Jamie knows after one probing look at her that his suspicions are justified*" (747), and Jamie's cynical words and attitude throughout the rest of the play are shaped by this knowledge. Although her condition remains unidentified in explicit terms, the symptoms are clearly those of some kind of chemically induced intoxication. Tyrone then comes into the house for lunch, and as soon as he observes his wife for an instant, it is clear that "*he knows*" (753), and he reacts with bitter resignation. It is only Edmund who still seems to deny all the evidence that Mary has resumed her addictive behavior. As the family exits into the dining room for lunch through the dark back parlor, their opening entrance is reversed; the sons go first, followed soon after by the parents, and the lightness and hope of their opening entrance have been replaced by darkness and disappointment.

The next scene begins with the family entering from the dining room as they had at the beginning of act 1, but this time, although the two generations walk in at the same time, each of the four Tyrones is alienated from the others. Whereas in act 1 there was laughter and conversation, in act 2, scene 2, there is only Mary's incessant chatter, which is met with silence from the men.

After a brief, tense confrontation about why this summer home has never felt like a real home, the first real "event" of the play occurs: there is a phone call from Dr. Hardy, asking Edmund to see him that afternoon. Mary advises against believing anything the doctor says, and then she exits upstairs, allegedly to find her glasses; by this point, however, it is fairly evident that the threat of bad news from the doctor provokes her to protect herself behind a deeper drug-induced haze. It is apparent enough for Jamie to predict as she exits, "Another shot in the arm!" (758), which is the first direct indication in the play that Mary is taking drugs. Once she is gone, the men resume the pattern of arguing about who is to blame, as Tyrone reveals to Jamie that Edmund has consumption, and Jamie accuses Tyrone of jeopardizing Edmund's prognosis by choosing inferior health care to save money.

As both Edmund and Jamie exit to prepare for their visit into town, Mary and Tyrone have a few moments alone together, during which they exchange accusations, mostly Mary accusing Tyrone of excessive drunkenness and of wasting his money on a car and chauffeur for her. Mary increasingly evokes the past to help explain the present: "The past is the present, isn't it? It's the future, too. We all try to lie out of that but life won't let us" (765), specifically recalling the death of her second child, Eugene. When Edmund returns, dressed for his visit to the doctor, Mary, afraid of learning the truth about his condition, pleads with him not to go; he, in turn, pleads with her to stop taking the drugs. She resumes her pattern of denial, however, so Edmund retreats, as all three men depart for town, leaving Mary by herself. She is glad to be left alone but feels lonely at the same time.

Act 3 begins with a rather long scene in which Mary invites Cathleen, the maid, to stay with her for company. As Cathleen accepts the invitation for an afternoon pick-me-up, Mary rambles on about her early infatuation with Tyrone, trying to justify to herself her own marriage, which has now become so sad. When Tyrone and Edmund return, the cycle of guilt, blame, and denial resumes, as Mary continues her reminiscences about the early years of their marriage, but the rose-tinted lens through which she relates her story to Cathleen now becomes tainted by resentment. Mary attacks Tyrone, primarily for his drinking, and she expresses her deep regrets about her disappointments, symbolized by her wedding gown, the whereabouts of which she cannot now recall. Her sad and angry reminiscences drive Tyrone away to replace the drained bottle of bourbon with a new one. While he is gone, Edmund tries to break through Mary's wall of denial in search of maternal concern for his failing health. Mary stands firm in denial, however, which leads Edmund to strike back at her with his most direct and poignant rebuff: "It's pretty hard to take at times, having a dope fiend for a mother!" (788). Act 3 ends with Edmund retreating from this painful confrontation with his mother, as he leaves the house, presumably to seek the comfort of the barroom in town. Mary ascends to the spare room upstairs to take yet more morphine ("that God-damned poison," as Tyrone calls it) to ease her pain. Tyrone walks off through the back parlor to the dining room again, but this time, for dinner, he is alone, "*a sad, bewildered, broken old man*" (791).

Act 4, the longest act in the play, opens with Tyrone sitting alone, drunk, playing solitaire in the living room around midnight. After a few moments, he is joined by Edmund, who returns from town, also drunk. While playing cards, they engage in a long conversation that revisits many of the sources of tension and conflict between them, including Edmund's poor health, Mary's condition, and the role that Tyrone's stinginess has played in both. Their discussion is punctuated by the sounds of Mary stirring above, to which they react with fear and anxiety. Much of this conversation reiterates issues raised previously in the play, but the difference here is that both characters venture into new territory as, in their intoxicated state, each launches into an extended, self-revealing monologue that strengthens the bond between them. Edmund tells his father of his visions of "nirvana" while at sea, his hopes to find meaning in life and the words to express it, while Tyrone reveals to his son that the great disappointment of his life has been that he sold away the chance to be one of the finest actors of his time for financial security, and now his life feels empty.

On the heels of these revelatory speeches, Jamie stumbles in, exaggeratedly drunk, and Tyrone leaves Edmund alone with him to avoid the inevitable conflict he expects if he were to stay. The two brothers then have an equally poignant exchange in which Jamie warns his younger brother that although he loves him more than he hates him, he does hate him, and he will seek to destroy him. All of these revelations of regret and resentment set the stage for the inevitable entrance of Mary from upstairs, now deeply lost behind a wall of morphine-induced intoxication that has taken her back to the time before she married James Tyrone. After clumsily playing the piano in the front parlor, she enters carrying her wedding dress, speaking as the young Mary who must decide between pursuing her dream of being a nun or marrying James Tyrone. She seems not to recognize the three men in her life, and she does not acknowledge them. Edmund makes one last attempt to reach her, to have her acknowledge his condition and his existence, but she rejects him. She rejects them all and the reality they represent. As the three men sit staring in front of them, Mary speaks the final words of the play:

> That was in the winter of senior year. Then in the spring something happened to me. Yes, I remember. I fell in love with James Tyrone and was so happy for a time. (828)

The play ends, but without resolution. The Tyrone family appears to be stuck in time, together yet alone on life's long anguished journey.

## CHARACTER DEVELOPMENT

There are four main characters in *Long Day's Journey Into Night*, the four members of the Tyrone family—Edmund, Jamie, James, and Mary. Although Edmund is clearly depicted as a version of the dramatist himself, the drama does not unfold from his perspective. Indeed, one of the great dramaturgical accomplishments of the play is that O'Neill presents multiple, and often conflicting, perceptions of the same events and circumstances by different members of the same family. As stated in his dedication, O'Neill wrote the play "*with deep pity and understanding and forgiveness for* all *the four haunted Tyrones*" (O'Neill's emphasis). Each character has his or her moments in the play; each one gets to make his or her claim for the audience's "pity and understanding and forgiveness." That said, there is no question that Mary is at the heart of this drama. She is the focus of the men's attention on this day, and much of what they say and do is in response to her. Each of the Tyrone men in his own way depends on her.

Edmund, the younger son, is 23 years old and in poor health. He is an alcoholic. He has been away from his family, traveling at sea, but has recently returned to their summer home, and through his father's connections, he has been working for the local newspaper. He aspires to be a writer, but does not believe in his own talent. When his father grudgingly admits that Edmund has "the *makings* of a poet," Edmund replies: "No, I'm afraid I'm like the guy who is always panhandling for a smoke. He hasn't even got the makings. He's got only the habit" (812).

As the youngster in the family, Edmund had been kept in the dark the longest about his mother's morphine addiction, but since discovering her "secret" at the age of 15, he has lost his religious faith, and he has spent the rest of his life searching for something in which to believe. In this regard, Edmund is something of a romantic, as indicated when he speaks beatifically of his transcendent experience at sea:

> I was set free! I dissolved in the sea, became white sails and flying spray, became beauty and rhythm, became moonlight and the ship and the high dim-starred sky! I belonged, without past or future, within peace and unity and a wild joy, within something greater than my own life, or the life of Man, to Life itself! To God, if you want to put it that way. (811–812)

Consistent with his romantic spirit, Edmund holds out hope the longest among the three Tyrone men that Mary can overcome her addiction and reject the morphine. In the course of the drama, while establishing close but complicated bonds with both his father and his brother, Edmund endures a series of telling blows to his spirit of romantic hopefulness: his father's confession of the deep regret of his life, his brother's confession of jealous hatred for him, and finally, his mother's retreat behind a hard, drug-induced wall of disappointment and shame.

Jamie, the older sibling, is 33 years old and suffers, at a more advanced stage and more visibly than does Edmund, from the debilitating effects of alcoholism. Like Edmund, Jamie has spent time away from his family, but he regularly returns to the family's summer home when he runs out of money. According to his father, Jamie has some talent as an actor, but because this is not only his father's profession, but one in which his father has gained fame and fortune, Jamie has rejected this path in life, only reluctantly accepting work when forced by circumstances of unemployment. He is a huge disappointment to his parents, and they blame him for having a bad influence on Edmund, especially when it comes to liquor and prostitutes. Jamie identifies strongly with his mother, especially her struggles with addiction, but this identification manifests itself in cynical sneering at both parents. As he confesses to Edmund, he hates himself, so he feels compelled to take revenge on everyone else in the family. Beneath his cynicism lies a fatal vulnerability to his mother's losing battle.

James Tyrone is 65 years old, and one of the most well-known theatrical stars of his time. He has made a fortune, for those days, by touring with the play he bought "for a song," but in doing so, he turned his back on artistic success as a serious actor. His money is all invested in real estate, and his sons ridicule him for his miserliness, which he justifies as a response to having grown up as a poor immigrant in America whose family had to work hard to survive. The only real estate that tangibly benefits the Tyrone family is the modest summer home in which the play takes place, which is furnished frugally.

Both of his sons and his wife blame Tyrone's miserliness for Mary's addiction, because he allegedly hired a cheap doctor to treat her when she gave birth to Edmund, which is when her dependence on morphine began. Both Jamie and Edmund also accuse Tyrone of compromising on Edmund's health care to save money. A lifetime of alcoholism has apparently inured him to its debilitating effects. He claims never to have missed a performance, and in the course of the play, in spite of consuming large quantities of liquor, he appears quite sober. He rationalizes his heavy drinking not only as "a good man's failing" but also as an understandable method of coping with the burden of a drug-addicted wife and disappointing sons who are still dependent on him. Tyrone is an optimist, often quoting (and misquoting) Shakespeare in defense against the pessimistic modern sensibilities of his sons. His innate optimism is seriously challenged in the course of the play, as his wife drifts further and further away from him, until she transports herself at the end of the play to the last time in her life when she was happy—when she first met and fell in love with James Tyrone.

Mary Tyrone is 54 years old. From the beginning of the play, the audience knows that something is not quite right with her. Her sons and husband treat her with caution and are highly solicitous of her at first. She seems nervous and high strung. As the play progresses, we notice a gradual change in her. Her eyes become brighter, and her voice and manner become more and more detached and aloof. She rambles on, increasingly oblivious to those around her. In her ramblings, she recalls past events as if they were happening again, and she repeatedly accuses her husband and sons of causing her misery. By the end of act 2, the audience knows that her demeanor is being influenced by morphine, to which she is addicted.

The four Tyrones work as an ensemble, both as characters in the drama and as co-dependent members of an addictive family, but Mary is clearly established as the central figure in this dysfunctional dynamic. At first, the three men try their best to comfort her and to keep her mind off the drugs. Once they know she is on morphine again, each one responds in his own way, and their responses trigger the conflicts among them. Each one of them invests his hope for his own peace of mind in Mary's successful efforts to find peace, and each is then doomed to failure when she fails. Mary is a constant presence in the play. Even when she is off stage, especially for the long stretch of most of the fourth act, the men talk about her and anticipate her return with dread and anxiety. Her entrance toward the end of act 4—"The Mad Scene. Enter Ophelia!" as Jamie introduces it—is the dramatic climax of the play. As she stands at the very end, obliviously carrying her wedding gown, and speaking as if she were still the happy and innocent girl she remembers being before she married James Tyrone, she forms the focal point of the concluding tableau of the play—the four Tyrones in the dark living room, each painfully alone, yet inextricably tied together for eternity.

The only other character in the play is Cathleen, the maid. She is a secondary character, to be sure, but she provides an outsider's view of this terribly insular family. She admires the Tyrones, reminding the readers and viewers of this play that they are getting a private glimpse behind the public façade of this family, and that all families, indeed all people, have private secrets unknown to the world outside.

## THEMATIC ISSUES

*Long Day's Journey Into Night* is the quintessential American family drama, even more so than Miller's *Death of a Salesman*. Miller's play views the American family through the father/husband's lens, but O'Neill's drama demands that the audience consider multiple perspectives on the family, not only that of each of the four Tyrones, but also that of the "outsider," Cathleen. As the Tyrones spin an endless cycle of guilt, blame, and denial, the audience cannot help but see how each member of the family simultaneously contributes to, and is a victim of, the family's trials and dysfunction. O'Neill explores many of the family dynamics that have been analyzed by Freud and his clinical disciples in the last century, including oedipal conflicts and sibling rivalry. His depiction of alcoholism and its effects on individuals reflects many contemporary insights into both addictive and enabling behaviors. The repetitious pattern of guilt, blame, and denial that defines the experience of the addictive Tyrone family is emblematic of patterns of behavior that define many families in which addiction is not an issue.

Through his depiction of family, O'Neill raises issues of gender roles and expectations, especially in terms of Mary's roles as wife and mother. Incapable of providing the kind of maternal nurturance so desperately sought by both of her sons, and caught in a trap of chemical dependency typically not associated with a woman of her station in life, Mary alternates in the course of the play between the gendered roles of virgin mother and whore. In their dependency on this seemingly fragile, yet manipulative woman, the men in the play struggle with the gendered notion of male power and success.

Through this dysfunctional family dynamic, O'Neill also raises issues of class conflict and the failures of American capitalism. Both Mary and Tyrone allude to the class differences in their upbringings, Mary having been reared in a well-to-do middle-class family, whereas Tyrone has struggled to rise up from the depths of immigrant poverty and discrimination. The summer home in which the play is set is rife with ironic social paradoxes as Mary complains not only about the cheap ways in which Tyrone has furnished it, but also about the poor quality of the help, which she insists on having. The one servant who appears in the play, the maid Cathleen, reminds the audience of the pretense of the Tyrone family in the face of the social pressures of the larger community.

Beyond the psychological and sociocultural themes of *Long Day's Journey*, there are also universal philosophical themes. O'Neill once said that, in his drama, he was less interested in the relationship between man and man than in the relationship between man and God (Berlin 162). O'Neill was interested in "big" issues, raising questions about the very nature of human existence. As this family is forced to cope with the disappointments of unfulfilled dreams and dashed hopes, they confront the audience with basic questions about the purpose of human life and its place in the grand scheme. Edmund sums it up:

> It was a great mistake, my being born a man. I would have been much more successful as a sea gull or a fish. As it is, I will always be a stranger who never feels at home, who does not really want and is not really wanted, who can never belong, who must always be a little in love with death! (O'Neill 812)

This theme of not belonging has been a constant in O'Neill's drama. It pervades *Long Day's Journey*, evoked in speeches like this one by Edmund and even in the setting of the play. This summer house is the closest the Tyrones (and the O'Neills) have to a home, but it lacks stability. It never provides the strong foundation needed by the family that lives in it, and especially by the son (who, in life, was to become the dramatist). The Tyrones (the O'Neills) never feel that they belong in, and are never accepted by, this community, which is emphasized in the play by the isolation of the house and family. Mary never leaves, and although the men do leave, they always return, and nothing positive or affirming happens to them while they are away (the exception perhaps being Edmund's walk through the fog). Over the course of the play, the fog thickens, so that by the fourth act, "the wall of fog appears denser than ever" (792), symbolically cutting the Tyrones off from other human beings and emphasizing how alone they are.

In this emphasis on "aloneness," O'Neill captures the essence of twentieth-century existentialist philosophy. Having lost his faith in God at age 15, O'Neill continued to search for some explanation of existence to replace the Catholic one. He struggled to understand human "fate." Mary says to Edmund: "It's wrong to blame your brother. He can't help being what the past has made him. Any more than your father can. Or you. Or I" (751). Later, Tyrone quotes Shakespeare to Edmund: "The fault, dear Brutus, is not in our stars, but in ourselves that we are underlings" (810–811). Yet Edmund laughs at life, because "it's so damn crazy" (810): "Then the hand lets the veil fall and you are alone, lost in the fog again, and you stumble on toward nowhere, for no good reason!" (812). Through the four characters in this drama, O'Neill presents a philosophical discourse that forces the audience to confront these difficult and complex questions of human existence. O'Neill does not necessarily provide an answer, but he heroically raises the questions in the most compelling of theatrical terms.

## STYLISTIC AND LITERARY DEVICES

After all the stylistic experimentation of his middle years, mostly in the interest of bringing the inner life of his characters on stage, O'Neill returned to naturalism in his late plays. Yet he had not abandoned his desire to plumb the depths of the human psyche. One naturalistic element that he discovered with which to achieve his goal was drinking and alcoholism, and as in *The Iceman Cometh*, in *Long Day's Journey Into Night*, his use of this device is most effective. All three male characters become increasingly intoxicated beginning in the second act and culminating in the monologues of the long fourth act, and throughout the play, Mary's behavior is increasingly influenced by the effects of morphine.

Just as O'Neill, in his stage directions, creates a highly naturalistic setting, down to the titles of the books in the bookcases, so his depiction of intoxication and addiction is remarkably realistic. He depicts behaviors and symptoms that psychologists and other professionals today have documented as clinically diagnostic. Unlike drunken characters in earlier drama, O'Neill's drunks are not comic characters who stumble around the stage and slur their words. When Jamie does this in act 4, he is actually exaggerating his symptoms in an effort to hide the true and debilitating impact that his heavy drinking has had. O'Neill's drunks become self-absorbed and depressed. They become uninhibited in action and speech, and they reveal truths about themselves and their feelings for others that they are much less likely to do when sober. This is best illustrated by Jamie's fourth-act confession of his hatred for his brother Edmund:

> Listen, Kid, you'll be going away. May not get another chance to talk. Or might not be drunk enough to tell you truth. So got to tell you now. Something I ought to have told you long ago—for your own good. *He pauses—struggling with himself. Edmund stares, impressed and uneasy. Jamie blurts out.* No drunken bull, but "in vino veritas" stuff. You better take it seriously. Want to warn you—against me. Mama and papa are right. I've been rotten bad influence. And worst of it is, I did it on purpose. (820)

Discarding the artificial asides and masks of his middle experimental period, O'Neill finds in the disease that he knew all too well the key to writing the kind of realistic drama he was determined to write, a drama that went beneath the surface of the "old naturalism," which, according to O'Neill, represents "our Fathers' daring aspirations toward self-recognition by holding the family Kodak up to ill-nature" (Bogard 187, first published in Provincetown Playbill, January 3, 1924).

The play is highly naturalistic; however, it is also highly poetic in its use of theatrical imagery that is both verbal and visual. Because the male characters are all heavily influenced by theatre and literature, they frequently quote from the authors who have influenced them. For Tyrone, it is primarily Shakespeare; his sons quote more modern writers, such as

Wilde, Baudelaire, and Swinburne. This in itself adds a lyrical quality to the text and a theatrical quality to productions, as the men recite their quoted verses with great flourish and take pride in the quality of their "performances."

Beyond this allusive lyricism, *Long Day's Journey* has a poetic quality of its own that is engendered by O'Neill's use of theatrical effects, most particularly the fog, foghorn, and bells in the harbor. These become textual metaphors for the refuge that both Mary and Edmund take in their respective escapes, literally for Edmund as he recalls his transcendental experiences at sea, and symbolically for Mary as she associates the fog with the protection from reality that the morphine provides her. The final tableau of the play creates a striking stage image through the increasing darkness that envelopes the four characters, as the foghorn blows and the harbor bells ring at regular intervals. This effect is demonstrated impressively in the 1962 film directed by Sidney Lumet, in which the camera pulls away from the four characters who remain in what seems to be a shrinking pool of light, as each character stares into the darkness and the foghorn wails in the background as a melancholy reminder of their apparently hopeless feeling of aloneness.

## ALTERNATE PERSPECTIVE: A DECONSTRUCTIONIST READING

There is an irony in seeking meaning in a text through a deconstructionist approach: the essence of deconstructionist theory is that it is impossible to establish a definitive meaning for any text. Deconstructionism challenges the notion that a text has a single, authoritative meaning. Rather, it assumes that a text is polysemic, having multiple, simultaneous, and often contradictory meanings. A deconstructionist approach examines "binary oppositions" within a text, ignoring its formal structure and finding in its contradictions indications of the uncertainties of human existence. The ambivalence O'Neill felt toward his family of origin, as established by several biographers, is reflected in a deconstructionist reading of *Long Day's Journey Into Night*.

Throughout the play, the Tyrone sons, Jamie and Edmund, accuse their father of being a "tightwad." His frugality or in their eyes his miserliness has allegedly contributed not only to his mother's unhappiness with the trappings of their summer residence, which, according to Mary, is not a "home," but also, and more significantly, to her addiction to morphine. As suggested by Jamie and Edmund, it will likely lead to Edmund's demise, as well. At the same time, Tyrone convincingly argues, and Edmund affirms, that their house can hardly ever feel like a normal "home" as long as the matriarch of the family is addicted to morphine and exhibits the numerous antisocial symptoms of an addict. Similarly, although it may be true that Mary's introduction to morphine came at the prescribing hands of Dr. Hardy (a "cheap old quack"), that prescription was not unusual at that time, and surely, not every young woman who took morphine to ease the pain of childbirth became addicted to it. Now, it is Mary herself who finds ways to obtain the drug, and it is she who injects herself with it. Each member of the family appeals to Mary to use her will power to resist the lure of the drug, but she cannot, or will not. Adding to the web of contradictions, however, is the observation that the Tyrone men do little to create an atmosphere conducive to Mary's recovery. Although Tyrone has made plans for Mary to receive rehabilitative treatment, and Mary has complied, it is virtually impossible to expect an addict to continue to live drug-free in a home environment in which all the other family members drink alcohol day and night, commencing just after noon. It is difficult to say with any certainty, then, that any one of the Tyrones alone is to blame for Mary's plight, including Mary herself.

The question of whether Tyrone's miserliness is exclusively, or even primarily, to blame for his wife's condition is, at best, unresolved, but there is concrete evidence throughout the play that he is cautious about how he spends his money. The most obvious example is his insistence on keeping most of the lights turned off at night, while the family sits in the dark "There's no reason to have the house ablaze with electricity at this time of night, burning up money!" he insists in act 4, even after his son *collides with something in the dark hall*" (O'Neill 792). Even when he defends himself against his sons' accusations that he will sacrifice Edmund's health for a few dollars and agrees to send Edmund anywhere he chooses to ensure successful treatment for consumption—"I don't give a damn what it costs" (806)—he cannot help but qualify his largesse: "You can choose any place you like! Never mind what it costs! Any place I can afford. Any place you like—within reason" (808).

Yet, at the same time as his frugality is implicated as the cause of many of the family's struggles, the text provides evidence of understanding, and even forgiveness. In his long monologue in act 4, Tyrone not only explains how he came to appreciate "the value of a dollar," but also expresses profound regret for having sacrificed his own potential for artistic accomplishment as a fine actor in the interest of financial security, represented by his success with the play he bought for a song. It is difficult to blame Tyrone unequivocally for his family's situation when he exhibits such an awareness of both the roots and consequences of his behavior.

A similar pattern of contradictions is apparent in the words and deeds of the other characters as well. Jamie is both his brother's best friend and most dangerous enemy. Throughout the play, he expresses concern for his brother's health, even challenging his father to prove he is not a miser by spending whatever it takes for Edmund to receive effective treatment. At the same time, he does nothing to prevent his brother from drinking alcohol, only paying lip service to it, while drinking with him on several occasions, which certainly is not part of an effective treatment plan. In his monologue in act 4, he expresses both pride in and jealousy of his brother's literary/journalistic accomplishments, such as they are. Finally, Jamie declares, "I can't help hating your guts—! . . . But don't get the wrong idea, Kid. I love you more than I hate you" (821). Jamie's love/hate relationship with his brother is yet another unresolved contradiction in the play, and again, it is difficult to blame Jamie for his hurtful words toward Edmund (and Edmund himself seems to accept them with understanding) when these words are based on such a profoundly painful sense of self-awareness.

Mary's contradictory words and behavior are the most extreme and pervasive of all. At one moment, she is overly concerned about her younger son's ill health; at the next moment, she is cold and unresponsive to him. At one moment, she defends her husband's concern about money; at the next moment, she is critical of his stinginess. At one moment, she accuses Jamie of having a bad influence on Edmund; at the next moment, she excuses Jamie because of the ill effect his father has had on him, especially with regard to drinking. In act 2, scene 1, she implores Edmund not to blame anyone for his or her words or deeds because an individual is simply a victim of "what the past has made him" (751), yet throughout the play she blames everyone, except herself, for what has happened to her.

Throughout the play, Mary's contradictory feelings toward her husband and sons are apparent in a repeated push-pull pattern of relating to each of them. This dynamic is constantly revealed in the dialogue, as well as in the stage directions, as in the following short scene from act 2, scene 2:

MARY      *In blank denial now.* Anyway, I don't know what you're refer- ring to. But I do know you should be the last one—Right after I returned from the sanatorium, you began to be ill. The doctor there had warned me I must have peace at home with nothing to upset me, and all I've done is worry about you. *Then distractedly.* But that's no excuse! I'm only trying to explain. It's not an excuse! *She hugs him to her—pleadingly.* Promise me, dear, you won't believe I made you an excuse.

EDMUND      *Bitterly.* What else can I believe?

MARY     *Slowly takes her arm away—her manner remote and objective again.*
             Yes, I suppose you can't help suspecting that. (769)

Numerous incidences of Mary embracing Edmund and then rejecting him, holding him close to her and then distancing herself from him, do not suggest that Mary cannot make up her mind about whether or not she loves her son. Rather, they indicate that her love for him is characterized by contradictory feelings, all of which are functioning simultaneously.

Even O'Neill's dedication of the published text of *Long Day's Journey Into Night* is subject to deconstructionist interpretation, as it is possible to argue that the play itself contradicts the dedication in that Mary Tyrone seems to receive much less of the "pity and understanding and forgiveness" cited there than do the other Tyrones. O'Neill does not offer the same kind of explanation for her life as he does for the father, and many find it difficult to excuse her for neglecting her "maternal responsibilities." Still, it is also difficult not to have some sympathy for her as she stands alone at the end of the play, holding her wedding dress in her arms, recalling the day long ago when she met and fell in love with James Tyrone and was "so happy for a time" (828).

Although there are numerous indications of sympathy for each of the Tyrones in the text of the play, there are also, simultaneously and paradoxically, numerous indications of blame and incrimination toward each one. In the end, the implication is not that any of these claims of responsibility is more valid than the others, but rather that all of them, although often contradictory, are equally valid (binary oppositions), which explains why the dynamics of the Tyrone family (and by extension, all families) are so complex and therefore so realistic.

## WORKS CITED

Berlin, Normand. *Eugene O'Neill.* London: The MacMillan Press, Ltd., 1982.

Bogard, Travis. *Contour in Time: The Plays of Eugene O'Neill* (Revised Edition). New York: Oxford University Press, 1988.

O'Neill, Eugene. *Complete Plays 1932–1943.* Ed. Travis Bogard. New York: Library of America, 1988.

# 9

# *A Moon for the Misbegotten* (1943)

If *Long Day's Journey Into Night* is the final chapter in O'Neill's story, *A Moon for the Misbegotten* is the epilogue without which the story would not be truly complete. Whereas in *Long Day's Journey* O'Neill was able to confront his family ghosts with understanding and forgiveness, in *Moon*, through his brother's sins and debilitation, he was able to confront his own ghosts and find forgiveness, not insignificantly, in the arms of a seductively maternal woman. Looked at through a biographical lens, this play seems to be about Jamie O'Neill, the profligate brother who drank himself to death at an early age. Looked at in the context of O'Neill's dramaturgy, however, it is yet another play in which a strong and complex female character becomes the dominant force.

O'Neill never saw a production of *Moon*. Although completed in 1943, it was not produced until 1947, by which time, O'Neill was in poor health. Plagued by casting controversies and uncertainties, it premiered on tour. O'Neill was unable to travel to the Midwestern locales, which was probably just as well, as his play faced condemnation and censorship there. A headline in the Detroit *Times* declared that the police censor found the "Whole Theme Too Smutty" (Gelbs, *O'Neill* 883). It was reported that the censor objected to the use of the word *mother* in the same sentence as the word *prostitute* (884). This objection is amusing because it is just this apparently paradoxical linkage that provides insight into O'Neill's relationships with women throughout his life and his depiction of women throughout his drama. Indeed, tweaked another way, the Detroit police censor's observation provides a crucial insight into understanding Josie, O'Neill's ultimate female character.

## SETTING AND PLOT DEVELOPMENT

The setting of this play is not a new one for O'Neill. It is similar to the setting of *Desire Under the Elms*—a Connecticut farmhouse. The house in *Moon*, however, is characterized by its contrast with the landscape: "It has been moved to its present site, and looks it" (O'Neill 856). It is run-down, weather-beaten, and tired. All four acts take place outside the farmhouse. A path runs through the property, suggesting that people will come and go from this place, which they do, except for Josie, who never leaves. The setting is also familiar because it is the backdrop for the story that Edmund tells in act 1 of *Long Day's Journey* about the tenant farmer Shaughnessy, his pigs, and the Standard Oil millionaire next door. This story, a mere diversion for the Tyrones (but revealing about their characters and the dynamic among them) in *Long Day's Journey*, is the comic centerpiece around which the drama of *Moon* unfolds. Although not characterized as explicitly harsh and unyielding as the stone landscape of *Desire*, the Hogan homestead is similarly inhospitable, characterized by a "dirt road," "a field of hay stubble," and "a scraggly orchard of apple trees" (856). It is to this environment, seemingly so hostile to human warmth, that O'Neill ironically brings Jim Tyrone (a version of his own brother, Jamie) to find understanding and forgiveness in the arms of a woman.

There is not much of a traditional plot in *A Moon for the Misbegotten*. Although as it begins, the story seems to revolve around the stock situation of a man lured into the bed of a woman to entrap him for marriage, it evolves into a poignant vignette of love denied and transformed. When the first act begins, Josie Hogan is helping the third of her three brothers, Mike, escape from this harsh landscape and especially from the hold of its irascible taskmaster, their father, Phil Hogan. This scene immediately identifies Josie as a strong, controlling character, who cares for her brothers and her father, and keeps them apart, for their own good, as well as for her own best interests. Reminiscent of the use of exposition in the opening scene of *Desire Under the Elms*, the exposition here establishes the hatred of sons toward their controlling father, which leads them to flee. Here, however, instead of a son who remains to exact revenge, in this case a daughter remains to care for the old man. Instead of, as in *Desire*, a love interest (i.e., Abbie) for the father, in *Moon*, it is Josie who has the love interest, Jim Tyrone. It is autobiographically interesting that, in this much later play written many years after his father's death, O'Neill is able to depict the child/parent relationship with a much greater degree of understanding and compassion for the father. Phil Hogan is a much more appealing character than Ephraim Cabot, and this is established upon his entrance in act 1, when he and his daughter exchange joking insults with each other. In their disdain for the self-righteousness of the recently departed son/brother Mike, Hogan and Josie take their places comfortably at the table of modern moral relativism, as they "innocently" plant the seeds of a plot to deceive Jim Tyrone for both mutually beneficial financial and romantic/marital ends.

By the time Jim Tyrone enters in act 1, the audience knows that 1) Phil Hogan has been a tyrant to his sons, but in his daughter, he has met his match; 2) Josie Hogan has a reputation as a "loose woman," but harbors a true love interest in Jim Tyrone; 3) Phil and Josie Hogan may have reason to distrust their landlord, Jim Tyrone, especially when he is under the influence of alcohol; and 4) Phil Hogan is a clever and deceitful rascal who will do almost anything to ensure his and his daughter's financial well-being.

When Tyrone enters, he, Hogan, and Josie engage in what is clearly a routine and mutually amusing repartee that reinforces the strong bond among them, a bond that has been forged around money, alcohol, and, in the case of Josie and Tyrone, physical attraction and flirtation. While Tyrone and Hogan playfully bicker about the value of the land owned by Tyrone on which the Hogans live, Josie rather brazenly presents herself as an alternative to the New York prostitutes with whom she assumes to compete for Tyrone's attention. Before too long, Tyrone, a confirmed alcoholic, focuses on his growing constitutional need for a drink, which leads to another playful exchange in which Hogan holds the upper hand, that is, the alcohol, until Tyrone reveals his knowledge about the imminent visit of the Hogans' millionaire neighbor, Harder. Tyrone knows the Hogans would give anything (even liquor) to wreak vengeance on Harder (for the general sins of the haves/Yankees against the have-nots/Irish). His insight into his tenant family's psyche proves to be sharp indeed, as they respond to his news with near delirium, as well as a drink (which he had explicitly sought) and a kiss from Josie (which he had only implicitly sought).

What follows is as fine a bit of comedic dramaturgy as can be found in any play, as O'Neill sets up the situation so that the audience roots for the Everyman underdogs to gain power over an upper-class scoundrel who deserves his comeuppance. Making the most of their "home field advantage," the underdogs prevail by being both physically and verbally more adroit than their opponent. Harder's original complaint, that Hogan's pigs are contaminating his ice pond, is turned against him as Hogan accuses him of killing his pigs by luring them into his ice cold pond to die of pneumonia. As they bully Harder, who appears in all the trappings of an elitist aristocracy, and rout him off of their property, much to the enjoyment of the unseen landlord, Tyrone, it appears to be a victory for the common people (represented here by the Irish) and for American populist democracy itself. As the three of them celebrate the victory with food and drink, Josie expresses her concern for Tyrone's well-being, even as he arouses their suspicions about his intentions by suggesting that their antics against Harder have now made their property more valuable to the Standard Oil millionaire. Indeed, Harder may make Tyrone an offer for the property that he will not be able to refuse. Thus, act 1 ends with both the promise of Tyrone's moonlight rendezvous with Josie and the threat of Tyrone's betrayal of both Josie and her father.

Act 2 begins at 11:00 that night, and Josie, who has changed into nicer clothing in anticipation of her date with Tyrone, waits in the moonlight for him, disappointed because he had promised to visit her at around 9:00. After a few moments, her father arrives, noticeably drunk, and he tells her of Tyrone's betrayal of them at the Inn, where he has agreed to sell their land to Harder for $10,000. At first, she refuses to believe that Tyrone would betray them in this way, but when her father reminds her of his betrayal of her by missing their date, and then fuels the fire of her regret and anger by suggesting that he purposely did not show up to avoid being tempted by his attraction to her, she hatches a plot that recalls the one that her brother Mike had suggested when he departed in act 1. She conspires with her father to get Tyrone drunk and in bed with her, so that her father can arrive in the morning with witnesses and then blackmail Tyrone into selling the land to them at a lower price, as well as giving Josie a portion of his estate. Throughout this scene, it is never clear whether Hogan is telling the truth about what Tyrone has said or done. Tyrone's appearance on the road walking toward the Hogan property then adds further suspicion about Hogan's truthfulness, but Josie is determined to move ahead with her plan. So she has her father pretend to be too drunk to remember what has allegedly occurred at the Inn, or to have informed Josie of it, and she pretends to kick him out of the house to go sleep it off. The second act ends with Josie inviting Tyrone to sit with his head at her breast, raising the possibility of taking him to bed with her, while he expresses hope that his night with her will be different from the time he spends with Broadway whores. When Josie leaves to get a bottle of liquor, she appears to be moving her plan forward, while Tyrone, when left alone, trembles with self-hatred. As the curtain falls, the audience is left to wonder, who is tricking whom, who has been telling the truth, and who is the victim.

Act 3 begins without any lapse of time. Tyrone is still fumbling with the cigarette he had taken out at the end of act 2. He continues to struggle with his inner demons until Josie returns after a few moments carrying a quart of whiskey, which brings Tyrone relief, although he also, significantly, welcomes Josie's return in itself as an antidote for his intense feeling of loneliness. As they continue their parrying repartee, now accompanied by alcohol, the uncertainties and complications intensify. Now Josie is pouring generous drinks for Tyrone with the intention of getting him drunk enough to fall asleep, while she is pouring drinks for herself as well, with the intention of diminishing her natural inhibitions and also encouraging Tyrone to continue to drink. At the same time, Tyrone strikes several potentially romantic/seductive notes in his banter with Josie; yet whenever Josie responds in kind, Tyrone recoils as he is reminded of his sordid behavior when he is with prostitutes.

Josie finds herself in a difficult situation. She is driven toward revenge by her disappointment and anger at Tyrone for the betrayal to which her father has attested, yet she is also strongly drawn to Tyrone and still hopes that they can consummate a romantic engagement with each other. To achieve this second goal, she must believe in Tyrone's loyalty to her and her father. As she watches for evidence of his guilt or innocence, so does the audience. An offhand, probing comment by Josie (suggesting jealousy) about Tyrone's plans to return to New York (and the prostitutes there) leads to a discussion about Hogan's drunkenness, during which Tyrone proclaims his loyalty to Josie and her father with a conviction that leads Josie to believe him. With her faith in Tyrone restored, Josie is able to resolve her conflicted feelings and pursue Tyrone's love without suspicion. She thus abandons her father's scheme to "trap" Tyrone and she pursues his love unequivocally. She admits to him that she is a virgin, appealing to him to overcome his "honorable scruples" and let himself succumb to the passion that she knows he feels for her: "It's in your kisses!" (924). To her horror, however, Tyrone responds to her as if she were a whore, and this reaction pushes her away for the last time. As he turns to leave, declaring their "moonlight romance...a flop" (926), he reveals a vulnerability and desperate need for love that Josie cannot resist, and she runs to him to offer a different kind of love, a maternal love, which is really what he has been after all along.

As Josie comforts him, he lays his head on her breast and confesses the awful truth about his relationship with his mother, and especially about his behavior surrounding her death. During her final illness, he returned to heavy drinking. Upon her death, he was left numb, but pretended to be distraught ("Once a ham, always a ham!" [930]). On the train journey back East with her body, he got drunk and paid a prostitute 50 dollars a night to be with him, while always aware of his mother's body in a coffin in the baggage car, unable to shake from his mind the haunting lyrics of a song: "'And the baby's cries can't waken her/In the baggage coach ahead.'" Finally, he confesses that he was too drunk to attend her funeral (931–932). Josie at first withdraws from him, offended and horrified by what he has confessed to her, but her love and compassion for him allow her to overcome these feelings and offer him her love and forgiveness on behalf of his mother:

> I understand now, Jim, darling, and I'm proud you came to me as the one in the world you know loves you enough to understand and forgive—and I do forgive!...—As *she* forgives, do you hear me! As *she* loves and understands and forgives! (933)

With that, Tyrone falls asleep in her arms, and Josie realizes that their night together has indeed been quite different from what she ever imagined, either in her romantic yearnings or her paranoid, vengeful scheming at her father's instigation. She realizes that the comfort and forgiveness she has provided Tyrone have been at the expense of her hopes for an enduring loving relationship, and she sees the ironic humor in it: "God forgive me, it's a fine end to all my scheming, to sit here with the dead hugged to my breast, and the silly mug of the moon grinning down, enjoying the joke!" (934).

Act 4 begins at dawn. Josie has been sitting for several hours with Tyrone asleep on her breast when Hogan returns. That he is alone (without the promised witnesses) suggests that there was a scheme within his conspiracy with Josie to entrap Tyrone. He seems surprised to see the two of them sitting on the steps. Josie remains protective of Tyrone, insisting that her father remain quiet so as not to wake him up from his seemingly peaceful rest. At the same time she reveals to Hogan that she has solved the riddle of his scheming behavior, accusing him of using her, and her love for Tyrone, to get Tyrone's money: she and Tyrone would get drunk; she would learn the truth about Tyrone's loyalty to them, increasing her desire to sleep with him; Tyrone would then discover that she was a virgin; given his affection for her, Tyrone would offer to marry her, even if he continued to consort with prostitutes; Tyrone would soon die from all of his overindulgences, leaving his estate (going out of probate within days) to his legal widow, Josie.

As the sun rises magnificently in the eastern sky, Josie banishes her father to the house so that she can be alone with Tyrone when he awakens. At first, Tyrone seems too hung over to remember anything about the night before, but gradually he recalls leaving the Inn to visit Josie, and what a beautiful night it was. He worries about what he might have said to her, but she assures him that he said nothing to be ashamed of. He marvels at the cleansed feeling he has, so different from most mornings when he awakens, but he still seems uncertain about why he has this feeling. It is only when he has a drink of the "honest-to-God bonded Bourbon" (943) that the events of the previous evening come flooding back on his consciousness, and he resists acknowledging them, as he turns to leave. Josie pleads with him to recognize the profound love that has connected them, and finally, he does so: "Forgive me, Josie. I do remember! I'm glad I remember! I'll never forget your love!...I'll always love you, Josie!" (944). After a final embrace, Josie sadly watches him leave.

Hogan returns at this moment, and as they both watch Tyrone's figure recede from view, he begs for his daughter's forgiveness, explaining that, although he would not deny that he wanted Tyrone's money to ensure Josie's comfort, he was mostly motivated by his desire to see her happy, "by hook or crook, one way or another, what did I care how?" (944). Josie forgives him and promises that she will not leave him (which she had previously threatened to do, "to punish [him] for a while" [944]). With the tension between them eased, they return to their usual loving exchanges of insults and attacks, as Hogan demands, and Josie agrees to provide, his breakfast. As she enters the house, though, the final word is a prayer for Jim Tyrone, as she turns and looks after him down the road for the last time: "May you have your wish and die in your sleep soon, Jim, darling. May you rest forever in forgiveness and peace" (946). The drama concludes with the disappointment of the unconsummated romantic relationship, the sadness of a ruined life, and yet, the hope for inner peace that comes with forgiveness.

## CHARACTER DEVELOPMENT

A Moon for the Misbegotten is essentially a three-character play, but two secondary characters—Mike Hogan and T. Stedman Harder—make brief appearances that are important to O'Neill's development of the three main characters. Conveniently enough, O'Neill has spaced their scenes in the play so that in a production with limited funds the same actor can play both roles. This approach will reinforce the common dramaturgical purpose of the two characters—to provide a foil for the main characters. Josie's brother Mike is escaping from his father's tyranny when the play begins, following in the footsteps of two brothers who have done so before him and leaving Josie as Hogan's sole companion and heir apparent. Mike is the first one to call attention to Josie's local reputation as a whore, and he is the one who first (unintentionally) plants the seeds for the scheme to trick Tyrone into marrying Josie. As he sets himself apart moralistically from Josie and her father, scolding them for their devious behavior, he also sets himself apart from them charismatically, as it quickly becomes clear that he lacks the wit and resourcefulness of either his sister or his father (or, as the audience will eventually discover, of Tyrone). This contrast tightens the bond between Josie and Hogan, making their shaky alliance all the more compelling. As he did in *Desire Under the Elms*, by having the other siblings abandon the farm and the family, O'Neill intensifies the connection between the one sibling who remains and the father. In *Desire*, Eben is motivated by jealous hatred, while in *Moon*, Josie is motivated by love, for both her father and Jim Tyrone. In both plays, this motivation is symptomatic of a powerful need for personal redemption.

The bond between Josie and Hogan is also secured by the other secondary character, Harder, who makes only a brief appearance in the play. O'Neill depicts Harder as a stereotype of the wealthy Standard Oil baron whom O'Neill's father detested for his wealth, privilege, and superciliousness. He is an easy comic foil for Josie and Hogan as they humiliate him and send him running for his life to escape from their proletarian clutches. Although the treatment he receives at the hands of the Hogans is both inhospitable and rude, O'Neill renders Harder such an unlikable symbol of upper class arrogance that it is impossible not to root for Josie and Hogan. Thus O'Neill makes a sociopolitical statement that places the poor tenant farmer above the wealthy businessman in the audience's sympathies. As with Mike, the contrast establishes both of the Hogans, as well as Jim Tyrone, as more likable than those around them, in spite of their behavior, which by traditional social standards might be deemed unacceptable. O'Neill uses these two minor characters to help challenge the audience's notions about morality.

Hogan is a rascal, a mischievous force in the play that demonstrates O'Neill's ability to create a character in the tradition of the best comic characters, one who exhibits what George Bernard Shaw called the "life force." And like many of Shaw's characters, with his defiance of traditional notions of morality, he has the power to turn morality on its head. Although he expresses his admiration for Jim Tyrone and a basic degree of trust in him as a landlord that he shares with his daughter, he is a more seasoned player in the field of economic relations than she is, as his motto conveys: "never trust anyone too far, not even myself" (868). This motto, worthy of Shaw, underlies Hogan's behavior in the play, as he manipulates Josie to set a trap for Tyrone to protect their interests, at the same time raising Josie's suspicions about his own motives. As it turns out, his emotions in relation to Tyrone and Josie may be even more complicated than he himself suspects.

Hogan sets himself apart from the morally self-righteous, whether of his own class or those of greater means. He disparages his wife's family as a "pious lousy lot":

> They wouldn't dare put food in their mouths before they said grace for it. They was too busy preaching temperance to have time for a drink. They spent so much time confessing their sins, they had no chance to do any sinning. (*He spits disgustedly.*) The scum of the earth! (864)

Even as he schemes to deceive and trap Jim Tyrone, Hogan establishes himself as a clever and life-affirming character. The comic high point of the play occurs in the middle of act 1 when he and Josie conspire to humiliate Harder, (884–889). When Harder arrives to complain about Hogan's pigs bathing in his ice pond, Hogan soon turns the tables on the helpless Harder, complaining that it is his pigs, dying from the cold, that are the victims of Harder's enticing ice pond.

Hogan's penchant for practical jokes and good-humored kidding is crucial to the bond he has forged with Jim Tyrone, best exemplified in the ritualized game they play when Tyrone arrives and tries to tease a drink out of Hogan (878–879). The alliance between them is further reinforced when Tyrone encourages Harder's humiliation while watching and enjoying the spectacle from inside Josie's bedroom. The bond between the Hogans and Tyrone, both individually and collectively, builds the suspense and intrigue, as Josie puts into action her father's plan to trap Tyrone in act 2. When Hogan returns in act 4 to discover that although his scheme has failed, his daughter has been profoundly transformed by the events of the moonlit night, he subordinates his desire for financial security to his care and concern for his daughter and, to some extent, for Jim Tyrone:

> But it wasn't his money, Josie. I did see it was the last chance—the only one left to bring the two of you to stop your damned pretending, and face the truth that you loved each other. I wanted you to find happiness—by hook or crook, one way or another, what did I care how? I wanted to save him, and I hoped he'd see that only your love could— (944)

In the end, Hogan is more than just a scheming rascal; there is sincerity in this confession of his true motives. Beneath the mischievous scheming and abusive jokes is a good friend and a loving father, which is why Josie finds peace in the face of her romantic disappointment when she returns to her familiar life with her father, jokingly complaining that she cannot live with any other man because "there'd never be the same fun or excitement" (945).

Jim Tyrone enjoys the repartee with Hogan because it provides an escape for him from his intense internal turmoil. On the surface, he presents a devil-may-care attitude toward life, but beneath the surface, he is wracked by guilt and uncertainty. The connection he has made with the Hogans offers him companionship to ward off loneliness, and in the virgin/whore Josie, he discovers the possibility of confession, repentance, and maternal forgiveness.

Tyrone is a likable character. When he enters in act 1, he immediately joins in on the knowingly amusing banter between Hogan and Josie, and in the pleasure he derives from the Hogans' humiliation of Harder, he casts himself with the "good guys" in the battle between the classes (even though he is a landowner). There is no question that he genuinely likes Phil Hogan and his daughter Josie, although there is some question about the nature of his affection for Josie. His declarations of romantic love for her are most often diluted and tainted by his cynicism, nurtured and finely honed over the years by a profligate lifetime of drunken sex with whores; yet there is something sincere behind his words. One of the most compelling mysteries of the play lies in whether Tyrone is a good guy or a bad guy. The audience wonders along with Josie whether or not Tyrone will betray, or be true to, his friendship with the Hogans and his love for Josie. During the long encounter between Josie and Tyrone that overlaps acts 2 and 3, after it becomes evident that Tyrone's intentions toward Josie and her father are good and true, Josie responds in kind, offering Tyrone the maternal forgiveness he seeks.

O'Neill wrote *Moon* as a kind of sequel to *Long Day's Journey*, in which, as the Gelbs explain, he "[carried] the story of Jamie O'Neill to its bitter conclusion" (*O'Neill* 848). O'Neill claimed that the play was "otherwise entirely imaginary" (*O'Neill: Life* 508). The most obvious parallel between the real-life brother and the fictional character is that Jim Tyrone is ravaged by the effects of alcoholism, just as Jamie O'Neill was in the final stages of his life. From the moment Tyrone enters, he needs a drink, and in the course of the ensuing drama, he has quite a few. A glass or bottle is never too far from his hands or mouth, and his dialogue is punctuated with constant references to the drink he has just had or the one he is about to have. His physical appearance bespeaks his condition. The stage directions indicate, for example, that his *"physique has become soft and soggy from dissipation*" (O'Neill 874–875). In addition, as he drinks more, his mood swings become more extreme and erratic, until he finally succumbs to a state of self-absorbed depression.

It is, of course, the depressive and uninhibiting effects of alcohol that enable him to plumb the depths of his tortured soul and confess his "sins" to Josie. In his tortured soul and need for forgiveness lie even deeper parallels to O'Neill's brother Jamie, at least as perceived by the playwright. Tyrone is wracked by guilt about his disappointing retreat to liquor when his mother became ill and to a whore after she died, as well as his failure to cry at her wake, all symptomatic of his self-loathing over this failed relationship. Physically debilitated and on the verge of death himself, Tyrone seeks and receives absolution at the breast of the surrogate mother, Josie. In the end, Tyrone departs from the Hogan farm a sad, yet sympathetic figure—a broken man, but a saved soul, the former being the true condition of O'Neill's brother when he died, and the latter being the condition that the sibling/artist perhaps wished he could have bestowed upon his deceased brother as he contemplated his own mortality.

In his effort to write a play about his brother, however, O'Neill created a strong, rich, and compelling female character who becomes the real heart and soul of this drama. As O'Neill conceived her, Josie Hogan seems an impossible role for any actress to play:

> She is so oversize for a woman that she is almost a freak—five feet eleven in her stockings and weighs around one hundred and eighty. Her sloping shoulders are broad, her chest deep with large, firm breasts, her waist wide but slender by contrast with her hips and thighs. She has long smooth arms, immensely strong, although no muscles show. The same is true of her legs....She is more powerful than any but an exceptionally strong man, able to do the manual labor of two ordinary men. But there is no mannish quality about her. She is all woman. (857)

Several extraordinary actresses, large and small, have demonstrated over the years that these stage directions need not be taken literally. Rather, they provide an extraordinary blueprint for the depiction of character.

Josie Hogan is larger than life. On the surface, with her brother and father, and especially in the scene with Harder, she is brash and brazen. She is clearly the dominant figure in a family of men. She overwhelms her brothers, and her life force is a match for that of her wily father. She anticipates with relish the confrontation with Harder, and she joins her father in battle against him with gusto. She stands by her father when her brothers abandon the farm, yet she stands up to her father when she suspects his motives. She struggles to balance her need for security, represented by her father and the land, with her need for love, represented by Tyrone and the moon.

When Tyrone first appears, she joins in the repartee with him and her father, but when the banter turns to matters of the flesh, Josie becomes more subdued and seemingly uncomfortable, behaving in ways that contradict her local reputation for promiscuity. It turns out that her promiscuity is all talk. In fact, Josie is a virgin, and if her body is Tyrone's for the asking, it comes along with her big heart. It does not take long to see that Josie loves Tyrone. She is jealous of his "Broadway tarts," and she becomes self-conscious about her appearance only when he is around. She nervously anticipates her moonlight rendezvous with Tyrone as if she were a schoolgirl awaiting her date for the prom.

Josie's relationship with Tyrone is complex. When their long scene in the moonlight begins in act 2, Hogan has planted enough suspicions in Josie's mind that she approaches Tyrone with cautious deceitfulness, yet her flirtation with him is driven more by her real attraction to him than by cunning. She drinks with him as part of the plan to entrap him, but getting him in bed would, at the same time, fulfill her heart's desire. So when he affirms his loyalty to her and her father, it relieves her of the burden of her father's plot so that she can freely declare her deep affection for Jim, hugging him "*passionately*" and kissing him on the lips (922–923).

It is ironic, then, that the only remaining obstacle to the consummation of her love with Jim Tyrone in the romantic moonlight is Jim Tyrone himself, who is unable to give his love to any woman because he is trapped by self-hatred over his unresolved and guilt-ridden relationship with his mother. When this reality becomes evident to Josie, however, she discovers that she has "all kinds of love" for Tyrone and gives him the understanding, forgiving maternal love he needs, even though it "costs [her] so much" (927). Josie is a sadly heroic character because she saves the soul of Jim Tyrone, but at the expense of her own happiness. Even when she returns to the fun-loving bickering with her father at the end of the play, there is an empty feeling that she will merely be biding her time with her father for the rest of her days, while her hope for true wholeness has died with the departure of Jim Tyrone.

## THEMATIC ISSUES

In his final drama, O'Neill had his final say on many of the issues that he wrestled with throughout his creative life. *A Moon for the Misbegotten* is the last in a long line of family dramas, focusing most apparently on a father/daughter relationship. The landlord, Jim Tyrone, who also figures prominently in the drama, is unrelated to the Hogans by blood; he is, however, the vehicle through which O'Neill represents the mother/son relationship, the family dynamic with which he most closely identified and which plays a central role in several of his other dramas, most notably *Long Day's Journey*. Through Tyrone's long, tortured confession in act 3, O'Neill depicts a son who is wracked by guilt over his inability to mourn the loss of his mother and at the same time seeks her forgiveness. Tyrone loves his mother intensely, and his attachment to her has inhibited him from forming any meaningful relationships with other women. The only way he can have a meaningful relationship with Josie is to re-create the maternal dynamic. When O'Neill remarked in 1925 that all the evidence needed to see that he had an Oedipus complex was in his plays (Sheaffer 190), the plays that he had in mind at that time pale in their development of oedipal themes when compared to the as yet unwritten *A Moon for the Misbegotten*. Based on the intensity of the oedipal feelings in this final play of his career, one can only conclude that O'Neill took his Oedipus complex with him to the grave.

The primary dramatized relationship in *Moon*, however, is the father/daughter relationship between Hogan and Josie. Although O'Neill was one of two sons in his own family of origin, several daughter/father relationships preceded this one in his canon, most notably Anna and Chris in *Anna Christie*, Nina and Professor Leeds in *Strange Interlude*, and Lavinia and Mannon in *Mourning Becomes Electra*. The relationship in *Moon* is closest in spirit to the one in *Anna Christie*. In fact, the interaction between Josie and Hogan could well be a vision of what might have become of the interaction between Anna and Chris after many years of living together.

Josie is loyal to her father. Although she encourages and helps her three brothers to leave their father and the farm behind and strike out on their own, she remains with him. She does the work of three brothers and also cooks and cares for her father. They forge a bond that is founded on mutual admiration and understanding; they enjoy each other's company. Hogan exhibits typical fatherly concern for his daughter's welfare when he seizes an opportunity to bring her happiness, as well as material comfort, by encouraging her relationship with Jim Tyrone. Although his devious strategy may be suspect, his parental intentions are good. Although his behavior angers Josie, she ultimately understands and forgives him. The loss of Tyrone's love is somewhat less traumatic for her because she has the foundation of her father's love to support her: "Sure, living with you has spoilt me for any other man, anyway. There'd never be the same fun or excitement" (O'Neill 945). It is interesting that the "fun and excitement" of the barroom camaraderie with which both A Touch of the Poet and The Iceman Cometh conclude is found within the family in A Moon for the Misbegotten, in sharp contrast to the stagnation and death-in-life aura that pervades the Tyrone family at the end of Long Day's Journey Into Night. This contrast suggests that although O'Neill may not have experienced this kind of "safe harbor" within his own family, it may be part of the human experience for some people.

Even this family, though, with all of its "fun and excitement," is still characterized by deceit and betrayal. Josie can never be certain about her father's behavior or motives. He deceives her about Tyrone's intentions to sell their farm, although he does so to serve her best interests, as he sees them. Josie speaks of herself in a way that promotes a false impression of her identity and morals. Josie and Hogan conspire to get the best of Harder by spinning a comic web of twisted facts regarding Hogan's pigs and Harder's ice pond. These patterns of deceit and betrayal are consistent with O'Neill's vision of a world in which people survive the trials of the human condition by lying to others and to themselves. In this world, appearances are often different from reality, and one must pay close attention to discover the truth. It is only with the intense concentration of their encounter in the second and third acts that Josie and Tyrone are able to recognize and acknowledge the difficult and painful truth about each other and themselves. What others see is just pretense.

A Moon for the Misbegotten is a spiritual play with religious undertones characterized by a lengthy confessional monologue toward the end, and a self-consciously designed Pièta image of mother cradling son in her bosom. After Tyrone confesses and repents for his sins, Josie blesses him with peace: "Sleep in peace, my darling" (935–936). She then proclaims the scene a miracle—"A virgin who bears a dead child in the night, and the dawn finds her still a virgin. If that isn't a miracle, what is? (936)—reinforcing the ironic significance of the Pièta in this context. Finally, the play ends with a prayer: "May you have your wish and die in your sleep soon, Jim, darling. May you rest forever in forgiveness and peace" (946). With this, Josie has, in effect, performed the last rites for Jim Tyrone, whose death is inevitable and assured, thus suggesting that peace and salvation are attainable for even the most lost souls, not necessarily through the rituals of Catholicism or other organized religions, but through the understanding and forgiveness of loved ones.

A Moon for the Misbegotten is a love story that recognizes how love manifests itself in many ways. Josie and Tyrone's love for each other is at first expressed in playful, flirtatious ways, very much focused on physical attraction (Tyrone repeatedly admires Josie's beautiful breasts), but suggesting a deeper emotional attraction within (reiterating the appearance/reality theme discussed previously). Under the influence of alcohol in act 3 and relieved to learn of his loyalty to her and her father, Josie declares her love for Tyrone and kisses him passionately (922–923). Blocked from loving Josie (or any woman) romantically by his intense feelings of guilt about his mother, and poisoned by a life of loveless sex, Tyrone asks for a different kind of love from Josie. Josie, in an immense display of the potential of the human heart, finds the capacity to offer him "all the love" he needs: "for I have all kinds of love for you—and maybe this is the greatest of all—because it costs so much" (927). As she sits back and comforts the man she loves, accepting that he will never be able to love her in the way that she needs, Josie becomes emotionally the larger-than-life character that O'Neill describes physically in the initial stage directions. In her capacity for self-sacrificing love, she demonstrates the potential strength and grandeur of the human heart.

Although much of the thematic focus of this play is on the human heart and soul, O'Neill did not ignore the social context of the human condition. Even in this most personal of plays, he found room for social commentary in the confrontation between the Hogans and Harder, the oil millionaire. His depiction of Harder as an uptight, arrogant, and humorless representative of the privileged American elite makes Harder easy prey for the fun-loving, clever, and free-spirited representatives of the American working class, the Hogans. True to his Irish immigrant roots, O'Neill takes his stand with the ethnic American Everyman against the Yankee aristocracy.

Finally, *A Moon for the Misbegotten* is yet another example of O'Neill's brand of existentialist drama, a precursor of the theatre of the absurd, a drama in which characters confront the essential emptiness of human existence and face the challenge of moving forward with life in spite of it. In this case, Tyrone finds salvation in the forgiving breasts of Josie Hogan and departs along the dusty road that inevitably leads him toward death, leaving the Hogans alone with each other. In their final moments together, they surely foreshadow Samuel Beckett's famous characters Vladimir and Estragon in the quintessentially absurdist drama, *Waiting for Godot.* Like Beckett's characters, the Hogans appear to have little reason to go on living. In Josie's case, her only hope for a purpose in life—her love for Jim Tyrone—has departed, unlikely to ever return. There is no evidence in the play that anyone or anything else new will enter the lives of these characters. Like Vladimir and Estragon, they have only each other; and like Vladimir and Estragon, their companionship—the "fun and excitement," as Josie calls it—is what keeps them going. O'Neill's existentialist drama suggests that human companionship (in this case, rather unexpectedly, within the family) may be the only hope for people in the face of the apparent meaninglessness of human existence.

## STYLISTIC AND LITERARY DEVICES

In his later years, O'Neill claimed to sense "a feeling around...of fate. Kismet, the negative fate; not in the Greek sense....It's struck me as time goes on, how something funny, even farcical, can suddenly without any apparent reason, break up into something gloomy and tragic" (Sheaffer 577). He said that he used this sense of fate in particular in *The Iceman Cometh*: "The first act is hilarious comedy...the comedy breaks up and the tragedy comes on" (577–578). In fact, it is a device he used in all of his later full-length plays, including *A Moon for the Misbegotten*. Not only does this device convey O'Neill's vision of "Kismet, the negative fate," but it also contributes to the emotional impact of these later plays. The comedy of the first act draws in the audience and builds sympathy and affection for the characters, so that when "the tragedy comes on," the audience feels the pain and sadness that much more intensely.

In the first act of *Moon*, the comic banter between Josie and Hogan, Hogan and Tyrone, and Tyrone and Josie is entertaining and establishes an easy camaraderie among the characters. Although there are some signs of tension, stemming from Hogan's apparent mistrust of Tyrone's intentions regarding his farm, and from Josie's real affection for Tyrone, for the most part, act 1 moves at a fast pace, punctuated by sarcasm and friendly insults.

For instance, Tyrone calls Hogan a "lucky old bastard to have this beautiful farm, if it is full of nude rocks," to which Hogan replies, "I like that part about the rocks. If cows could eat them this place would make a grand dairy farm" (O'Neill 875). A few moments later, Tyrone attempts to wangle a drink from Hogan by playfully claiming that he has a weak heart and his doctors have recommended a large alcoholic drink after a long walk in the hot sun has strained his heart, to which Hogan replies, teasingly, "Walk back to the Inn, then, and give a good strain, so you can buy yourself two big drinks" (879). Throughout all this, Tyrone knows that he will get his drink, and Hogan knows that he will give it to him, but the fun for them is in the banter, in the game. The same holds true for Josie and Tyrone as they play a similar verbal game, although owing to the awkward romance lurking beneath the surface of their banter, it often gets derailed.

All the fun and games culminate in the confrontation with Harder, in which Hogan and Josie combine verbal and physical bullying to intimidate their enemy; the witty dialogue and slapstick comedy combine for hilarious theatrical effect (884–889). Although this comic *tour de force* unites the three characters in the class war against the Standard Oil millionaire, it also establishes them in the audience's minds and hearts as the protagonists of the drama. The audience identifies not only with their revolt against arrogance and elitism, but also with their life-affirming comic spirit. So when the interplay between Tyrone and Josie reaches its complicated and wrenching conclusion, Tyrone's guilty misery, Josie's unselfish disappointment, and even Hogan's sheepish regret, all take on corresponding poignancy. O'Neill uses comedy as a theatrical device to intensify the audience's reaction to the tragic in his characters' lives.

Language is another important device in this play. Several critics, most notably Eric Bentley and Mary McCarthy, have disparaged O'Neill's ear for dialogue, but these critics seem to miss the point that O'Neill's dialogue is true to his characters. If the language lacks eloquence, that is because the characters are not eloquent; if the language seems strained, that is because the characters strain to express themselves effectively. If his characters attempt to speak poetically, it often sounds like a person awkwardly reaching for lyrical effect, and he or she may even be conscious of the strain, as with Josie in *Moon*. In her dialogue with her father and with Tyrone, she speaks in the straightforward, plain vernacular and with the lilt of her Irish roots. Her words are concrete and often blunt. For example, when her father calls her an "overgrown cow," she responds with "I'd rather be a cow than an ugly little buck goat" (862), the latter being a reference to her father's physical appearance. Yet, at the end of act 3, after her moonlit rendezvous with Tyrone, during which she has sacrificed her dreams of a romantic relationship with him so that he could find forgiveness and solace falling asleep at her breast, she waxes poetic: "You're a fine one, wanting to leave me when the night I promised I'd give you has just begun, our night that'll be different from all the others, with a dawn that won't creep over dirty windowpanes but will wake in the sky like a promise of God's peace in the soul's dark sadness" (933). Josie herself recognizes the implications of her linguistic shift: "Will you listen to me, Jim! I must be a poet. Who would have guessed it? Sure, love is a wonderful mad inspiration! (933). O'Neill uses language, then, to establish character, as well as to signal the deep, transformative feelings that one human being may have for another, in this case, of Josie for Tyrone.

Finally, O'Neill effectively uses verbal and theatrical imagery in *A Moon for the Misbegotten*, particularly in the pattern of symbolic references to the moon. The long, central part of the drama (acts 2 and 3) unfolds on "*a clear warm moonlight night*" (892). First, the moon represents romance: toward the end of act 1, Josie invites Tyrone to "Come up tonight and we'll spoon in the moonlight" (883), and later, during their scene together, they make explicit reference to the moon's romantic aura several times, as when Josie coaxes Tyrone into having another drink: "There's only tonight, and the moon, and us—and the bonded bourbon" (914). Josie's repeated reminders to Tyrone about the moonlight signify the effort it takes for Josie to help Jim overcome his psychic obstacles to romance and succumb to her seduction. When she gives up and turns her attention from his heart to his soul, it is the moon, again, that provides the appropriate aura, this time an aura of death:

JOSIE—    It's the moonlight. It makes you look so pale, and with your
          eyes closed—
TYRONE— (*simply*) You mean I look dead? (927)

Throughout Tyrone's long confession, the stage directions several times refer to the moonlight as a reminder of Tyrone's death-in-life condition. In the end, the moon becomes symbolic of O'Neill's sense of irony about life when Josie refers to "the silly mug of the moon grinning down, enjoying the joke!" (934) as she cradles the "dead" Tyrone at her breast. So much for the romantic moonlit night of Josie's dreams.

## ALTERNATE PERSPECTIVE: FEMINIST ANALYSIS

Feminist criticism is often concerned with understanding how male writers have depicted female characters within an oppressive patriarchal social context. O'Neill's plays are populated by a number of complex and interesting female characters. Often, in fact, a female is the central character of the play, as in *Anna Christie, Strange Interlude, Mourning Becomes Electra,* and somewhat surprisingly, *A Moon for the Misbegotten.* The latter is ostensibly O'Neill's final effort to come to terms with his feelings about his brother, yet the maternal female character is the dominant figure in the play. Of course, given its autobiographical roots and knowing about O'Neill's relationships with women, especially with his mother, it is not entirely surprising that this transference of dramaturgical dominance occurred. As a number of feminist scholars have observed, there is no question that the female, and especially the mother, lies front and center within O'Neill's male line of vision. There is perhaps no better depiction of O'Neill's tortured obsession with, and keen ambivalence toward, women than Josie Hogan.

O'Neill hated his mother for being a drug addict, a condition that he associated only with prostitutes, and he longed for her to comfort and understand him as he felt a mother should. As a result of his conflicted relationship with his mother and, to some extent, his philosophical struggle with Catholicism, he came to see women as either whores or virginal maternal figures, and Josie Hogan is both. Josie is reputedly a whore, but during the course of the play, she admits to being a virgin. She tries to relate to Tyrone as if she were a prostitute, yet he ultimately needs her to relate to him as if she were his mother, which she does in the end.

From the outset, Josie is described as "*so oversize for a woman that she is almost a freak*" (857). She is not only large, but she is also strong—"*able to do the manual labor of two ordinary men*" (857)—and it is not insignificant that O'Neill describes this strong female character as "almost a freak." Josie either dominates or holds her own with every male in the play, whether they are weak or ridiculous, like her brother Mike and Harder, respectively, or more confident, yet vulnerable, like both Hogan and Tyrone. Josie lords it over all of these men, and in this regard, she is a strong character, one that debunks the traditional stereotype of the weak, dependent female. Josie is independent, brazen, and beholden to no one.

Yet for all the strength of character that Josie demonstrates, she also behaves in some stereotypical female ways, and in the end, she submits to the patriarchal hierarchy. She initially agrees to her father's scheme to have her seduce Tyrone to trap him into marrying her, and although she falters from time to time, she moves ahead with this scheme, placing her in the stereotypical role of the evil temptress. Then she sacrifices her own longing for romantic fulfillment with Jim Tyrone when she agrees to hear his confession and grant him forgiveness, recognizing the pathetic position she has created for herself when she refers to the "silly mug of the moon…enjoying the joke" (934).

At the very end, having lost her only hope for a romantic relationship with a man, she watches sadly as Tyrone leaves her, and although she stands up fearlessly to her father, she still resumes a stereotypical place as her father's keeper:

HOGAN—    There'll be excitement if I don't get my breakfast soon, but it won't be fun, I'm warning you!

JOSIE—    (*forcing her usual reaction to his threats*) Och, don't be threatening me, you bad-tempered old tick. Let's go in the house and I'll get your damned breakfast. (945)

Although there is resistance in her role-playing and a winking acknowledgment that they both know that she is in complete control, still it is undeniable that at the end of *A Moon for the Misbegotten*, O'Neill's strong earth mother is a lonely young woman who has sacrificed her independence, her dreams, indeed her life, to save the soul of one man and to nurture the body of another.

## WORKS CITED

Gelb, Arthur and Barbara. *O'Neill*. New York: Harper & Row, 1962.
———. *O'Neill: Life with Monte Cristo*. New York: Applause Books, 2000.
O'Neill, Eugene. *Complete Plays 1932–1943*. Ed. Travis Bogard. New York: Library of America, 1988.
Sheaffer, Louis. *O'Neill: Son and Artist*. Boston: Little, Brown, & Co., 1973.

# Bibliography

## WORKS BY EUGENE O'NEILL

*The Calms of Capricorn: A Play*. Developed from O'Neill's scenario by Donald Gallup, with a transcription of the scenario. New Haven, CT: Ticknor & Fields, 1982.

*Complete Plays*. Ed. Travis Bogard. New York: Library of America, 1988. 3 vols.

*Eugene O'Neill at Work: Newly Released Ideas for Plays*. Ed. Virginia Floyd. New York: Ungar, 1981.

*More Stately Mansions: The Unexpurgated Edition*. Ed. Martha G. Bower. New York: Oxford University Press, 1988.

*The Unknown O'Neill: Unpublished and Unfamiliar Writings of Eugene O'Neill*. Ed. Travis Bogard. New Haven, CT: Yale University Press, 1988.


## INTERVIEWS AND LETTERS

*"As ever, Gene": The Letters of Eugene O'Neill to George Jean Nathan*. Ed. Nancy L. Roberts & Arthur W. Roberts. Rutherford, NJ: Fairleigh Dickinson University Press, 1987.

*Conversations with Eugene O'Neill*. Ed. Mark W. Estrin. Jackson: University of Mississippi Press, 1990.

*Selected Letters*. Eds. Travis Bogard & Jackson R. Bryer. New Haven, CT: Yale University Press, 1988.

*"The Theatre We Worked for": The Letters of Eugene O'Neill to Kenneth Macgowan*. Ed. Jackson R. Bryer. New Haven, CT: Yale University Press, 1982.

A *Wind Is Rising: The Correspondence of Agnes Boulton and Eugene O'Neill.* Ed. William D. King. Madison, NJ: Fairleigh Dickinson University Press, 2000.

## BIOGRAPHIES

Black, Stephen A. Eugene *O'Neill: Beyond Mourning and Tragedy.* New Haven, CT: Yale University Press, 2000.
Clark, Barrett H. *Eugene O'Neill: The Man and His Plays.* Rev. ed. New York: Dover, 1947.
Gelb, Arthur & Barbara Gelb. *O'Neill.* Enlarged ed. New York: Harper, 1973.
———. *O'Neill: Life with Monte Cristo.* New York: Applause Books, 2000.
Sheaffer, Louis. *O'Neill, Son and Playwright.* Boston: Little, Brown, 1968.
———. *O'Neill, Son and Artist.* Boston: Little, Brown, 1973.

## DOCUMENTARY FILMS

*Eugene O'Neill: A Documentary Film.* Directed by Ric Burns. Written by Arthur & Barbara Gelb and Ric Burns. PBS, March 27, 2006. American Experience/ WGBH, 2006.
*Eugene O'Neill: A Glory of Ghosts.* Directed by Perry Miller Adato. PBS/American Masters Series, 1986.

## BIBLIOGRAPHIES

Carpenter, Charles A. "O'Neill Play by Play: A Selective, Classified International Bibliography of Publications about the Drama of Eugene O'Neill." July 2006. <http://www. eoneill.com/library/playbyplay/contents.htm>.
Miller, Jordan Y. *Eugene O'Neill and the American Critic: A Bibliographical Checklist.* 2d ed. Hamden, CT: Archon, 1973.
Smith, Madeline C., & Richard Eaton. *Eugene O'Neill: An Annotated International Bibliography, 1973 through 1999.* Jefferson, NC: McFarland, 2001.

## COLLECTIONS OF CRITICAL ESSAYS

Cargill, Oscar, et al., eds. *O'Neill and His Plays: Four Decades of Criticism.* New York: New York University Press, 1961.
Frenz, Horst, & Susan H. Tuck, eds. *Eugene O'Neill's Critics: Voices from Abroad.* Carbondale: Southern Illinois University Press, 1984.
Gassner, John, ed. *O'Neill: A Collection of Critical Essays.* Englewood Cliffs, NJ: Prentice-Hall, 1964.
Griffin, Ernest G., ed. *Eugene O'Neill: A Collection of Criticism.* New York: McGraw-Hill, 1976.

Houchin, John H., ed. *The Critical Response to Eugene O'Neill*. Westport, CT: Greenwood Press, 1993.

Liu, Hai-Ping, & Lowell Swortzell, eds. *Eugene O'Neill in China: An International Centenary Celebration*. New York: Greenwood Press, 1992.

Manheim, Michael, ed. *The Cambridge Companion to Eugene O'Neill*. Cambridge: Cambridge University Press, 1998.

Martine, James J., ed. *Critical Essays on Eugene O'Neill*. Boston: G. K. Hall, 1984.

Maufort, Marc, ed. *Eugene O'Neill and the Emergence of American Drama*. Amsterdam: Rodopi, 1989.

Miller, Jordan Y. *Playwright's Progress: O'Neill and the Critics*. Chicago: Scott, Foresman, 1965.

Moorton, Richard F., ed. *Eugene O'Neill's Century: Centennial Views on America's Foremost Tragic Dramatist*. New York: Greenwood Press, 1991.

Stroupe, John H., ed. *Critical Approaches to O'Neill*. New York: AMS Press, 1988.

## CRITICAL STUDIES

Berlin, Normand. *Eugene O'Neill*. London: Macmillan, 1982.

———. *O'Neill's Shakespeare*. Ann Arbor: University of Michigan Press, 1993.

Bloom, Harold. *Eugene O'Neill*. Broomall, PA: Chelsea House, 2000.

Bogard, Travis. *Contour in Time: The Plays of Eugene O'Neill*. Rev. ed. New York: Oxford University Press, 1988.

Brietzke, Zander. *The Aesthetics of Failure: Dynamic Structure in the Plays of Eugene O'Neill*. Jefferson, NC: McFarland, 2001.

Chothia, Jean. *Forging a Language: A Study of the Plays of Eugene O'Neill*. Cambridge: Cambridge University Press, 1979.

Dubost, Thierry. *Struggle, Defeat or Rebirth: Eugene O'Neill's Vision of Humanity*. Jefferson, NC: McFarland, 1997.

Eisen, Kurt. *The Inner Strength of Opposites: O'Neill's Novelistic Drama and the Melodramatic Imagination*. Athens: University of Georgia Press, 1994.

Engel, Edwin A. *The Haunted Heroes of Eugene O'Neill*. Cambridge, MA: Harvard University Press, 1953.

Falk, Doris V. *Eugene O'Neill and the Tragic Tension: An Interpretive Study of the Plays*. New Brunswick, NJ: Rutgers University Press, 1958.

Floyd, Virginia. *The Plays of Eugene O'Neill: A New Assessment*. New York: Ungar, 1985.

Manheim, Michael. *Eugene O'Neill's New Language of Kinship*. Syracuse, NY: Syracuse University Press, 1982.

Miliora, Maria T. *Narcissism, the Family, and Madness: A Self-psychological Study of Eugene O'Neill and his Plays*. New York: Lang, 2000.

Pfister, Joel. *Staging Depth: Eugene O'Neill and the Politics of Psychological Discourse*. Chapel Hill: University of North Carolina Press, 1995.

Porter, Laurin R. *The Banished Prince: Time, Memory, and Ritual in the Late Plays of Eugene O'Neill*. Ann Arbor, MI: UMI Research Press, 1988.

Raleigh, John H. *The Plays of Eugene O'Neill*. Carbondale: Southern Illinois University Press, 1965.

Ranald, Margaret L. *The Eugene O'Neill Companion*. Westport, CT: Greenwood Press, 1984.

Richter, Robert A. *Eugene O'Neill and Dat Ole Davil Sea: Maritime Influences in the Life and Works of Eugene O'Neill*. Mystic, CT: Mystic Seaport, 2004.

Robinson, James A. *Eugene O'Neill and Oriental Thought: A Divided Vision*. Carbondale: Southern Illinois University Press, 1982.

Shaughnessy, Edward L. *Down the Nights and Down the Days: Eugene O'Neill's Catholic Sensibility*. Notre Dame, IN: University of Notre Dame Press, 1996.

Tiusanen, Timo. *O'Neill's Scenic Images*. Princeton, NJ: Princeton University Press, 1968.

Törnqvist, Egil. *A Drama of Souls: Studies in O'Neill's Super-naturalistic Technique*. New Haven, CT: Yale University Press, 1969.

Viswanathan, R. *O'Neill and the Sea*. Calicut: Poorna, 2000.

## REVIEWS AND SELECTED CRITICISM

### The Emperor Jones

*Reviews*

Macgowan, Kenneth. "The New Season." *Theatre Arts*, 5 (January 1921) 5–7. (Original production after move to Broadway).

Shand, John. "The Emperor Jones." *New Statesman*, 25 (September 19, 1925): 628–29.

Woollcott, Alexander. "The New O'Neill Play." *New York Times*, November 7, 1920, VII, 1: 3.

———. "The Emperor Jones Revived." *New York Sun*, May 8, 1924: 20 (Revival with Paul Robeson).

*Criticism*

Callens, Johan. "'Black is white, I yells it out louder 'n deir loudest': Unraveling The Wooster Group's *The Emperor Jones*." *Eugene O'Neill Review* 26 (2004): 43–69.

Hinden, Michael. "*The Emperor Jones*: O'Neill, Nietzsche, and the American Past." *Eugene O'Neill Newsletter* III.3 (1980): 2–4.

Murphy, Brenda. "McTeague's Dream and *The Emperor Jones*: O'Neill's Move from Naturalism to Modernism." *Eugene O'Neill Review* 17 (1993): 21–29.

Nolan, Patrick J. "*The Emperor Jones*: A Jungian View of the Origin of Fear in the Black Race." *Eugene O'Neill Newsletter* IV.1–2 (May-September 1980): 6–9.

Smith, Madeline C. "The Emperor Jones and Confession." *Bulletin of the West Virginia Association of College English Teachers* 8 (1983): 17–22.

Viswanathan, R. "*The Jungle Books* and O'Neill." *Eugene O'Neill Newsletter* XI.2 (1987): 3–7.


## The Hairy Ape

### Reviews

Brantley, Ben. "A Lug Against the Universe In Up-to-the-Minute O'Neill." *New York Times*, April 4, 1997: C1. (Wooster Group revival).

Lewisohn, Ludwig. "The Development of Eugene O'Neill." *Nation*, 114 (March 22, 1922): 349–50.

Macgowan, Kenneth. "Broadway at the Spring." *Theater Arts*, 6 (July 1922): 182.

Woollcott, Alexander. "Eugene O'Neill at Full Tilt." *New York Times*, March 10, 1922, 18:2.

Young, Stark. "The Hairy Ape." *New Republic*, 30 (March 22, 1922):112–13.


### Criticism

Connolly, Thomas F. "*The Hairy Ape* in the Context of Early 20th Century American Modernism." *Eugene O'Neill Review* 25 (2001): 76–79.

Floyd, Virginia. "The Search for Self in *The Hairy Ape*: An Exercise in Futility." *Eugene O'Neill Newsletter* I.3 (January 1978): 4–7.

Hinden, Michael. "Ironic Use of Myth in *The Hairy Ape*." *Eugene O'Neill Newsletter* I.3 (January 1978): 2–4.

Murray, Keat. "O'Neill's *The Hairy Ape* and Rodin's *The Thinker*." *Journal of Evolutionary Psychology* 19.i-ii (1998): 108–15.

Robinson, James A. "The Masculine Primitive and *The Hairy Ape*." *Eugene O'Neill Review* 19 (1995): 95–109.

Roy, Emil. "Eugene O'Neill's *The Emperor Jones* and *The Hairy Ape* as mirror plays." *Comparative Drama* 2 (1968): 21–31.


## Anna Christie

### Reviews

Atkinson, Brooks. "Anna Christie." *New York Times*, January 10, 1952, 33:1. (City Center revival).

Benchley, Robert. Untitled review. *Life*, 78 (November 24, 1921): 18.

Krutch, Joseph Wood. "Anna Christie." *Nation*, 174 (January 26, 1952): 92. (City Center revival).

Rich, Frank. "A Fierce View of Tragic Lives." *New York Times*, January 15, 1993: C1. (Roundabout Theater Company revival / Liam Neeson and Natasha Richardson).

Woollcott, Alexander. "The New O'Neill Play." *New York Times*, November 3, 1921, 22:1.


## Criticism

Brietzke, Zander. "Tragic Vision and the Happy Ending in *Anna Christie*." *Eugene O'Neill Review* 24 (2000): 43–60.

Frazer, Winifred L. "Chris and Poseidon: Man Versus God in *Anna Christie*." *Modern Drama* 12 (1969): 279–85.

Garvey, Sheila H. "*Anna Christie* and the 'Fallen Woman Genre.'" *Eugene O'Neill Review* 19 (1995): 66–80.

Hall, Ann C. "'Gawd, you'd think I was a piece of furniture': O'Neill's *Anna Christie*." Katherine Burkman & Judith Roof, eds. *Staging the Rage: The Web of Misogyny in Modern Drama*. Madison, NJ: Fairleigh Dickinson University Press, 1998: 171–82.

Holmberg, Arthur. "Fallen Angels at Sea: Garbo, Ullmann, Richardson, and the Contradictory Prostitute in *Anna Christie*." *Eugene O'Neill Review* 20 (1996): 43–63.

McAleer, John J. "Christ Symbolism in *Anna Christie*." *Modern Drama* 4 (1962): 389–96.

Westgate, Chris. "Staging the 'poor, wicked lot': O'Neill's Rebuttal to Fallen Women Plays." *Eugene O'Neill Review* 28 (2006): 62–79.


## *Desire Under the Elms*

*Reviews*

Atkinson, Brooks. "At the Theatre." *New York Times*, January 17, 1952, 23:4. (ANTA revival).

Gibbs, Wolcott. "Desire Under the Elms." *New Yorker*, 27 (January 26, 1952): 53. (ANTA revival).

Nathan, George Jean. "The Kahn-Game." *Judge*, 87 (December 6, 1924): 17.

Siegel, Ed. "A Desolate Love Triangle Drives ART's Visceral 'Desire.'" *Boston Globe*, May 20, 2005: D17. (American Repertory Theatre revival).

Skinner, Richard Dana. "Decay 'Under the Elms.'" *Commonweal*, 1 (December 17, 1924): 163.

Young, Stark. "Eugene O'Neill's Latest Play." *New York Times*, November 12, 1924, 20:7.


## Criticism

Hartman, Murray. "*Desire Under the Elms* in the Light of Strindberg's Influence." *American Literature* 33 (1961): 360–69.

Hays, Peter L. "Biblical Perversions in *Desire Under the Elms.*" *Modern Drama* 11 (1969): 423–28.

Hinden, Michael. "*Desire Under the Elms:* O'Neill and the American Romance." *Forum* (Houston) 15.i (1977): 44–51.

Mandl, Bette. "Family Ties: Landscape and Gender in *Desire Under the Elms.*" *Eugene O'Neill Newsletter* XI.2 (Summer-Fall 1987): 19–22.

Mossman, Mark A. "Eugene O'Neill and 'the Myth of America': Ephraim Cabot as the American Adam." *Eugene O'Neill Review* 23 (1999): 48–59.

Weiss, Samuel A. "O'Neill, Nietzsche, and Cows." *Modern Drama* 34 (1991) 494–98.

Winther, Sophus K. "*Desire Under the Elms:* a Modern Tragedy." *Modern Drama* 3 (1960): 326–3.

## Ah, Wilderness!

### Reviews

Atkinson, Brooks. "Eugene O'Neill's 'Ah, Wilderness!' Restaged." *New York Times*, October 3, 1941, 26: 2. (New York revival).

———. "In which Eugene O'Neill Recaptures the Past. . ." *New York Times*, 3 October 1933, 28:2.

Gibbs, Wolcott. "Ah, Wilderness!" *New Yorker*, 17 (October 11, 1941): 47. (New York revival).

Krutch, Joseph Wood. "Mr. O'Neill's Comedy." *Nation*, 137 (October 18, 1933): 458–59.

Nathan, George Jean. "A Turn to the Right." *Vanity Fair*, 41 (November 1933): 66.

Rich, Frank. "O'Neill's Idealistic 'Ah, Wilderness!'" June 24, 1988: C3. (First New York International Festival of the Arts Revival / Jason Robards and Colleen Dewhurst).

### Criticism

Adler, Jacob H. "The Worth of *Ah, Wilderness!*" *Modern Drama* 3 (1960): 280–88.

Bermel, Albert. "O'Neill's Funny Valentine." *Eugene O'Neill Newsletter* XII.2 (Summer-Fall 1988): 18–22.

Fisher, James. "The Man Who Owned Broadway: George M. Cohan's Triumph in Eugene O'Neill's *Ah, Wilderness.*" *Eugene O'Neill Review* 23 (1999): 98–126.

Frank, Glenda. "Fun house Mirrors: The Neil Simon-Eugene O'Neill Dialogue." Gary Konas, ed. *Neil Simon: a casebook*. New York: Garland, 1997: 109–26.

Shaughnessy, Edward L. "A Connecticut Yankee in the Wilderness: The Sterner Stuff of O'Neill's Comedy." *Recorder* 3.ii (1989): 89–99.

Van Laan, Thomas F. "Singing in the Wilderness: The Dark Vision of Eugene O'Neill's Only Mature Comedy." *Modern Drama* 22 (1979): 9–18.

## The Iceman Cometh

*Reviews*

Atkinson, Brooks. "Four Hour O'Neill." *New York Times*, October 20, 1946, II, 1:1.
———. "O'Neill Tragedy Revived." *New York Times*, May 9, 1956, 38:1. (Circle-in-the-Square revival/José Quintero, dir., w/Jason Robards).
Bentley, Eric. "The Return of Eugene O'Neill." *Atlantic* 178 (November 1946): 64–66.
Brantley, Ben. "Bottoms Up to Illusions." *New York Times*, April 9, 1999: E1. (New York revival / Howard Davies, dir. w/Kevin Spacey).
Gibbs, Wolcott. "Good Old Hickey." *New Yorker*, 32 (May 26, 1956): 72–74. (Circle-in-the-Square revival / José Quintero, dir., w/Jason Robards).
Hayes, Richard. "Waiting for Hickey." *Commonweal*, 64 (August 24, 1956): 515–16, (Circle-in-the-Square revival / José Quintero, dir., w/Jason Robards).
Krutch, Joseph Wood. "Drama." *Nation*, 163 (October 26, 1946): 481–82.
McCarthy, Mary. "Dry Ice." *Partisan Review*, 13 (November-December 1946): 577–79.
Rich, Frank. "Jason Robards in 'The Iceman Cometh.'" *New York Times*, September 30, 1985: C11. (American National Theater Revival; José Quintero, dir.).

*Criticism*

Raleigh, John H., ed. *Twentieth Century Interpretations of* The Iceman Cometh: *A Collection of Critical Essays*. Englewood Cliffs, NJ: Prentice-Hall, 1968.
Bentley, Eric. "Trying to Like O'Neill." *Kenyon Review* 14 (1952): 476–92.
Black, Stephen A. "Tragic Anagnorisis in *The Iceman Cometh*." *Eugene O'Neill Review* 28 (2006):147–64.
Bloom, Steven F. "Drinking and Drunkenness in *The Iceman Cometh*: A Response to Mary McCarthy." *Eugene O'Neill Newsletter* IX.1 (Spring 1985): 3–12.
Day, Cyrus. "The Iceman and the Bridegroom: Some Observations on the Death of O'Neill's Salesman." *Modern Drama* 1 (1958): 3–9.
Frazer, Winifred L. "O'Neill's Iceman—Not Ice Man." *American Literature* 44 (1973): 677–78.
———. "'Revolution' in *The Iceman Cometh*." *Modern Drama* 22 (1979): 1–8.
Larner, Daniel. "Dionysus in Diaspora: O'Neill's Tragedy of Muted Revelries." *Eugene O'Neill Review* 24 (2000): 13–19.
Lee, Robert C. "Evangelism and Anarchy in *The Iceman Cometh*." *Modern Drama* 12 (1969): 173–86.
Mandl, Bette. "Absence as Presence: The Second Sex in *The Iceman Cometh*." *Eugene O'Neill Newsletter* VI.2 (Summer-Fall 1982): 10–15.

Murphy, Brenda. "*The Iceman Cometh* in Context: An American Saloon Trilogy." *Eugene O'Neill Review* 26 (2004): 214–25.

Porter, Laurin R. "*The Iceman Cometh* as Crossroad in O'Neill's Long Journey." *Modern Drama* 31 (1988): 52–62.

Vena, Gary A. *O'Neill's* The Iceman Cometh: *Reconstructing the Premiere.* Ann Arbor, MI: UMI Research Press, 1988.

## Long Day's Journey Into Night

### Reviews

Atkinson, Brooks. "O'Neill's Journey." *New York Times,* November 18, 1956, II, 1:1.

Bloom, Steven F. "*Long Day's Journey Into Night*." *The Eugene O'Neill Newsletter* X.2 (Summer-Fall, 1986): 33–39. (New York revival / Jonathan Miller, dir. w/Jack Lemmon).

Brantley, Ben. "A Mother's Haunting Presence in O'Neill's Unraveling Family." *New York Times,* May 7, 2003: E1. (New York revival / Robert Falls, dir. w/ Vanessa Redgrave).

Clurman, Harold. "Theatre." *Nation,* 183 (November 24, 1956): 466.

Gibbs, Wolcott. "Doom." *New Yorker,* 32 (November 24, 1956): 120.

Hayes, Richard. "A Requiem for Mortality." *Commonweal,* 65 (February 1, 1957): 467–468.

Hewes, Henry. "O'Neill: 100 Proof—Not a Blend." *Saturday Review,* 39 (November 24, 1956): 30–31.

Rich, Frank. "The Stars Align for 'Long Day's Journey.'" *New York Times,* June 15, 1988: C21. (First New York International Festival of the Arts Revival / Jason Robards and Colleen Dewhurst).

### Criticism

Black, Stephen A. "Reality and its Vicissitudes: The Problem of Understanding in *Long Day's Journey Into Night*." *Eugene O'Neill Review* 16.2 (Fall 1992): 57–72.

Bloom, Steven F. "'The mad scene: enter Ophelia!': O'Neill's Use of the Delayed Entrance in *Long Day's Journey Into Night*." *Eugene O'Neill Review* 26 (2004): 226–38.

Brietzke, Zander. "Too Close for Comfort: Biographical Truth in *Long Day's Journey Into Night*." *Eugene O'Neill Review* 25 (2001): 24–36.

Bryer, Jackson R. "Hell Is Other People: *Long Day's Journey Into Night*." Warren French, ed. *The Fifties: Fiction, Poetry, Drama.* Deland, FL: Everett/Edwards, 1970: 261–70.

Garvey, Sheila H. "Desecrating an Idol: *Long Day's Journey Into Night* as Directed by José Quintero and Jonathan Miller." *Recorder* 3.i (1989): 73–85.

Kerr, Christine. "Eugene O'Neill: An American Playwright's Contribution to Family Therapy." *Arts in Psychotherapy* 27 (2000): 115–22.

Mandl, Bette. "Wrestling with the Angel in the House: Mary Tyrone's Long Journey." *Eugene O'Neill Newsletter* III.3 (Winter 1988): 19–24.

Murphy, Brenda. *O'Neill: Long Day's Journey Into Night.* Cambridge: Cambridge University Press, 2001.

Wertheim, Albert. "Gaspard the Miser in O'Neill's *Long Day's Journey Into Night.*" *American Notes and Queries* 18 (1979): 39–42.

Winther, Sophus K. "O'Neill's Tragic Themes: *Long Day's Journey Into Night.*" *Arizona Quarterly* 13 (1957): 295–307.

## A Moon for the Misbegotten

*Reviews*

Atkinson, Brooks. "O'Neill's Finale." *New York Times,* May 12, 1957, II, 1:1. (First New York production).

Barnes, Clive. "Landmark *Moon for the Misbegotten.*" *New York Times,* December 31, 1973: 22. (Quintero revival / Jason Robards and Colleen Dewhurst).

Brantley, Ben. "A Love Story to Stop the Heart." *New York Times,* March 20, 2000: E1. (New York Revival / Cherry Jones).

Darrach, Henry B. "Moon in Columbus." *Time,* 49 (March 3, 1947): 47. (Tryout production).

Gibbs, Wolcott. "A Tired Tyrone." *New Yorker,* 33 (May 11, 1957): 84. (First New York production).

Hewes, Henry. "Requiem for a Roué." *Saturday Review,* 40 (May 18, 1957): 34. (First New York production).

"New Play by O'Neill Opens in Columbus." *New York Times,* February 21, 1947, 16:2. (Tryout production).

Nightingale, Benedict. "A Moon for the Misbegotten." *The London Times,* September 27, 2006. <http://www.eoneill.com/artifacts/reviews/mfm6_times.htm>. (Old Vic Revival / Howard Davies, dir. w/Kevin Spacey).

Rich, Frank. "Kate Nelligan in 'Moon for the Misbegotten.'" *New York Times,* May 2, 1984: C21. (New York revival).

*Criticism*

Black, Stephen A. "Letting the Dead Be Dead: A Reinterpretation of *A Moon for the Misbegotten.*" *Modern Drama* 29 (1986): 544–55.

Fitzgerald, John J. "Guilt and Redemption in O'Neill's Last Play: A Study of *A Moon for the Misbegotten.*" *Texas Quarterly* 9.i (1966): 146–58.

Garvey, Sheila H. "New Myths for Old: A Production History of the 2000 Broadway Revival of *A Moon for the Misbegotten.*" *Eugene O'Neill Review* 24 (2000): 121–33.

Hinden, Michael. "O'Neill and Jamie: A Survivor's Tale." *Comparative Drama* 35 (2001–02): 435–45.

Lee, Robert C. "Eugene O'Neill's Remembrance: The Past is the Present." *Arizona Quarterly* 23 (1967): 293–305.

Smith, Madeline C. "The Truth about Hogan." *Eugene O'Neill Review* 18 (1994): 163–70.

## *Related Secondary Sources*

Adler, Thomas P. *American drama, 1940–1960: A Critical History.* New York: Twayne, 1994.

Ben-Zvi, Linda. *Susan Glaspell: Her Life and Times.* New York: Oxford University Press, 2005.

Berlin, Normand. *The Secret Cause: A Discussion of Tragedy.* Amherst: University of Massachusetts Press, 1981.

Bigsby, C.W.E. *A Critical Introduction to Twentieth-Century American Drama, I: 1900–1940.* Cambridge: Cambridge University Press, 1982.

Brustein, Robert. *The Theatre of Revolt.* Boston: Little, Brown, 1964.

Dardis, Tom. *The Thirsty Muse: Alcohol and the American Writer.* New York: Ticknor & Fields, 1989.

Egan, Leona R. *Provincetown as a Stage: Provincetown, the Provincetown Players, and the Discovery of Eugene O'Neill.* Orleans, MA: Parnassus, 1994.

Hall, Ann C. *"A Kind of Alaska": Women in the Plays of O'Neill, Pinter, and Shepard.* Carbondale: Southern Illinois University Press, 1993.

Krasner, David. "Eugene O'Neill: American Drama and American Modernism." Krasner, ed. *A Companion to Twentieth-Century American Drama.* Malden, MA: Blackwell, 2005: 142–58.

Manheim, Michael. *Vital Contradictions: Characterization in the Plays of Ibsen, Strindberg, Chekhov and O'Neill.* Brussels: Lang, 2002.

Orlandello, John. *O'Neill on Film.* Rutherford, NJ: Fairleigh Dickinson University Press, 1982.

Porter, Thomas E. *Myth and Modern American Drama.* Detroit: Wayne State University Press, 1969.

Quintero, José. *If You Don't Dance They Beat You.* Boston: Little, Brown, 1974.

Sarlós, Robert K. *Jig Cook and the Provincetown Players: Theatre in Ferment.* Amherst: University of Massachusetts Press, 1982.

Scanlan, Tom. *Family, Drama, and American Dreams.* Westport, CT: Greenwood Press, 1978.

Schroeder, Patricia R. *The Presence of the Past in Modern American Drama.* Rutherford, NJ: Fairleigh Dickinson University Press, 1989.

Shafer, Yvonne. *Performing O'Neill: Conversations with Actors and Directors.* New York: St. Martin's Press, 2001.

Sievers, W. David. *Freud on Broadway: A History of Psychoanalysis and the American Drama.* New York: Hermitage House, 1955.

# Index

in, 125, 127, 145; pipe dreams in, 14, 15, 112, 128–31, 133–35, 137–44, 146–49; prostitute in, 132, 136, 149; racism in, 132; repetition in, 14, 126, 135, 145, 146, 148; symbolism in, 127, 132, 137, 139, 143, 146, 147; 141, 143, 182; women in, 138, 142, 149

"Ile," 6, 36

Illusion, 42, 59, 138, 143, 144, 145, 150

"In the Zone," 6

Individualism, 35

Intoxication, 37, 80

Irish, 2, 12, 15, 25, 34, 42, 48, 55, 56, 66, 96, 111, 145, 169, 170, 181, 183

Irony, 6, 34, 139, 163, 184

Jimmy-the-Priest's, 4

Jones, Brutus (The Emperor) (*The Emperor Jones*), 35, 65, 66, 69–71, 76, 78, 82–84; relationship to plot, 67–76, 79, 80; relationship to themes, 78–81

Jones, Robert Edmond, 88, 90

Jung, Carl, 40, 84

Krutch, Joseph Wood, 64

Kushner, Tony, 44

Lady Macbeth, 30

"The Last Supper," 143

*Lazarus Laughed*, 9, 26, 38

Le Plessis, 11, 16

Leeds, Nina (*Strange Interlude*), 10, 32, 179

London, Jack, 31, 35

*Long Day's Journey Into Night*, 2, 3, 4, 7, 14, 17, 20, 21, 23, 24, 26, 29, 30, 33, 36, 37, 38, 39, 42, 47, 87, 100, 103, 104, 110, 112, 113, 114, 117, 118, 125, 151–66, 167, 168, 176, 179, 180; addiction in, 14, 42, 157, 158, 160, 162, 163; alcoholism in, 158, 160, 162; capitalism in, 160;

chemical dependency in, 160; class in, 160; confession in, 158, 162; consumption (*also* tuberculosis) in, 14, 153, 155, 164; denial in, 14, 112, 153, 155, 160; family in, 24, 153–54, 156–64, 166; fog in, 29, 36, 104, 153, 161, 163; foghorn in, 35, 118, 163; hope in, 153, 154, 157, 159; imagery in, 162; intoxication in, 154, 156, 162; irony in, 160, 163; liquor in, 158; morphine in, 14, 42, 152, 153, 155, 156, 157, 158, 159, 162, 163, 164; posthumous publication and production of, 20–21, 152; repetition in, 112, 153, 160; the sea in, 157, 161, 163; tragic in, 112

"The Long Voyage Home," 6

Lumet, Sidney, 20, 163

Macbeth, 30

Mamet, David, 38, 42

Mannon, Lavinia (*Mourning Becomes Electra*), 11, 27, 28, 30, 32, 40, 179

Mannon, Orin (*Mourning Becomes Electra*), 27, 28, 30, 40

Marblehead, Massachusetts, 18

*Marco Millions*, 9, 26, 35, 38, 39

Marthy (*Anna Christie*), 49–50, 53–55, 57, 58

The Marx Brothers, 43

Marxist, 39, 147, 150

Masks, 9, 12, 28, 29, 34, 37, 81, 162

McCarthy, Mary, 43, 143, 183

Medea, 27, 88

Melodrama, 24, 25–26

Melville, Herman, 36; *Moby Dick*, 35, 36; *Typee*, 36

Miller, Arthur, 27, 41, 43, 44; *Death of a Salesman*, 41, 42, 159

Miller, Essie (*Ah, Wilderness!*), 106–10, 117–20, 122

Miller, Lily (*Ah, Wilderness!*), 107, 109, 111–13, 115–19, 122

Miller, Nat (*Ah, Wilderness!*), 105–10, 116, 120–22

Miller, Richard (*Ah, Wilderness!*), 23, 109–14, 120–22; relationship to plot, 104–9; relationship to themes, 114–17

Miscegenation, 8

Monologue, 14, 30, 32, 33, 92, 133, 140, 156, 164, 165, 180

Monte Cristo Cottage, 104

*A Moon for the Misbegotten*, 1, 7, 8, 14, 15, 17, 19, 26, 32, 113, 125, 167–86; alcoholism in, 176; betrayal in, 170, 171, 180; class in, 169, 174, 175, 181, 183; comic in, 168, 174, 175, 180, 182, 183; confession in, 175, 176, 179, 184, 185; family in, 174, 175, 177, 179–80, 182; hope in, 170, 173, 178, 181, 182, 185; imagery in, 183; irony in, 172, 178, 180, 184; liquor in, 169, 170, 177; moonlight in, 170, 171, 175, 178, 183, 184; New York City in, 169, 171; Pièta in, 180; prostitute in, 167, 172, 185; symbolism in, 183, 184; tragic in, 183; women in, 179

"The Moon of the Caribbees," 6, 117

Moral relativism, 94, 95, 169

*More Stately Mansions*, 19, 36

Morphine, 139. See also *Long Day's Journey Into Night*; O'Neill, Mary Ellen

*Mourning Becomes Electra*, 11, 12, 24, 26, 27–28, 29, 30, 32, 36, 40, 47, 179, 184

Mythic, 84, 89, 97

Naturalism, 31–34, 38, 47, 49, 60, 61, 65, 88, 96, 97, 117, 127, 143, 145, 146, 162

New England, 11, 27, 35, 36, 88, 92, 94, 97, 98, 99, 103, 109, 110, 111, 113

New London, 1, 2, 3, 4, 5, 23, 66, 104, 105, 111, 152

New York City, 2, 3, 4, 5, 6, 8, 9, 10, 11, 12, 14, 15, 16, 17, 18, 20, 34

Nietzsche, Friedrich, 9, 23, 36, 37, 104, 105; *Thus Spake Zarathustra*, 4, 37, 38; *The Birth of Tragedy*, 37

Nobel prize, 13, 14, 19, 31, 40

O'Casey, Sean, 34, 35

Oedipus complex, 26, 27, 39, 40, 87, 91, 98, 160, 179

O'Neill, Agnes Boulton (2nd wife), 6, 8, 9, 10, 11, 33

O'Neill, Carlotta Monterey (3rd wife), 10–21, 151

O'Neill, Edmund (brother who died in infancy), 2

O'Neill, Eugene Gladstone: alcoholism, 9–11, 18, 42–43, 143, 160, 162; birth and childhood, 2–3; children, 4, 6, 9, 16; death, 19; early plays, 5–7; education, 3, 5; family, 1–4, 7, 8, 10, 12, 14, 24, 103, 104, 109, 121, 125, 151, 167; ideas and themes, 36–40, 58–60, 78–80, 94–96, 114–17, 141–45, 159–61, 178–82; illness, 5, 17–19; influences on, 40–44; language, 30, 40, 42, 43, 61, 65, 66, 68, 97, 183; late plays, 12–17; religious faith, 3, 7, 12, 161; marriages, 4, 6, 9–10, 11–14, 15–19; middle plays, 7–12; others influenced by, 23–40; popular culture, 43–44; the sea, 4, 6, 18, 34, 36, 66; suicide, 4, 100; women, 4, 32, 167, 184, 185. *See also individual titles*

O'Neill, Eugene III (Shane's son), 16

O'Neill, Eugene Jr. (son by Kathleen Jenkins), 4, 16, 18, 20; and alcohol, 18; and suicide, 18

O'Neill, James (father), 2, 3, 7, 24, 25, 110

O'Neill, James Jr. (brother "Jamie"), 3, 7, 14, 24, 72, 105, 111, 167, 168, 176, 177; and alcoholism, 2, 7, 167, 176

## About the Author

STEVEN F. BLOOM is the President of the Eugene O'Neill Society (2006–2007) and a member of the Society's Board of Directors since 2000. He was the Book Reviews Editor of The Eugene O'Neill Review from 1988 until 2004. He has published numerous articles and reviews on O'Neill in The Eugene O'Neill Review and elsewhere, and he has spoken on O'Neill at many professional conferences and other public forums. He has taught courses in drama, media studies, literature, and writing for over thirty years. He is currently Dean of Undergraduate Education and Professor of English at Lasell College in Newton, Massachusetts.